Sandy read
Insufficient Belief – P. 42 *
Faith and Obedience 43

To Mom and Dad,

who have given me a love for the Word of God, a desire for excellence, an appreciation for the power of the printed page, a burden to communicate sound doctrine to a needy world, and most of all a living example of true Christianity.

Brian,

The Root Brings Life
to the Tree.

Remember your Roots!

Pastor Jeff Harpole

TABLE OF CONTENTS

TABLES AND CHARTS

AUTHOR'S PREFACE

In the apostolic movement today there is a great need for comprehensive books in important doctrinal areas. It is the author's hope that *The New Birth* will help to meet this need with respect to the doctrine of salvation. This book does not cover all concepts relative to salvation, but it focuses on one aspect: the conversion experience or regeneration. This book is Volume II of the *Series in Pentecostal Theology.* Volume I, *The Oneness of God,* was published in 1983, and Volume III, *In Search of Holiness,* was published in 1981.

The New Birth attempts to present biblical truth in an understandable yet scholarly way, not from the viewpoint of denominational dogma but from the viewpoint of what the Bible itself says. Numerous biblical references have been included so that the reader can search these things out and come to his or her own conclusions. If the reader approaches this subject with a prayerful, sincere, truth-seeking, studious attitude (rather than with a prejudiced or even a gullible mind), God will illuminate the truth of His Word as it relates to salvation.

All biblical quotations are from the *King James Version* unless otherwise indicated. Abbreviations used are KJV for *King James Version, NIV* for *New International Version,* and *TAB* for *The Amplified Bible.* If not specified otherwise, definitions of Greek words are taken from *Strong's Exhaustive Concordance.*

I would like to express special thanks to my mother, Loretta A. Bernard, for offering numerous suggestions, particularly for Chapters 3, 5, and 6. Also, I would like to express appreciation to my father, Elton D. Bernard, who gave inspiration and desire to undertake this project, and to my wife, Connie, who gave much encouragement and support.

The purpose of this book is not to condemn anyone who does not agree with or who has not experienced what is taught, but rather to encourage all to receive the fulness of salvation that God has provided in Jesus Christ.

David K. Bernard

Jackson, Mississippi

1

AN HONEST QUESTION

"Men and brethren, what shall we do?" (Acts 2:37).
"Sirs, what must I do to be saved?" (Acts 16:30).

Every human being is a sinner and stands in need of salvation. Through the centuries many people have realized this fact and have asked, "How can I be saved?" Christianity proclaims that God has provided salvation through Jesus Christ. However, the question remains, "How can I receive the salvation that Jesus Christ provides?"

We believe the Bible provides the answer to this simple yet vital question. The goal of this book is to find the biblical answer to the question just posed, and to discuss the many issues arising out of this subject. We will attempt to lay aside the doctrines of men and man-made denominations and see what the Bible itself teaches.

The Universal Need for Salvation

The Bible emphatically declares that all human beings are sinners. "Who can say, I have made my heart clean, I am pure from my sin?" (Proverbs 20:9). "But we are all as an unclean thing, and all our righteousnesses are as filthy rags; and we all do fade as a leaf; and our iniquities, like the wind, have taken us away" (Isaiah 64:6). "There is no man that sinneth not" (I Kings 8:46; II Chronicles 6:36).

The first three chapters of Romans affirm that both Jews and Gentiles stand condemned in God's sight. Those who did not have the law of Moses are condemned by conscience, and those who had the law of Moses are condemned by the law (Romans 2:12-16). In short, all mankind is under sin (Romans 3:9). "There is none righteous, no, not one" (Romans 3:10; see Psalm 14:1-3). All the world is guilty before God (Romans 3:19). "For all have sinned, and come short of the glory of God" (Romans 3:23).

Because of this, all mankind is under the sentence of death. "For the wages of sin is death" (Romans 6:23). "Sin, when it is finished, bringeth forth death" (James 1:15).

Salvation Comes Only Through Faith in Jesus Christ

Not only does each man need salvation, there is nothing man can do to save himself. No amount of good works or adherence to law can save a man. Ephesians

2:8-9 proclaims, "For by grace are ye saved through faith; and that not of yourselves: it is the gift of God: not of works, lest any man should boast." This means salvation is a free gift from God. The death, burial, and resurrection of Jesus Christ made this free gift of salvation available, and the only way to receive salvation is to have faith in Jesus and in the sufficiency of His sacrifice. Of course, saving faith in Christ includes obedience to His gospel and application of His gospel to our lives. (See Chapter 2 for further discussion of grace and faith.)

We must stress that salvation can come only through faith, and that faith must be in the Lord Jesus Christ. Jesus asserted, "I am the way, the truth, and the life: no man cometh unto the Father, but by me" (John 14:6). He also said we must believe He is God manifested in the flesh as our Savior. "I said therefore unto you, that ye shall die in your sins: for if ye believe not that I am he, ye shall die in your sins" (John 8:24).

Why is reliance upon Christ absolutely necessary? Since all men are sinners, the holiness of God demanded that He separate Himself from sinful man and also required death as a penalty for man. God chose to bind Himself by the principle of death for sin. Without the shedding of blood (the giving of a life) there can be no remission or release from this penalty (Hebrews 9:22) and no restoration to fellowship with the holy God. (See Ephesians 2:13-17; Colossians 1:19-22.) The death of animals is not sufficient to remit the sin of man (Hebrews 10:4), because man is much greater than the animals in that he was created in the spiritual, mental, and moral image of God (Genesis 1:27). Neither can an ordinary man become the substitutionary sacrifice for another, for all deserve eternal death for their own sins.

In order to provide a suitable substitute, God manifested Himself in flesh through the man Jesus Christ. Christ is the only sinless man who has ever lived, so He was the only One who did not deserve to die and who could be a perfect substitute. Therefore, His death became a propitiation or an atonement—the means by which God can pardon sins without violating His holiness and justice (Romans 3:23-26). God does not excuse our sins, but He has inflicted the penalty for those sins on the innocent man Christ. This substitution avails to us when we place our faith in Christ and apply His gospel to our lives. Thus the substitutionary, atoning death of Christ was made necessary by (1) the sinfulness of man, (2) the holiness of God, and (3) God's law requiring death as the punishment for sin. This is why there can be no salvation outside Jesus Christ.

What Is Salvation?

At the outset, we should establish what we actually mean by the word *salvation*. In general, *salvation* can refer to any kind of deliverance, preservation, or liberation. In a theological context, it means deliverance "from the power and effects of sin."[1] From the Bible it is apparent that salvation has past, present, and future aspects. We can say we *were* saved, meaning that at a past point in time we received forgiveness of sin, freedom from sin's control, and power to live for God. For example, Paul said, "Not by works of righteousness which we have done, but according to his mercy he saved us" (Titus 3:5).

We can also say we *are* saved, because we presently enjoy forgiveness of sins, power to live for God, and freedom from the power and effects of sin. Thus Paul said, "By grace ye are saved" (Ephesians 2:5). The resurrection and life of Christ effect present salvation. Not only did His death purchase past salvation from sin, but His life provides present victory over sin through His Spirit that dwells in us (Romans 5:10; I John 4:4).

In another sense of the word, however, salvation is still future. We have not yet received final and complete deliverance from all the curse of sin. We still live in this sinful and imperfect world, have mortal bodies, have the sinful nature within us, face temptation, and have the ability to sin. Our salvation will be complete only when we receive glorified, immortal bodies like that of the resurrected body of Jesus (Romans 8:23; Philippians 3:20-21). At that time we will no longer be subject to sickness, pain, the temptation of sin, or the possibility of death (I Corinthians 15:51-57). This last stage in God's salvation plan for us is called glorification (Romans 8:30), and it will occur when Christ comes back for His church (I Thessalonians 4:14-17; I John 3:2). Thus the Bible often speaks of salvation as a future event: "But we believe that through the grace of the Lord Jesus Christ we shall be saved" (Acts 15:11). "For now is our salvation nearer than when we believed" (Romans 13:11). "So Christ was once offered to bear the sins of many; and unto them that look for him shall he appear the second time without sin unto salvation" (Hebrews 9:28).

The Relation Between Past, Present, and Future Salvation

Obviously, the three tenses of salvation are closely related. Future salvation will come only to those who have experienced past and present salvation in this life. Those who are saved in the present have full assurance of salvation in the future. However, a one-time past experience does not automatically guarantee future salvation. We are responsible for keeping our salvation until the end. Just as we have received past salvation through faith in Jesus, we will receive future salvation only if we continue to live by faith in Jesus. We can forfeit our present salvation and our promise of future salvation by a voluntary return to sin and unbelief. The link between past and future salvation is continuance in present salvation.

Many scriptural passages emphasize this truth. Jesus taught the absolute necessity of abiding in Him and keeping His commandments (John 15:1-14). He said, "He that endureth to the end shall be saved" (Matthew 10:22). "Whosoever believeth in him should not perish, but have everlasting life" (John 3:16). In this last verse, "believeth" is in the present tense, implying that continued present belief is necessary.

Likewise, Paul said the gospel of Christ is "the power of God unto salvation to every one that believeth. . .For therein is the righteousness of God revealed from faith to faith: as it is written, The just shall live by faith" (Romans 1:16-17). Salvation will come to those who move from faith to faith, to those who continue to live by faith.

Paul also stated, "Work out your own salvation with fear and trembling" (Philippians 2:12). This does not mean we can save ourselves by our own plan or earn our own salvation. Rather, it means we must consciously abide in and keep our salvation. We should view salvation with awe and respect, realizing we can lose it if we do not value it. We should be watchful of Satan's tricks and timid of doing evil.

Many other verses give similar admonitions. "Take heed unto thyself, and unto the doctrine; continue in them: for in doing this thou shalt both save thyself, and them that hear thee" (I Timothy 4:16). "Behold therefore the goodness and severity of God: on them which fell, severity; but toward thee, goodness, if thou continue in his goodness: otherwise thou also shalt be cut off" (Romans 11:22). "I declare unto you the gospel. . .By which also ye are saved, if ye keep in memory what I have preached unto you, unless ye have believed in vain" (I Corinthians 15:1-2). Many other passages teach that we can lose salvation through unbelief and disobedience. (Galatians 5:4; I Timothy 5:12; Hebrews 12:14-15; James 5:19-20; II Peter 1:10; 2:1; 2:20-21; Revelation 3:5).

In short, we have not yet received all the eternal benefits of salvation, and therefore our future salvation is still a hope. "We are saved by hope," and we have "the hope of salvation" (Romans 8:24; I Thessalonians 5:8). The hope of future salvation is more than a mere wish, however, for we have the promise and assurance of salvation if we continue to walk in the gospel. The one way to obtain eternal salvation is to find present salvation from sin in this life.

This brings us to the question: How can we be saved from sin in this life? Let us look at three crucial New Testament passages relating to this subject. The first passage we will consider comes from the ministry of Christ. The other two passages are the only two places in the New Testament church where someone asked how to be saved.

The Lord's Statement to Nicodemus

John 3 records an important conversation between a Jewish religious leader named Nicodemus and Jesus. Nicodemus came to Jesus one night and acknowledged Him as a teacher from God. Jesus replied, "Verily, verily, I say unto thee, Except a man be born again, he cannot see the kingdom of God" (John 3:3). Nicodemus did not understand this, for he asked the Lord how a man could be born a second time from his mother's womb. Jesus explained, "Verily, verily, I say unto thee, Except a man be born of water and of the Spirit, he cannot enter into the kingdom of God" (John 3:5). Jesus was pointing towards a new age in which the kingdom of God would soon be revealed, and every person who wished to enter that kingdom would have to be born again, that is, born of water and the Spirit.

The Kingdom of God

What is the kingdom of God? How does it relate to salvation? The words themselves express the sovereign rule of God in the universe. In analyzing this concept more closely, we find that the kingdom of God has both present and future aspects, just as salvation does. In the present tense, the kingdom of God is the rule of God in the hearts of men. Jesus came preaching that the kingdom of God was at hand (Mark 1:14-15). Once, the Pharisees asked Jesus when the kingdom of God would come. He replied, "The kingdom of God cometh not with observation: Neither shall they say, Lo here! or, lo there! for, behold, the kingdom of God is within you" (Luke 17:20-21). This aspect of the kingdom came into existence when God sent His Spirit to dwell in the hearts of believers. Thus Paul said, "For the kingdom of God is not meat and drink; but righteousness, and peace, and joy in the Holy Ghost" (Romans 14:17). The present aspect of God's kingdom actually consists of the riches of His eternal kingdom temporarily come down to this world through the Spirit (Ephesians 1:13-14; Hebrews 6:4-5).

The kingdom of God also has a future aspect in that one day God will completely destroy all opposition to His rule and will display His kingship in every facet of the universe. His kingdom will come physically to this earth in the thousand year reign of Christ (Revelation 20:4-6). It will be established throughout eternity by the judgment of all sinners and by the creation of a new heaven and a new earth without sin. Sin is rebellion against God, so God's kingdom will find perfect expression only when all sin is judged and eliminated.

The Book of Revelation describes the future aspect of the kingdom. "The kingdoms of this world are become the kingdoms of our Lord, and of his Christ; and he shall reign for ever and ever" (Revelation 11:15). In that day, voices will proclaim, "The Lord God omnipotent reigneth" (Revelation 19:6). Jesus will be "King of kings, and Lord of lords" and will occupy the throne throughout eternity

(Revelation 19:16; 22:1-3).

Applying Christ's words in John 3 to the concept of the kingdom of God, we find that one must be born again in order to partake of either its temporary, present manifestation or its eternal manifestation. No one can have the spiritual rule of God in his life until he is born of water and the Spirit. No one can have joy, peace, and righteousness in the Spirit until he is born of water and the Spirit. No one in the present age can enter into God's eternal kingdom—the new heaven and the new earth—unless he is born of water and the Spirit.

In short, the Lord's words to Nicodemus tell us how to be saved. Present salvation consists of freedom from the dominion and penalty of sin, and this simply means entering into the present aspect of the kingdom of God (submitting to His rule and receiving His righteousness). Future salvation consists of eternal life free from sin and its consequences, and this simply means entering into the future aspect of the kingdom of God (the new heaven and new earth that will be free of rebellion against God's rule). The question, "How can I be saved?" has the same answer as the question, "How can I enter the kingdom of God?" The answer of Jesus Himself is, "You must be born again of water and the Spirit."

Peter's Answer on the Day of Pentecost

In Acts 1 Jesus gave His disciples last minute instructions just before His ascension into heaven. He told them to go to Jerusalem and wait for the promise of the Father, namely the baptism of the Holy Ghost. About 120 disciples obeyed Him and gathered in an upper room in Jerusalem.

Acts 2 records that on the Jewish feast day of Pentecost the promised Spirit baptism came. Soon, many people in the city began to gather around the disciples, attracted by the supernatural sound that had accompanied this first outpouring of the Spirit as well as by the foreign languages supernaturally being spoken by those who had just received the Spirit.

Peter seized the opportunity to preach to the crowd. Standing with the other eleven apostles, he began to explain what had just happened and proceeded to preach about Jesus. He proclaimed to the multitude that Jesus of Nazareth, whom they had crucified, was both Lord and Christ (Messiah).

When the crowd heard this, they began to feel guilt and conviction of sin, for undoubtedly many of them had demanded the crucifixion of Jesus less than two months before. Consequently, they asked Peter and the rest of the apostles, "Men and brethren, what shall we do?" (Acts 2:37). As the context shows, they were asking, "How can we receive forgiveness for our sin? How can we correct the wrong we have done in rejecting Jesus and crucifying Him? How can we now accept Jesus as Lord and Messiah?" The essence of salvation is receiving forgiveness of sins through faith in Christ, so their question simply meant, "What must we do to be saved?"

Here is the answer that Peter gave, with the support of all the apostles: "Repent, and be baptized every one of you in the name of Jesus Christ for the remission of sins, and ye shall receive the gift of the Holy Ghost" (Acts 2:38). In our search for a biblical answer to the question of how to be saved, we must attach great significance to this verse. It is a plain, simple, unambiguous answer to a direct inquiry. It is an answer that had the full endorsement of all the apostles. It is the climax of the first sermon of the New Testament church—the first sermon preached after the outpouring of the Spirit. As *The Pulpit Commentary* states, "We have in this short verse the summary of Christian doctrine as regards man and God."[2] In short, Acts 2:38 is the authoritative answer of the apostolic church to the question, "What must I do to be saved?"

Paul's Answer to the Philippian Jailer

We find only one other situation in the New Testament church that directly poses the question, "What must I do to be saved?" Acts 16 records that the magistrates of Philippi, a city in Macedonia, jailed Paul and Silas for preaching the gospel. At midnight Paul and Silas prayed and sang praises to God. Suddenly, an earthquake shook the prison and opened the doors. When the jailer awoke and realized what had happened he assumed the prisoners had all escaped. Apparently faced with the penalty of death for allowing this to happen, he decided to commit suicide. As he drew his sword, Paul shouted, "Do thyself no harm: for we are all here" (Acts 16:28). When he heard this, the jailer called for a light and went to investigate for himself. He came trembling and fell down at the feet of Paul and Silas, realizing that they were the ones responsible for the miraculous earthquake. He brought them out and asked, "Sirs, what must I do to be saved?"

They replied, "Believe on the Lord Jesus Christ, and

thou shalt be saved, and thy house" (Acts 16:30-31). The Bible further records, "And they spake unto him the word of the Lord, and to all that were in his house. And he took them the same hour of the night, and washed their stripes; and was baptized, he and all his, straightway. And when he had brought them into his house, he set meat before them, and rejoiced, believing in God with all his house" (Acts 16:32-34).

In this passage, Paul and Silas told the jailer that the path to his future salvation was through faith in the Lord Jesus Christ. Presumably the jailer was a Gentile and did not know very much about God. Unlike the Jews on the Day of Pentecost he probably did not understand terminology such as repentance, baptism, and the Holy Ghost. Furthermore, this was a crisis situation with no time for a long sermon or a detailed explanation; he needed to be shown the right direction quickly. Paul and Silas told him in the most simple way possible how he could receive future salvation, namely, by believing on Jesus instead of on pagan gods and idols.

At this, the jailer took them to his home and gave them the opportunity to speak to his whole household. They did not stop with the general statement quoted above, but they preached the Word of the Lord with specificity. As a result of their message, the jailer was baptized that same hour and received an experience that caused him to rejoice. One translation says, "He leaped much for joy and exulted" (Acts 16:34, *TAB*). All of this happened when he believed on the Lord and the Word of the Lord.

It is very instructive to study the Greek word translated as *believe* in this passage. It does not denote merely mental understanding and assent but asserts absolute reliance and adherence. (See Chapter 2.) The biblical definition of belief includes acceptance of God's Word and obedience to it. The publisher's foreword to *The Amplified Bible* explains that the phrase "believe on the Lord Jesus Christ" really means "to have an absolute personal reliance upon the Lord Jesus Christ as Saviour." Consequently, *The Amplified Bible* translates Acts 16:31 as, "And they answered, Believe in and on the Lord Jesus Christ—that is, give yourself up to Him, take yourself out of your own keeping and entrust yourself into His keeping and you will be saved; [and this applies both to] you and your household as well."

In order to gain a better understanding of this passage, we should examine the significance that Peter attached to the phrase "believe on the Lord Jesus Christ." On one occasion he explained that the Gentiles had received the Holy Ghost the same as the Jews who "believed on the Lord Jesus Christ" (Acts 11:15-17). Thus he linked faith in Jesus Christ with receiving the Spirit. Paul taught that the kingdom of God includes joy in the Holy Ghost (Romans 14:17). Although it is not specifically stated in Acts 16 that the Philippian jailer received the Holy Ghost, the reference to his joy may indicate that he received the baptism of the Holy Ghost. (See also Acts 8:39.)

Comparison of the Three Answers

We have discussed the biblical answer to the question, "How can I be saved?" in light of the three most prominent passages on the subject. The Bible uses different language in each passage. Since the Bible is the inspired, infallible Word of God, we know it does not contradict itself. Since God wants everyone to find salvation, we know the Bible must be clear and unambiguous on the subject. Therefore, despite differences in wording, the three passages we have analyzed cannot be contradictory or confusing. Instead, we must believe that each answers the question correctly. In other words, each gives the same answer in different terms, from different viewpoints, and in different situations, but it is the same answer nonetheless. Let us briefly demonstrate how this is so.

When Jesus spoke to Nicodemus He was not answering a direct question about salvation. Instead, He was describing God's plan of salvation for the future New Testament church that was about to come into existence. The Spirit was not yet given at that time and would not be given until after Christ's ascension (John 7:39; Acts 1:4-5). Christ's purpose was to give Nicodemus information and to motivate him to believe in His person and mission (John 3:16), not to impart the Spirit to him immediately.

The situation on the Day of Pentecost was different in that Peter gave a direct answer to a direct question about salvation. The Spirit had been poured out, so Peter did intend for his answer to give explicit instructions and to produce an immediate new birth. His listeners were Jews and Jewish proselytes, most (if not all) of whom had heard about Jesus of Nazareth. Since they were well acquainted with religious concepts and terminology, Peter was able to give them a precise, thorough answer in a single statement.

In Acts 16, Paul and Silas confronted a man who knew little if anything about God. He had just attempted suicide. He was recovering from the fright of an earthquake and was awestricken in the presence of the supernatural. They answered his question in a simple, general way that would be understandable and reassuring. They let him know that the way of salvation is through Jesus Christ. Then they explained the gospel in detail to him and his household.

The differences in these three passages stem from the different situations, but the content of each is consistent with the others. Two passages speak of water baptism, and the third refers to the birth of water. Two passages speak of the work of the Spirit in salvation, and the third describes an experience that caused rejoicing, which is experienced when a person receives the Spirit. Only one of the three passages explicitly mentions repentance and only one explicitly mentions faith in Christ, but many other verses teach that both faith and repentance are prerequisites to salvation.

We conclude from these three passages that salvation comes only through repentance from sin and faith in Jesus Christ. Repentance and faith will lead to water baptism in the name of Jesus (birth of water) and to the baptism of the Spirit (birth of the Spirit).

Other verses that mention salvation support this conclusion. For example, it is stated that salvation comes through: (1) the name of Jesus (Acts 4:12); (2) confession of Jesus as Lord, belief in His resurrection, and calling on His name (Romans 10:9-13); (3) grace through faith (Ephesians 2:8-9); (4) repentance (II Corinthians 7:10); (5) sanctification of the Spirit and belief of the truth (II Thessalonians 2:13); and (6) obedience to Christ

(Hebrews 5:9).

We can view salvation from two complementary, not contradictory, points of view: (1) It has a minimum requirement, namely, the new birth; (2) It is a process of progressively appropriating God's grace throughout a continual life of faith and holiness. We will see both aspects fulfilled in our lives if we are to inherit eternal salvation.

From start to finish, our salvation rests on faith in Jesus Christ. If we have faith in Him we will repent of sin, be baptized in His name, receive His Holy Spirit, and continue to live a holy, Christian life by faith. In this way we will receive both present salvation from sin and future salvation from all the eternal consequences of sin.

Understanding and Obeying the Gospel

The next few chapters will examine all the above elements in detail. If some have already experienced salvation as explored in this book, we hope they will understand the importance and necessity of what they have received. They should learn exactly what has happened to them and why. If some have not been baptized in the name of Jesus or have not received the baptism of the Holy Ghost, we ask them to read with an open mind, open heart, and open Bible. We do not wish to minimize or deny what God may have already done in their lives; however, we want them to see the importance of the birth of water and Spirit. It is biblical, it is for us today, and God wants everyone to experience it. The new birth is not something strange, nor is it difficult to receive from God. Rather it is a privilege that every Bible-believing person can and should enjoy.

All of us should seek to draw closer to God at all times. We should seek to know more about Him and to be more and more obedient to His Word. We must let God lead us further and further into the truth of His Word. We must seek to receive everything God has for us today.

Instead of dwelling so much on the question, "Do I have to receive this?" we should ask, "Can I receive this?" If God has something more for us that we have not received, or if God's Word reveals something that we have not yet obeyed, then we should not be distracted by a debate over whether it is necessary or optional. Instead, we should seek to receive all that God has for us and seek to obey all that God's Word teaches. This is the attitude of one who truly has faith in the Lord Jesus Christ.

FOOTNOTES

[1]*Webster's Third New International Dictionary of the English Language,* unabridged, Philip Gove et al, eds. (Springfield, Mass.: G. & C. Merriam Co., 1976), p. 2006.

[2]H. D. M. Spence and Joseph Exell, eds., *The Pulpit Commentary* (Rpt. Grand Rapids: Eerdmans, 1977), XVIII (Acts), 54.

2

GRACE AND FAITH

"For by grace are ye saved through faith; and that not of yourselves: it is the gift of God: Not of works, lest any man should boast" (Ephesians 2:8-9).

This chapter lays a foundation for all subsequent discussion of salvation. Before proceeding to analyze the various aspects of salvation, we need to understand what grace and faith are and how they relate to each other.

Grace Defined

Grace is the unmerited favor of God towards man. It is God's free gift to man. It is God's work in man. The word expresses that salvation is an undeserved, unearned blessing that God bestows freely. God does all the work involved in saving a soul. Man cannot aid God in his own salvation or contribute to it; he can only accept or reject the work that God has done and is willing to do on his behalf.

Man's Salvation Stems from God's Grace

Ephesians 2:8-9 emphasizes that salvation comes by God's grace and not by any works on man's part. Specifically, God has made salvation available to us through the death of Jesus Christ. We are "justified freely by his grace through the redemption that is in Christ Jesus: Whom God hath set forth to be a propitiation through faith in his blood" (Romans 3:24-25). Not only did God give His Son to die for us and to purchase through His death our salvation, but He now extends everything necessary to preserve our salvation. As Paul asked, "He that spared not his own Son, but delivered him up for us all, how shall he not with him also freely give us all things?" (Romans 8:32).

Philippians 2:13 teaches that God works in us to bring about salvation: "For it is God which worketh in you both to will and to do of his good pleasure." In Philippians 2:12 Paul admonished us to work out our salvation with awe, reverence, and watchfulness. Then in the next verse he explained that we cannot save or help save ourselves; rather we can either reject or submit to God's work in us. If we let Him, God will give us both the desire (willingness) and the power (ability) to perform His will.

God, who purchased our right to be saved, now freely provides all things necessary for us to receive and retain salvation. Thus man's salvation is a product of God's grace from start to finish. Of course, grace does not eliminate our choice. God has given us the freedom either to surrender to Him or reject Him, but we can contribute nothing positive to earn our own salvation.

Grace and Works

We are not saved by works in the sense of earning, meriting, or purchasing salvation by good works. However, the grace of God will lead to good works and holiness of life. After Ephesians 2:8-9 emphatically teaches salvation by grace and not works, the next verse continues, "For we are his workmanship, created in Christ Jesus unto good works, which God hath before ordained that we should walk in them." God gives us grace expressly to enable us to produce good works. "And God is able to make all grace abound toward you; that ye, always having all sufficiency in all things, may abound to every good work" (II Corinthians 9:8). God's grace has come to show us how to live righteous, holy lives and to give us power to do so. "For the grace of God that bringeth salvation hath appeared to all men, teaching us that, denying ungodliness and worldly lusts, we should live soberly, righteously, and godly, in this present world" (Titus 2:11-12).

Grace does not give license to sin. "Shall we continue in sin, that grace may abound? God forbid" (Romans 6:1-2). "Shall we sin, because we are not under the law, but under grace? God forbid" (Romans 6:15). On the contrary, grace makes the power of the Spirit available to us. If we follow the Spirit, we can fulfill all the righteousness that the law of Moses demanded but could not give (Romans 8:3-4).

In sum, God's grace brings salvation as a free gift, including the power to live righteously. Although we cannot earn the gift of salvation, once we receive it our lives will change and we will begin to do good works as a result. If we do not manifest righteous and godly attributes, then we are not letting God's saving grace work in us. We cannot separate grace from a life of devotion and obedience to Christ.

Grace and Faith

If the doctrine of grace teaches that God does all the work in man's salvation, are all men automatically saved? This cannot be true because many will receive eternal damnation at the last judgment (Revelation 20:11-15). If the doctrine of grace teaches that man cannot assist God in providing salvation, does God unconditionally choose certain ones to be saved regardless of their own attitudes and responses? This cannot be true either because God is no respecter of persons (Acts 10:34). If He chose some unconditionally, His fairness would cause Him to choose all. The doctrine of faith helps us understand the answer to both of the above questions.

Faith is the means by which man accepts and receives God's saving grace (Romans 3:21-31; Ephesians 2:8). Man cannot help God in providing salvation, but man does have the responsibility to accept or reject what God offers. Man's response to God in accepting His work of salvation is called faith. Thus faith is the channel through which God's grace comes to man. Both God's grace and man's faith are necessary for salvation. "Without faith it is impossible to please him [God]" (Hebrews 11:6). One Protestant author stated, "That man must do something to take advantage of God's provision of salvation through Christ does no violence to the doctrine of grace. Theologically as well as etymologically there are two aspects of *charis* (grace): unmerited provision and thankful reception."[1]

However, we must avoid saying that salvation comes partly from man. When man accepts grace the credit belongs wholly to God and the power of His grace, but when man rejects grace the blame falls wholly upon man and his unbelief. Thus we affirm both salvation by grace alone and the responsibility of man to accept salvation.

Justification by Faith

To be justified means to be counted or declared righteous by God. The Bible clearly teaches justification by faith: "The just shall live by faith" (Habakkuk 2:4; Romans 1:17; Galatians 3:11; Hebrews 10:38).

Paul preached this doctrine: "Be it known unto you therefore, men and brethren, that through this man [Jesus] is preached unto you the forgiveness of sins: And by him all that believe are justified from all things, from which ye could not be justified by the law of Moses" (Acts 13:38-39).

Paul emphasized justification by faith in his writings: "By the deeds of the law there shall no flesh be justified in his sight. . .But now the righteousness of God without the law is manifested, being witnessed by the law and the prophets; Even the righteousness of God which is by faith of Jesus Christ unto all and upon all them that believe. . .Being justified freely by his grace through the redemption that is in Christ Jesus: whom God hath set forth to be a propitiation through faith in his blood" (Romans 3:20-25). "Knowing that a man is not justified by the works of the law, but by the faith of Jesus Christ, even we have believed in Jesus Christ, that we might be justified by the faith of Christ, and not by the works of the law: for by the works of the law shall no flesh be justified" (Galatians 2:16). Romans 4 and Galatians 3 contain much additional teaching on this subject.

The bottom line is this: no one can be justified by observing the law of Moses or by doing good works. Instead, the only way to salvation is through faith in Jesus Christ and His sacrifice for us. Having established this, we must next determine what true faith in Christ is and how to have it. For a start, we note the words of Benjamin Warfield: "Justification by faith does not mean. . .salvation by believing things instead of doing right. It means pleading the merits of Christ before the throne of grace instead of our own merits."[2]

The Source of Faith

Before discussing faith in detail, we need to answer the question, "What is the origin of faith?" If man manufactures faith on his own, then he would seemingly be his own savior, at least partially. This would negate the doctrine of grace. The answer is that the ability to possess faith comes from God's grace.

However, this raises a second problem. If God gives potential faith to everyone, will everyone be saved? On the other hand, if God gives potential faith only to some, He would arbitrarily condemn the rest to hell without giving them any ability to choose. The answer is that God does give potential faith to everyone, but He leaves it up to each individual whether or not to accept and apply faith to his life. Another way to phrase this is to say God gives everyone the ability to have faith in Him. Every human being has the capacity to believe, but not everyone chooses to believe in God; nevertheless, everyone believes or can believe in something, whether it be God, the devil, false gods, self, other people, or material things. In creation God left a clear witness of Himself so that everyone would have a chance to believe in God and would have no excuse for failure to do so (Romans 1:19-20).

The Scriptures teach that God gives everyone the ability to believe and therefore He is the source of a Christian's faith. "God hath dealt to every man the measure of faith" (Romans 12:3). Jesus is the author and finisher of our faith (Hebrews 12:2). Even after the new birth, the Spirit continues to impart faith as a supernatural gift in moments of crisis and as an element of daily Christian life (I Corinthians 12:9; Galatians 5:22).

Due to our sinful natures, none of us could ever seek God on our own in the absence of His drawing power (John 3:27; 6:44; Romans 3:10-12). No one would ever have faith if God did not grant it. However, Christ died for the whole world so that He could bestow grace upon all (John 3:16). Although man on his own is so depraved and sinful that he cannot of himself choose God, God gives every man the ability to seek after Him and respond to Him. This grace that precedes salvation and is given to all mankind is what theologians call "universal prevenient grace."

The Bible teaches that universal grace precedes salvation, enabling and encouraging all mankind to accept God's work of salvation: "For the grace of God that bringeth salvation hath appeared to all men" (Titus 2:11). God commands all men everywhere to repent (Acts 17:30), and He gives the ability to fulfill what He requires (Philippians 2:13; I John 5:3). God wants all to repent, and He gives all a chance to do so (II Peter 3:9). The goodness of God leads men to repentance (Romans 2:4), so He extends to everyone the goodness or grace that leads to repentance. The call goes to all (Matthew 11:28; Revelation 22:17), but only those who respond are saved. Many are called but few are chosen (Matthew 20:16; 22:14).

We also find that faith comes by the Word of God (Romans 10:17). There are many instances recorded in Scripture in which the hearing of the Word of God inspired faith. Such was the case with the Samaritans, with Cornelius and his household, and with the Corinthians (Acts 8:12; 10:44; 18:8).

Thus everyone receives an initial measure of faith from God. We can increase our faith by hearing the Word of God and by operation of the Holy Spirit. We are responsible for letting God develop faith in us and for using the faith He has placed in our hearts.

Faith Defined

We have already identified faith as man's positive response to God and the means by which man accepts God's saving grace. It is the means by which we yield to God, obey His Word, and allow Him to perform His saving work in us. This accurately states the function of faith, but now we will try to define more precisely what faith is. *Webster's Dictionary* defines *belief* as "a state or habit of mind in which trust or confidence is placed in some person or thing," and it defines *faith* as "allegiance to duty or a person; loyalty. . .belief and trust in and loyalty to God. . .something that is believed esp. with strong conviction."[3]

When we turn to the Greek language, we find an even greater depth of meaning. The publisher's foreword to *The Amplified Bible* contains a significant discussion of the word *believe.* As it points out, most people believe in Christ in the ordinary English meaning of the word. That is, most people believe that Christ lived, was the Son of God in some sense, and died on the cross to save sinners. However, according to *The Amplified Bible* no single English word can adequately convey the intended meaning of the Greek word *pisteuo,* which most translations render *believe.* Here is *The Amplified Bible's* definition of *pisteuo:* "It means 'to adhere to, trust, to have faith in; to rely on.' Consequently, the words, 'Believe on the Lord Jesus Christ. . .' really mean to have an absolute personal reliance upon the Lord Jesus Christ as Saviour."[4]

W. E. Vine, in his *An Expository Dictionary of New Testament Words,* defines *pisteuo* as follows: "to believe, also to be persuaded of, and hence, to place confidence in, to trust, signifies, in this sense of the word, reliance upon, not mere credence."[5] The *King James Version* sometimes translates it as "commit" or "trust." The noun form of *pisteuo* is *pistis,* which is usually translated as "faith."

Vine defines *pistis* as "primarily, firm persuasion, a conviction based upon hearing."[6] He states that *pisteuo* and *pistis* include a total acknowledgement of God's revelation, a personal surrender to Him, and a lifestyle inspired by that surrender:

> "The main elements in faith in its relation to the invisible God, as distinct from faith in man, are especially brought out in the use of this noun and the corresponding verb, *pisteuo;* they are (1) a firm conviction, producing a full acknowledgement of God's revelation or truth, e.g., 2 Thess. 2:11, 12; (2) a personal surrender to Him, John 1:12; (3) a conduct inspired by such surrender, 2 Cor. 5:7. . .All this stands in contrast to belief in its purely natural exercise, which consists of an opinion held in good faith without necessary reference to its proof."[7]

The well-known Bible commentator Charles Erdman confirms that biblical faith embraces a personal relationship to Christ reflected in a person's trust, obedience, and holy conduct:

> "If faith denotes mere assent to dogmas, or the repetition of a creed, then to accept one as righteous, in view of his faith, would be absurd and unjust; but faith describes a personal relationship to Christ. For a believer, it means a trust in Christ, obedience to Christ, love for Christ, and such trust and obedience, and love inevitably result in purity and holiness and a life of unselfish service."[8]

Protestant theologian Donald Bloesch makes a number of illuminating remarks with respect to biblical faith. He speaks of the "heresy of cheap grace whereby salvation became a passport to heaven that was assured to one simply through baptism or a public affirmation of faith or by birth in the covenant community."[9] In opposition to the concept of "cheap grace," he states that "the free gift of salvation demands not simply an outward intellectual assent or a voluntary submission to the Gospel but a total commitment and lifelong discipleship under the cross."[10] Furthermore, he presents a definition of faith as "a radical commitment of the whole man to the living Christ, a commitment that entails knowledge, trust, and obedience."[11]

Three Components of Saving Faith

In other words, saving faith means much more than mental knowledge or assent. In fact, we can identify three key components of saving faith: knowledge, assent, and appropriation.[12]

To have faith in something, a person must first have a certain degree of knowledge or mental understanding. He must know what he professes to believe. Saving faith does not require us to understand everything about God or life, but it does require that we realize our need of salvation and know that Jesus Christ is our only Savior.

Second, to have faith there must be assent or mental acceptance. Knowledge is not enough, for a person can understand a certain proposition and yet disbelieve it. In addition to understanding, there must be an acknowledgement that the profession is correct.

Finally, there must be an appropriation of what is

believed. In other words, there must be a practical application of truth. The only way we can believe another person is by accepting and following his word. Saving faith in Jesus Christ, then, involves more than mentally acknowledging Him as the Savior. We must appropriate this truth and make it the guiding principle of our lives. We do this by obeying the gospel of Jesus, by identifying with Him, by totally committing ourselves to Him, and by establishing a relationship of total trust in and adherence to and reliance upon Him.

Our study of the Greek words *pistis* and *pisteuo* emphasized this third component. Without it, there is no saving faith. Many will acknowledge Jesus to be Lord and Savior and yet admit they have not obeyed the gospel. Although they have both knowledge and assent, they have not appropriated the gospel to their lives. They have not acted upon the truth. They have not committed themselves to Christ or identified with Him. In sum, saving faith is an active reliance upon God and His Word. We cannot separate it from reliance, obedience, and commitment.

Examples of Insufficient Belief

The Scripture gives many examples of people who had some degree of faith in Christ but who were not saved. This demonstrates that a person can have a mental belief in Jesus as Lord and Savior and yet not obey Him, rely upon Him, or commit himself to Him to the point of salvation.

For example, many people in Israel believed on Jesus when they saw the miracles He performed. However, Jesus did not commit Himself to them because He knew their hearts. They had not fully committed themselves to Him as Lord of their lives (John 2:23-25).

Similarly, many of the Jewish religious leaders believed on Jesus but they did not confess Him for fear of being put out of the synagogues. They loved the praise of men more than the praise of God (John 12:42-43). God did not accept them because they did not act upon their belief.

According to Jesus, some people do great miracles in His name, yet if they refuse to do God's will, they will not be saved (Matthew 7:21-27). They will have enough faith for miracles but not enough faith to obey God's Word in all things. They will have faith but not saving faith.

The Samaritans believed Philip's preaching and were baptized, yet they did not receive the Spirit of God until Peter and John came (Acts 8:12-17). Simon the magician was one who believed and was baptized, but he later tried to buy spiritual power and blessings with money (Acts 8:18-19). Peter rebuked him and told him to repent of his wickedness, saying, "Thou hast neither part nor lot in this matter: for thy heart is not right in the sight of God. . .For I perceive that thou art in the gall of bitterness, and in the bond of iniquity" (Acts 8:21-23). He was not saved at this point, even though he had believed to some extent.

Even the devils believe in one God (James 2:19), which is more than some do. Not only do they believe, but they confess Jesus to be the Son of God (Matthew 8:29). Despite their belief and confession, however, they do not have saving faith.

In each of these cases, there was mental understanding and assent, but there was also a lack of total commitment to Jesus and obedience to His Word. The people possessed a degree of faith but not enough to bring about salvation. Saving faith, then, is inseparably linked with obedience.

Faith and Obedience

Paul emphasized justification by faith more than any other writer, yet he strongly insisted that saving faith is inseparably bound up with obedience. He taught that the mystery of God's redemptive plan, the church, has been "made known to all nations for the obedience of faith" (Romans 16:26). The *New International Version* translates this last phrase as "made known. . .so that all nations might believe and obey him." God's grace brings "obedience to the faith" (Romans 1:5). Christ worked through Paul to "make the Gentiles obedient" (Romans 15:18). Similarly, Luke recorded that a great number of priests were "obedient to the faith" (Acts 6:7). Faith and obedience are so closely linked that a lack of obedience to God is proof of a lack of faith: "But they have not all obeyed the gospel. For Esaias saith, Lord, who hath believed our report?" (Romans 10:16).

Many other passages reiterate the essential link between obedience and salvation. Jesus said, "Not every one that saith unto me, Lord, Lord, shall enter into the kingdom of heaven; but he that doeth the will of my Father which is in heaven" (Matthew 7:21). Only the man that both hears and does the Lord's Word will be saved (Matthew 7:24-27). Jesus also said, "If ye love me, keep my commandments" (John 14:15); "If a man love me, he will keep my words" (John 14:23).

The Lord will punish with everlasting destruction those who "obey not the gospel of our Lord Jesus Christ" (II Thessalonians 1:7-10). Christ has become "the author of eternal salvation unto all them that obey him" (Hebrews 5:9). Peter said, "For the time is come that judgment must begin at the house of God: and if it first begin at us, what shall the end be of them that obey not the gospel of God?" (I Peter 4:17).

John gave the following test for a Christian: "And hereby we do know that we know him, if we keep his commandments. He that saith, I know him, and keepeth not his commandments, is a liar, and the truth is not in him. But whoso keepeth his word, in him verily is the love of God perfected: hereby know we that we are in him" (I John 2:3-5). We know God, have the love of God perfected in us, and are in God only when we obey God. The true believer will obey God's commandments and will thereby know that he has love (I John 5:1-3).

When God sent the death angel to visit every household in Egypt, the Israelites were not automatically protected simply on the basis of their mental attitude. They had to apply the blood of the Passover lamb to their doorposts (Exodus 12). Only when they expressed their faith through obedience to God's command were they safe. "Through faith he [Moses] kept the passover, and the sprinkling of blood, lest he that destroyed the firstborn should touch them" (Hebrew 11:28). Likewise, saving faith today includes active obedience. We must apply the blood of the Lamb to our lives by obedience to His gospel of repentance, water baptism in His name, and receiving His Spirit.

Someone who really believes God's Word will obey it.

God's Word teaches water baptism, so the Bible believer will be baptized. God's Word promises the gift of the Spirit, so the true believer will expect, seek, and receive this gift. One Protestant writer has stated, "Christians have historically affirmed that to enjoy a life-transforming relationship with God a person must believe and obey the gospel."[13] Another Protestant theologian wrote, "The content of faith can in fact be caught in one sentence: Jesus is Lord (I Cor. 12:3). . . .Therefore, to say in faith that 'Jesus is Lord' is also to commit one's self to obedience. To believe the fact is to obey the summons implicit in the fact; and only in obedience is the fact truly acknowledged. . . .For Paul obedience is the same as faith, just as disobedience is a lack of faith."[14] Theologian Dietrich Bonhoeffer said, *"Only he who believes is obedient, and only he who is obedient believes."*[15]

Faith and Works

The Bible also teaches that faith cannot be separated from good works. "This is a faithful saying, and these things I will that thou affirm constantly, that they which have believed in God might be careful to maintain good works" (Titus 3:8).

There is no faith apart from or without works. James wrote of the inseparableness of faith and works: "What doth it profit, my brethren, though a man say he hath faith, and have not works? can faith save him? . . .Even so faith, if it hath not works, is dead, being alone. Yea, a man may say, Thou hast faith, and I have works: shew me thy faith without thy works, and I will shew thee my faith by my works. Thou believest that there is one God; thou doest well: the devils also believe, and tremble. But wilt thou know, O vain man, that faith without works is dead? Was not Abraham our father justified by works, when he had offered Isaac his son upon the altar? Seest thou how faith wrought with his works, and by works was faith made perfect? And the scripture was fulfilled which saith, Abraham believed God, and it was imputed unto him for righteousness: and he was called the Friend of God. Ye see then how that by works a man is justified, and not by faith only. . .For as the body without the spirit is dead, so faith without works is dead also" (James 2:14, 17-24, 26).

Some people see a contradiction in Paul's teaching about faith and James' teaching about works. Martin Luther disliked the Book of James and even questioned its place in the Bible because he thought it contradicted justification by faith. However, Paul's epistles and James' epistle are equally part of the Word of God, and God's Word does not contradict itself. The writings of Paul and James complement each other and fit together into a harmonious whole.

Paul emphasized that we are saved by faith in Jesus, not by our works. God has purchased salvation for us and we accept it by faith; we do not purchase salvation by good works. In particular, Paul emphasized that keeping the law of Moses cannot save anyone, because ceremonial observances do not have the power in themselves to cleanse sin.

James likewise recognized that "every good gift and every perfect gift is from above" (James 1:17), including salvation. He pointed out that the kind of faith that saves will necessarily produce works. In other words, we cannot demonstrate faith in the abstract apart from works; the only way God or anyone else sees our faith is through our response. Faith is not just a condition of the mind but a life-changing force.

Paul cited Abraham as a example of justification by faith (Genesis 15:6; Romans 4:1-3). James used the same example to show that faith can only be demonstrated by works. Without works Abraham's faith would have been dead. What if Abraham had said, "I believe God," but he would have refused to offer up Isaac? According to James, he would not have had true faith and so would not have been justified. God Himself told Abraham after he had willingly offered Isaac, "I will bless thee. . .because thou hast obeyed my voice" (Genesis 22:16-18). Paul's description of Abraham's faith leads to the same conclusion. Against hope Abraham believed in hope. He did not consider human limitations, he did not stagger at the promise of God, he was strong in faith, he gave glory to God, and he was fully persuaded (Romans 4:18-21). This passage does not describe mental assent apart from works but rather active faith that supported Abraham in his conduct for many years—faith that caused him to trust and commit himself wholly to God.

Any remaining confusion clears when we realize that Paul and James used the same terms in somewhat different ways and contexts. In Romans, *faith* means true faith in God with all this entails; in James it means mental assent that could fail to affect conduct, which would not be true, living faith at all. In Romans, *works* means dead works that can be done apart from faith; in James it means living works that can be done only through faith and that will attest to the existence of faith. In Romans, *justified* means "declared righteous by God"; in James it means "shown to be righteous." Vine commented on this harmony between Paul and James:

> "In regard to justification by works, the so-called contradiction between James and the Apostle Paul is only apparent. . . .Paul has in mind Abraham's attitude towards God, his acceptance of God's word. . . .James (2:21-26) is occupied with the contrast between faith that is real and faith that is false, a faith barren and dead, which is not faith at all."[16]

It is evident that Paul and James both agreed that saving faith will produce a life-changing reliance upon God, evidenced by works. Paul taught that we are saved through faith; James taught that saving faith will produce works and is only demonstrated by works. If works do not come with a person's faith, there is something wrong with his faith.

Hebrews 11 beautifully illustrates the complementary relationship between faith and works. The main purpose of this chapter is to show how necessary faith is and to show what it will produce. It names many Old Testament heroes and records their deeds done "by faith." The passage demonstrates that faith will always produce works and that it can only be shown by works. Every time the writer described someone's faith, he listed those actions faith caused.

Certainly, we are saved by grace through faith. We rely on God's work and not our own works to bring salvation. However, this does not relieve us of our responsibility to respond to God, to obey Him, and to act upon our faith. Saving faith is a living faith that works.

Continuing Faith

Saving faith is not just a temporary condition but a continuing relationship with Jesus Christ. We are not saved by faith held only at one point in time. Rather, "the just shall live by faith" (Romans 1:17; Galatians 3:11; Habakkuk 2:4). Colossians 2:6 says, "As ye have therefore received Christ Jesus the Lord, so walk ye in him." Just as we received Him in faith, so must we continue to exercise faith in Him.

The Bible often speaks of faith in the present tense, indicating continuing faith. For example, the word *believeth* in John 3:16 indicates continuous faith: "For God so loved the world, that he gave his only begotten Son, that whosoever believeth in him should not perish, but have everlasting life." Salvation is not just a past tense experience; it is a present tense relationship that will lead to eternal salvation. We must live daily by faith in order to be saved in the end. It is much easier to see the close relationship between faith and works when we realize this fact. Faith is progressive; it leads further and further into God's will.

The Object of Faith

Just as there is no merit in faith apart from response, so there is no merit in faith apart from the object of faith. Faith in and of itself is of no value. If man's faith in itself were meritorious, then justification by faith would be simply another form of man saving himself.

The value of faith depends totally upon the object of faith. We are saved by the One in whom we have faith, not by the condition of having faith. When Paul used Abraham as an example of justification by faith, he pointed out that Abraham believed God, the omniscient and omnipotent Being who could fulfill His promises (Romans 4:16-17). Pagan religionists may have great faith, but they are not saved because they do not have faith in Jesus. Since salvation comes solely through Jesus, it is vitally important to have faith in Him.

This means we must have faith in His Word as well. Many people have great faith in certain religious systems that profess Christ, but they are not saved because their faith is not based on the Word of God and the gospel of Christ. Belief in a man-made system and sincerity in that belief are not enough. We must worship God in truth as well as in spirit (John 4:24). Jesus said, "He that believeth on me, as the scripture hath said, out of his belly shall flow rivers of living water" (John 7:38). We must believe in accordance with the teaching of Scripture. There is no saving power in man's mental faith apart from belief in and obedience to Jesus and His Word.

Faith and Repentance

Now let us analyze in greater detail exactly what faith in Jesus will produce. Faith and repentance work together in salvation. Jesus preached, "Repent ye, and believe the gospel" (Mark 1:15). A person must have some faith in order to repent. No one seeks to repent from sin unless he believes that sin is wrong and that repentance is both possible and necessary. God's Word declares that all will perish without repentance and that all men everywhere must repent (Luke 13:3; Acts 17:30). Certainly, then, faith in the Word of God will lead to repentance.

Some debate whether repentance precedes or follows faith. Lutheran theologians traditionally have viewed repentance as preceding faith, while Calvin described it as a product of faith. This all depends on the usage of the term *faith*. For example, if a person uses it to mean the moment of salvation, then repentance must precede it because repentance is a prerequisite for salvation. On the other hand, if he views faith as a continuous process as well as a point in time, then faith can both precede repentance and also follow it. This latter view finds the support of Scripture.

Faith can begin at the first hearing of the Word of God even though at this moment faith does not bring salvation. We have explored biblical examples that show that a person can have some degree of faith prior to the salvation experience. A person is not saved at the first moment faith begins, but rather salvation is experienced as faith matures, gains control of his heart, and leads him to a positive response to Christ and the gospel so that he obeys the Scriptures in repentance, water baptism, and seeking and receiving the gift of the Spirit.

Repentance, then, follows the first moment of faith but it precedes the full expression of saving faith (the new birth experience). Perhaps it is best to describe repentance as the first "faith reponse" to the gospel, for repentance stands at the beginning of a life of faith and is itself the initial act of faith.

Faith and Water Baptism

Faith in God will also lead to water baptism. Jesus said,

"He that believeth and is baptized shall be saved" (Mark 16:16). Obviously He taught that faith would lead to baptism, and the history of the Early Church affirms this truth. After Peter's sermon on the Day of Pentecost, "they that gladly received his word were baptized" (Acts 2:41). When the Samaritans "believed Philip preaching the things concerning the kingdom of God, and the name of Jesus Christ, they were baptized" (Acts 8:12). The Philippian jailer believed and was baptized in the same hour that Paul admonished him to believe (Acts 16:31-34). When Paul preached in Corinth, many people "believed, and were baptized" (Acts 18:8).

On many other occasions people were baptized when they heard and accepted the gospel (Acts 8:36-38; 9:18; 10:47-48; 16:14-15; 19:5). We conclude that water baptism is an act of faith—a faith response to God. True faith in God and His Word will cause the believer to submit to water baptism.

A Baptist scholar stated, "There is, indeed, much to be said for the contention, independently advocated by the theologians of various schools, that in the New Testament faith and baptism are viewed as inseparables whenever the subject of Christian initiation is under discussion. . .Baptism is. . .the divinely appointed rendezvous of grace for faith. It is. . .the indispensable external expression and crowning moment of the act of faith."[17]

Faith and the Holy Spirit

Faith also leads to receiving the gift of the Holy Ghost. Jesus said, "He that believeth on me, as the scripture hath said, out of his belly shall flow rivers of living water" (John 7:38). John explained that Jesus spoke of the Holy Ghost: "But this spake he of the Spirit, which they that believe on him should receive: for the Holy Ghost was not yet given; because that Jesus was not yet glorified" (John 7:39).

Peter taught that the gift, or baptism, of the Holy Ghost comes to all who believe on the Lord Jesus Christ. He identified Cornelius' experience as the Pentecostal Spirit baptism and asked, "Forasmuch then as God gave them the like gift as he did unto us, who believed on the Lord Jesus Christ; what was I, that I could withstand God?" (Acts 11:15-17). In other words, Peter identified "believing on the Lord Jesus Christ" with being baptized with the Spirit.

Paul also expected that believers would receive the Holy Ghost. When he found some disciples of John the Baptist at Ephesus he asked, "Have ye received the Holy Ghost since ye believed?" (Acts 19:2). The *New International Version* puts the question even stronger: "Did you receive the Holy Ghost when you believed?" Paul further taught in his epistles that we receive the Holy Spirit through faith: "That the blessing of Abraham might come on the Gentiles, through Jesus Christ; that we might receive the promise of the Spirit through faith" (Galatians 3:14). "In whom [Christ] also after that ye believed, ye were sealed with that Holy Spirit of promise'' (Ephesians 1:13).

The inescapable conclusion is that faith leads to receiving the Holy Ghost. In other words, the true believer will receive the Holy Ghost; his faith is shown to be genuine and complete when God grants him the gift of the Spirit.

Repentance, Water Baptism, and Works

Can repentance and water baptism be classified as works? They are not works in the sense of things man does to assist in earning his salvation, but they are saving works of God. Saving faith necessarily expresses itself through repentance, water baptism, and receiving the Spirit.

In himself man does not have power to turn from sin, but God leads him to repentance and grants power to repent. God works repentance in man, changing his mind and direction. Likewise, God remits sin at baptism. Without the work of God and faith in His work, baptism is a meaningless ritual. Finally, receiving the Holy Spirit is certainly not a work on man's part; the Spirit is a free gift of God that a person receives by faith.

Man's role in all of this is simply to believe the gospel, to seek repentance, to submit to water baptism, and to allow God to fill him with the Spirit. These elements are all part of the appropriation, response, commitment, reliance, and obedience that saving faith necessarily includes. This "faith response" on man's part does not earn or pay for salvation, but it is a necessary response for receiving salvation.

God offers salvation to all people freely on the basis of Christ's atonement, but only those who express faith in God receive salvation. Man either allows God to perform the work of salvation (by his faith and obedience) or he refuses to let Him work (by unbelief and disobedience). God calls a person, leads this person to Himself, changes the person's mind and direction (repentance), washes away his sins (at water baptism), baptizes him with His Spirit, keeps him in His grace, and empowers him for a holy life. This action on God's part constitutes His salvation of man in the present age.

Confession, Belief, and Salvation

Does this conclusion about saving faith contradict Romans 10:8-10? This passage reads, "The word is nigh thee, even in thy mouth, and in thy heart: that is, the word of faith, which we preach; that if thou shalt confess with thy mouth the Lord Jesus, and shalt believe in thine heart that God hath raised him from the dead, thou shalt be saved. For with the heart man believeth unto righteousness; and with the mouth confession is made unto salvation."

Some interpret this passage to mean that salvation comes automatically if one mentally assents that Jesus rose from the dead and verbally confesses that He is Lord. However, this interpretation contradicts the truth that saving faith includes appropriation and obedience. Under this view, many who do not even claim to be living for God would be saved. Even the devils would be saved, for they know Jesus is alive, confess Him verbally, and believe in one God (Matthew 8:29; James 2:19). Clearly, such a superficial understanding of Romans 10:8-10 is inadequate.

This becomes even more apparent as we continue reading Romans 10. Verse 13 says, "For whosoever shall call upon the name of the Lord shall be saved." Does this mean that everyone who verbalizes the name of Jesus is saved? Certainly not, or else the name of Jesus would be merely a magical formula. Moreover, verse 16 teaches that a lack of obedience indicates a lack of faith: "But they have not all obeyed the gospel. For Esaias saith, Lord, who hath believed our report?" Many will verbally confess Jesus as Lord and call on His name, but only those who actually do God's will shall be saved (Matthew 7:21-23). Despite one's verbal confession of faith, if he refuses to obey the gospel he does not have saving faith.

If this is so, what is the correct interpretation of Romans 10:8-10? First, we must realize that Paul was writing to Christians. His purpose was to remind them of how accessible salvation really is (verse 8). He did not have to explain the new birth in detail because his readers had already experienced it. He was simply reminding them that the foundation of salvation remains faith in Christ and the gospel and in public confession of this faith to the world in which they lived. A commentator on Romans noted that Paul in this passage referred to faith that brought us to a proper relationship with Christ and to confession as the means by which we maintain that relationship.

> "If we render 'salvation' by safety, we have perhaps the best equivalent. We receive righteousness through believing, and we realize that righteousness as 'safety' by continual confession of Christ as Lord. . .while believing in Christ brings man into a right relation to God, confession of faith maintains him in that right relation and keeps him continually safe until the final salvation."[18]

Second, we should read Deuteronomy 30:14, for this is the verse Paul quoted in Romans 10:8; "But the word is very nigh unto thee, in thy mouth, and in thy heart, that thou mayest do it." This verse demonstrates that confessing and believing necessarily includes obeying the Word of God.

Third, to "confess with thy mouth the Lord Jesus"

means to give a truthful, verbal confession that He is Lord. For this to be truthful, however, we must submit our lives to Him as Lord and be obedient to Him. When do we first confess Jesus as Lord? Verbal confession comes when we call His name at water baptism (Acts 22:16) and when we speak in tongues at the Spirit baptism (Acts 2:4). After all, no one can confess that Jesus is Lord except by the Holy Spirit (I Corinthians 12:3).

In the fullest sense of this passage, no one can truly confess Jesus as Lord of his life until he receives the Spirit and lives by the Spirit's power. Interestingly, F. F. Bruce in *The Tyndale New Testament Commentaries* also linked this passage in Romans 10 with I Corinthians 12:3. He also connected *confession* to water baptism: "If we are to think of one outstanding occasion for such a confession to be made, we should more probably think of that first confession. . .made in Christian baptism."[19]

Fourth, to believe in the heart that God has raised Christ from the dead means a true belief, which includes reliance. We must believe in the resurrection and rely upon this supernatural event for salvation. We rely on the resurrection to make Christ's atoning death effective (Romans 4:25) and to give us new life through the Spirit of the risen Christ (Romans 5:10; 6:4-5; 8:9-11). True belief in Christ's resurrection, therefore, will lead us to apply His atonement to our lives and then to receive His Spirit.

Calling on the Name of the Lord

When Romans 10:13 says, "Whosoever shall call upon the name of the Lord shall be saved," it means more than merely an oral invocation of the name Jesus. Otherwise, faith itself would not be necessary. Saving faith is more than oral confession of Christ, for that act alone is not enough. (See Matthew 7:21.) Obviously Romans 10:13 describes the sincere heart's cry of someone who belives on Jesus. Oral confession is a step in that direction, but living faith and obedience are required to validate this confession.

The main point of Romans 10:13 is not to give a formula for salvation but to teach that salvation is for all. The emphasis is on *whosoever.* Paul quoted this verse to support his statement that "there is no difference between the Jew and the Greek: for the same Lord over all is rich unto all that call upon him" (Romans 10:12). The quotation originally appears in Joel 2:32, which follows Joel's prophecy concerning the latter-day outpouring of the Spirit upon all flesh (Joel 2:28-29) and the latter-day judgment of God (verses 30-31). Joel 2:32 explains that *all* who call upon Jehovah will be delivered from this judgment.

Peter applied this prophecy to the outpouring of the Spirit at Pentecost (Acts 2:21). Furthermore, Ananias commanded Paul (the writer of Romans) to call on the name of the Lord at water baptism (Acts 22:16).

In summary, we draw two conclusions about "calling on the name of the Lord." First, it does not proclaim an "easy believism" but teaches that God's salvation is freely available to all who seek Him and call upon Him in faith. Second, if one truly calls on the Lord he will receive His Spirit and call on His name at baptism.

One Plan of Salvation

We believe that God has always made salvation available to mankind according to one plan, namely, by grace through faith based on the atoning death of Christ. God has dealt with man in various ways throughout the ages, but ultimately all His dealings rest upon this one plan. Although our age has seen the fulness of God's grace to the point that we can call it the age of grace (John 1:17), salvation in all ages has been a product of God's grace and not man's works. If man could have ever saved himself, he could still do so now, but God's Word declares he cannot.

Likewise, the principle of faith has become so clear in this age that we can call it the age of faith (Galatians 3:23-25), but God has always required faith. Abraham was justified by faith (Galatians 3:6). Even though some Jews thought their salvation rested in works of the law, keeping the law was never of any value without faith (Matthew 23:23; Romans 2:29; 4:11-16; 9:30-33).

Of course, faith has always included obedience. As part of faith in God, Abraham obeyed the command to leave his homeland, trusted in God's promises, and offered his son Isaac back to God (Romans 4:16-22; Hebrews 11:8-10, 17-18; James 2:20-24). As part of faith in God, the Jews adhered to God's law as revealed to Moses, including the system of blood sacrifices (Hebrews 11:28-29). As part of faith, we obey the gospel of Christ. All of this obedience was and is necessary, but salvation in every age has come through faith, not works.

Finally, salvation in every age has rested upon the atoning death of Christ. He was the only sacrifice that could ever remit sin (Hebrews 9:22; 10:1-18). Christ's death atoned for the sins of all ages. "God presented him as a sacrifice of atonement, through faith in his blood. He did this to demonstrate his justice, because in his forebearance he had left the sins committed beforehand unpunished"

(Romans 3:25, *NIV*).

The Old Testament saints were saved by faith in God's future plan of atonement, which they expressed (without fully comprehending it) by obedience to the sacrificial system God had ordained. The New Testament saints are saved by faith in God's past plan of atonement, which they express by obedience to the gospel of Jesus Christ. The Old Testament requirements of obedience, such as circumcision and blood sacrifice, were consistent with the principle of justification by faith, and the New Testament requirements of obedience, such as repentance and water baptism, are also consistent with justification by faith.

Saving Faith

Based on our discussion in this chapter, here is our definition of saving faith in our age. Saving faith is acceptance of the gospel of Jesus Christ as the sole means of our salvation and appropriation (application) of that gospel to our lives by obedience to its requirements. Saving faith *rests* in Jesus, His sacrificial death on the cross, His resurrection, and the teachings of His Word. Saving faith *expresses* itself in our obedience to Christ's gospel and by our identification with Him. It is a living faith that works.

The gospel of Jesus Christ is His death, burial, and resurrection (I Corinthians 15:1-4). We apply the gospel to our lives—we identify with Christ and His saving work—by repentance, water baptism in the name of Jesus, and receiving the gift of the Holy Ghost (Romans 6:3-5). No matter how we analyze it, saving faith finds expression through, leads to, produces, and includes these three elements.

An Analogy of Grace and Faith

Here is an analogy that may help to put what we have learned into perspective. Suppose David tells John, "Meet me at the bank tomorrow morning at 10:00 A.M. and I will give you $1,000." (This is a condition for receiving the gift.) If John really believes David, he will appear at the appointed place and time. (Faith necessarily produces trust, response, and reliance.) If John shows up, has he thereby earned the money? Of course not, because the money is a free gift. Yet his appearance is a necessary condition that must be met in order to receive the gift. (Grace on David's part, faith on John's part.) If John fails to show up, he will not receive the gift and the responsibility for the failure will fall totally upon him. (Lack of faith in the promise.)

Similarly, we must respond to God in faith by seeking repentance, remission of sins at water baptism, and the Spirit baptism. If we do, God will graciously grant our petition, and we will receive salvation totally as a free gift and not as an earned right. If we do not respond in obedience to God's Word, we will not receive salvation, and the blame will rest totally upon us.

Grace, Faith, and the New Birth

The doctrines of grace and faith do not eliminate the necessity of the new birth, but they explain how we experience it. The doctrine of grace teaches that the new birth is a free gift from God which we do not earn or deserve. The doctrine of faith teaches that we receive the new birth by relying totally and exclusively on Christ and

His gospel. Faith is the means by which we appropriate God's grace, yield to Him, and allow Him to perform His saving work in us.

Genuine faith in God always includes obedience to His Word. If we believe on Jesus, we will obey His commands to repent and to be baptized. If we have faith in Christ and His atoning death, He will remit our sins at water baptism; otherwise we simply get wet at baptism. If we believe on Jesus according to the Scriptures, He will fill us with His Spirit. After this, faith will keep the born-again believer in a continuing relationship with Christ that includes continued obedience and holiness of life through the power of the indwelling Spirit. In sum, the new birth experience is a free gift of God that we receive through faith in Jesus Christ.

FOOTNOTES

[1]David Hesselgrave, *Communicating Christ Cross-Culturally* (Grand Rapids: Zondervan, 1978), p. 106.

[2]Donald Bloesch, *Essentials of Evangelical Theology* (San Francisco: Harper & Row, 1978), II, 250, quoting Benjamin Warfield, "Justification by Faith—Out of Date?," *Present Truth,* Vol. 4, no. 4 (August 1975), p. 9.

[3]*Webster's,* p. 816.

[4]*The Amplified Bible* (Grand Rapids: Zondervan, 1965), publisher's foreword.

[5]W. E. Vine, *An Expository Dictionary of New Testament Words* (Old Tappan, N.J.: Fleming H. Revell, 1940), p. 118.

[6]*Ibid,* p. 411.

[7]*Ibid.*

[8]Charles Erdman, *The Epistle of Paul to the Romans* (Philadelphia: Westminster Press, 1966), p. 77.

[9]Bloesch, I, 207.

[10]*Ibid.*

[11]*Ibid,* p. 224.

[12]William Evans, *The Great Doctrines of the Bible* (Chicago: Moody Press, 1974), p. 145.

[13]Bruce Demarest, "How to Know the Living God," *Christianity Today,* March 18, 1983, p. 40.

[14]Lewis Smedes, *Union with Christ* (Grand Rapids: Eerdmans, 1983), p. 147.

[15]Dietrich Bonhoeffer, *The Cost of Discipleship,* 2nd ed., R. H. Fuller, trans. (New York: Macmillan, 1959), p. 69. Emphasis in original.

[16]Vine, pp. 625-26.

[17]G. R. Beasley-Murray, *Baptism in the New Testament* (Grand Rapids: Eerdmans, 1974), p. 272-74.

[18]W. H. Griffith Thomas, *St. Paul's Epistle to the Romans* (Grand Rapids: Eerdmans, 1974), p. 279.

[19]F. F. Bruce, *The Epistle of Paul to the Romans,* Vol. VI of *The Tyndale New Testament Commentaries* (Grand Rapids: Eerdmans, 1963), p. 205.

3

THE GOSPEL OF JESUS CHRIST

"Moreover, brethren, I declare unto you the gospel which I preached unto you. . .For I delivered unto you first of all that which I also received, how that Christ died for our sins according to the scriptures; And that he was buried, and that he rose again the third day according to the scriptures" (I Corinthians 15:1, 3-4).

What Is the Gospel?

The English word *gospel* means "good news" or "good message," and as such it is a correct translation of the original Greek word *euangelion.*[1] First Corinthians 15:1-4 gives us the basic biblical definition of the gospel—the death, burial, and resurrection of Jesus Christ.

Of course, for these historical facts to have meaning

today, it is essential to understand their doctrinal significance. Merely preaching the historical events without explaining their meaning does not convey what is good about the good news. The significance is that by these acts Christ purchased salvation and made it available to everyone who would believe on Him. He died for our sins, was buried, and rose again, thereby winning victory over sin and death and enabling us to have eternal life. W. E. Vine defines *gospel* as follows: "In the N. T. it denotes the good tidings of the Kingdom of God and of salvation through Christ, to be received by faith on the basis of His expiatory death, His burial, resurrection, and ascension."[2]

The good news, then, is that Christ's death, burial, and resurrection bring salvation to all who respond in faith. By definition saving faith includes the appropriation or application of the gospel to our lives.

In this chapter we will discuss the specific answer to these questions: How do we appropriate or apply the gospel to our lives? How do we respond to or obey the gospel? How do we identify personally with the gospel? Paul gave the answer to these questions in Romans 6:3-5, in which he explained how a person actually identifies with Christ's death, burial, and resurrection.

Death

First of all, we must identify with Christ's death. Just as Jesus Christ was crucified on the cross, so our "old man" must be crucified and put to death. The "old man" is not the ability to sin for this remains with the born-again believer. Nor does our experience of death with

Christ eradicate the carnal nature, for the Christian continues to war against his carnal nature (Galatians 5:16-17). What is put to death is the dominion and control that the sinful nature has over the unsaved (Romans 6:12-14). When we are saved, sin's and Satan's control over us is destroyed. Since the dominion of sin over us is lost in our death with Christ, we should treat sin itself as dead. Sin can no longer dictate to us or control us. We can overcome temptations and ignore sin's power. Although we can sin if we desire, we should not submit to sin but treat it as though it no longer exists.

Paul explained our freedom from sin's power to the Romans when he reminded them of what actually occurred when they were saved: "What shall we say then? Shall we continue in sin, that grace may abound? God forbid. How shall we, that are dead to sin, live any longer therein? . . .Knowing this, that our old man is crucified with him [Christ], that the body of sin might be destroyed, that henceforth we should not serve sin. For he that is dead is freed from sin. . . .Likewise reckon ye also yourselves to be dead indeed unto sin, but alive unto God through Jesus Christ our Lord. Let not sin therefore reign in your mortal body, that ye should obey it in the lusts thereof. . . .For sin shall not have dominion over you" (Romans 6:1-2, 6-7, 11-12, 14). Peter also mentioned our identification with Christ's death. Speaking of Christ, he wrote, "Who his own self bare our sins in his own body on the tree, that we, being dead to sins, should live unto righteousness" (I Peter 2:24).

A careful study will reveal that both Paul and Peter referred to a specific experience and a specific time at which death to sin occurred. The Greek wording in

Romans 6:2 indicates such specificity. This specification is clearly seen in the phrase "we are dead to sin" in the *KJV*, which is translated "we died to sin" in the *NIV* and "we who died to sin" in *TAB*.

When did this death to sin occur? An individual's death to sin, or the death of the old man, occurs when he repents from sin. This is apparent from the very definition of repentance, which is a turn away from sin and a turn to God. (See Chapter 5.) At repentance man confesses sin, decides to forsake it, turns his back on it, and refuses to accept its dominion. He dies to the lusts and desires of the old man, and decides to live for God. At that point, Christ's death on the cross becomes effective in his life to enable him to break the bondage of sin.

Of course, the decision to repent is not complete in itself, for it brings only limited, temporary power to turn from sin. The completion of the salvation process includes the burial of past sins that takes place at water baptism and the reception of power to remain victorious over sin through the Holy Ghost. Since to die with Christ does not eradicate the sinful nature in us, we must continue to kill the desires of the flesh (Romans 8:13) and die to self daily (I Corinthians 15:31); still, the turning point—the death of the old man—comes at repentance. We first apply the death of Jesus to our lives when we exercise enough faith to repent from our sins.

Burial

Next we identify with Christ's burial. Again, Paul explained how: "Know ye not, that so many of us as were baptized into Jesus Christ were baptized into his death?

Therefore we are buried with him by baptism into death" (Romans 6:3-4). Paul repeated this truth that Christians are "buried with him [Christ] in baptism" in Colossians 2:12. By water baptism, then, we identify with Christ when His body lay dead and buried in the grave.

This will become even more obvious when we study water baptism in Chapters 6 and 7. In our study we will find that water baptism is effective only after repentance, that immersion is the biblical mode, and that the name of Jesus is the biblical formula. Since baptism follows repentance, it actually does signify that the baptized person identifies with the dead state of the man Christ. Since baptism is a total submergence, it truly is a burial. Since baptism is done in the name of Jesus, it truly is an identification with Him. When a man receives water baptism, it signifies that he has died to sin and is burying that sin. When he emerges from baptism, his old lifestyle and his past sins are forever buried and forgotten. Water baptism, then, applies Christ's burial to our lives.

Resurrection

Paul also explained how we identify with Christ's resurrection: "Like as Christ was raised up from the dead by the glory of the Father, even so we also should walk in newness of life. For if we have been planted together in the likeness of his death, we shall be also in the likeness of his resurrection" (Romans 6:4-5). Some would limit this to future bodily resurrection and eternal life thereafter, but the focus is upon the new life in this present world. We should notice that Paul wrote, "Reckon ye also yourselves to be dead indeed unto sin, but alive unto God through Jesus Christ our Lord" (Romans 6:11).

The Holy Spirit is the Spirit of Christ (Romans 8:9), so when we receive the Spirit, Christ literally comes to live in us. The Holy Spirit brings into our lives the same power that resurrected Jesus from the dead (Romans 8:11). Those who walk after the Spirit have life in Christ (Romans 8:2). The "newness of life" in Romans 6:4 is none other than the "newness of spirit" in Romans 7:6. This "newness of spirit" is not just a renewal of the human spirit, but the indwelling of God's Spirit. It is "the new way of the Spirit" *(NIV),* or "the Spirit in newness of life" *(TAB).* The Spirit brings about a new birth (John 3:5) and will give new life (II Corinthians 3:6). Thus, the resurrection of Jesus Christ becomes effective to give us new life when we receive the Holy Spirit.

We will now analyze the messages of prominent New Testament preachers to see if their presentation of the gospel corresponds to I Corinthians 15 and Romans 6.

John the Baptist's Message

John's ministry was essentially one of preparation for the future arrival of the Messiah. His message was repentance and water baptism for the remission of sin: "John did baptize in the wilderness, and preach the baptism of repentance for the remission of sins" (Mark 1:4). "Bring forth therefore fruits worthy of repentance" (Luke 3:8). He also pointed to the baptism of the Spirit: "I indeed baptize you with water unto repentance: but he that cometh after me is mightier than I, whose shoes I am not worthy to bear: he shall baptize you with the Holy Ghost, and with fire" (Matthew 3:11). We can therefore discern three prominent elements of John's message: (1) repent, and show evidence of repentance; (2) after repentance, be baptized in water to signify your repentance; (3) look for the One who will baptize with the Holy Ghost and fire.

Christ's Message

The four Gospels record so many teachings of Jesus that we cannot reproduce them all here. However, let us identify His basic teachings and commands relative to salvation. Three such passages stand out because of the strong emphasis that Jesus Himself placed on them. One concerns His deity: "For if ye believe not that I am he, ye shall die in your sins" (John 8:24). The second is His comments to the Jews: "I tell you, Nay: but, except ye repent, ye shall all likewise perish" (Luke 13:3, 5). The third is His words to Nicodemus: "Except a man be born of water and of the Spirit, he cannot enter into the kingdom of God" (John 3:5).

The records in the Gospels of the last instructions of Jesus to His disciples before His ascension also deserve special attention. Matthew 28:19-20 records His commands and promises as follows: (1) go and teach all nations; (2) baptize them; (3) I will be with you always. This last statement is a reference to His abiding Spirit (John 14:16-18). Mark 16:15-18 records these elements: (1) go and preach the gospel to every creature; (2) he that believes and is baptized shall be saved; (3) numerous miraculous signs, including tongues, shall follow believers. This last promise is a reference to the power accompanying the Spirit baptism (Acts 1:8; 2:4). Luke's account of Christ's last words contains these basic points: (1) you are witnesses of my death and resurrection; (2) preach repentance and remission of sins among all nations (of course, remission of sins includes water baptism [Acts 2:38]); (3) wait until you receive power from on high, the promise of the Father, which is the baptism of the Holy Ghost (Luke 24:46-49; Acts 1:4-5). From the Gospels we can summarize Christ's commands relative to the experience of salvation as follows: (1) believe in His deity; (2) repent; (3) be born of water and the Spirit. This last command corresponds to His command to be baptized and to wait for the baptism of the Holy Ghost.

Peter's Message

Peter was the spokesman for the disciples and the Early Church on many occasions. When he confessed that Jesus was the Christ and the Son of God, Jesus gave him the keys of the kingdom of heaven as well as the power to bind and loose things in earth and heaven (Matthew 16:19). Jesus gave the power to bind and loose to all His disciples (Matthew 18:18), which is the power to receive answers in prayer (Matthew 18:19; John 14:12-14) and the power to extend salvation to others, the power which accompanies all preaching of the gospel.

The keys of the kingdom, however, refers to the power to open the kingdom of God to the world through preaching. By giving Peter the keys, Jesus acknowledged that Peter would possess the true salvation message. By this message, people could enter into the kingdom of God. The specific appointment of Peter apparently signified the vital role Peter would play in introducing the gospel to all classes of people. At Pentecost he preached the first sermon of the New Testament church and opened the door to the Jews (Acts 2:14-40). Then he was instrumental in helping the Samaritans (people of both Jewish and Gentile ancestry) to receive the Holy Ghost for the first time (Acts 8:14-17). Finally, he was the first to preach the gospel to the Gentiles (Acts 10:34-48). The Jews, Samaritans and Gentiles represented all races and nationalities of people.

What message did Peter use to open the door of the New Testament church to the Jews, Samaritans, and Gentiles? At Pentecost, he proclaimed, "Repent, and be baptized every one of you in the name of Jesus Christ for the remission of sins, and ye shall receive the gift of the Holy Ghost" (Acts 2:38). If a preacher today had the opportunity to preach the very first sermon to a group of people, would he preach this? If sinners under conviction asked him what they needed to do, would he answer in this way? Peter did.

In Acts 3:19 Peter preached, "Repent ye therefore, and be converted, that your sins may be blotted out, when the times of refreshing shall come from the presence of the Lord." The blotting out of sins includes water baptism (Acts 2:38; 22:16), and the times of refreshing refer to receiving the Holy Ghost with speaking in tongues (Isaiah 28:11-12).

In Acts 10, the Gentiles received the Holy Ghost while Peter was preaching to them. Afterward, he commanded them to be baptized in the name of Jesus (Acts 10:44-48). When he reported this to the Jewish Christians, they rejoiced that God had granted the Gentiles "repentance unto life" (Acts 11:16-18).

Philip the Evangelist's Message

Philip brought the gospel to the Samaritans. The Bible simply says Philip "preached Christ" and "the things concerning the kingdom of God, and the name of Jesus" (Acts 8:5, 12). His message included water baptism because when the people believed Philip's preaching they were baptized. Moreover, preaching Christ and the kingdom of God includes the baptism of the Spirit because the Samaritans specifically sought this gift and ultimately received it. Peter and John "prayed for them, that they might receive the Holy Ghost: (For as yet he was fallen upon none of them: only they were baptized in the name of the Lord Jesus.) Then laid they their hands on them, and they received the Holy Ghost" (Acts 8:15-17).

Ananias' Message

God used Ananias of Damascus to preach the gospel to Saul of Tarsus, who became known as the Apostle Paul. What did Ananias tell Paul to do? "The Lord, even Jesus, that appeared unto thee in the way as thou camest, hath sent me, that thou mightest receive thy sight, and be filled with the Holy Ghost" (Acts 9:17). "And now why tarriest thou? arise, and be baptized, and wash away thy sins, calling on the name of the Lord" (Acts 22:16).

Paul's Message

Paul adhered to the message he received from Ananias. When he met twelve disciples of John the Baptist and heard that they were "believers, questions: (1) "Have ye received the Holy Gho believed?" (Acts 19:2); (2) "Unto what then were y tized?" (Acts 19:3). Would a preacher today ask these tw questions if confronted with professing believers? Paul did. When he found out that they did not know that the Holy Ghost was given and were only baptized unto repentance, he rebaptized them in the name of Jesus (Acts 19:5). Then he laid hands upon them and they received the Holy Ghost (Acts 19:6).

In several of Paul's epistles he reminded his readers that they had been saved through repentance, water baptism in Jesus' name, and the infilling of the Holy Ghost, as he did in Romans 6:3-4. He told the Corinthians, "But ye are washed, but ye are sanctified, but ye are justified in the name of the Lord Jesus, and by the Spirit of our God" (I Corinthians 6:11). He described God's work in salvation as follows: "Not by works of righteousness which we have done, but according to his mercy he saved us, by the washing of regeneration, and renewing of the Holy Ghost" (Titus 3:5).

The Message of Hebrews

The Book of Hebrews does not identify its author, although tradition names Paul. Hebrews 6:1-2 lists the basic doctrines of the church. The writer desired for his readers to go beyond spiritual babyhood and learn more than these foundational doctrines: "Therefore let us leave the elementary teachings about Christ and go on to maturity, not laying again the foundation. . ." (Hebrews

6:1, *NIV*). In other words, the doctrines listed here are fundamental, foundational truths that even newborn Christians understand. Among the doctrines in this category are "repentance from dead works," "faith toward God," and "baptisms" (plural).

The Book of Hebrews also teaches that the Holy Ghost is a witness of the new covenant (Hebrews 10:15-16). A few verses later, we are admonished to draw near to God, "having our hearts sprinkled from an evil conscience, and our bodies washed with pure water" (Hebrews 10:22), a reference to our prior repentance and water baptism.

The Apostle John's Message

First John contains a significant reference to the salvation message: "Who is he that overcometh the world, but he that believeth that Jesus is the Son of God? This is he that came by water and blood, even Jesus Christ; not by water only, but by water and blood. And it is the Spirit that beareth witness, because the Spirit is truth. . .And there are three that bear witness, in earth, the Spirit, and the water, and the blood: and these three agree in one. . . .He that believeth on the Son of God hath the witness in himself" (I John 5:5-6, 8, 10).

John identified three inseparable elements that bear witness of salvation and agree (work together) in the one purpose of salvation—the Spirit, the water, and the blood. Those who believe on the Son of God will have this witness in themselves. In other words, the true believer will have Christ's blood applied to his life at baptism of water and the infilling of the Spirit.

The Gospel of New Testament Preachers

All the New Testament writers and preachers taught the same salvation message in answer to the question of what a person must do to be saved. The elements, excluding faith, in appropriating salvation are shown in the table below.

Preacher	Repentance	Water Baptism	Spirit Baptism
John the Baptist	Matthew 3:2, 8; Luke 3:8	Matthew 3:6; Mark 1:8; Luke 3:3	Matthew 3:11; Mark 1:8; Luke 3:16
Jesus Christ	Matthew 4:17; Mark 1:15; Luke 13:3-5	Matthew 28:19; Mark 16:16; John 3:5; 4:1	Luke 11:13; John 3:5; 7:38-39; 20:22; Acts 1:4-8
Peter	Acts 2:38; 3:19	Acts 2:38; 10:48	Acts 2:38; 11:15-17
Philip		Acts 8:12, 16	Acts 8:15-16
Ananias		Acts 22:16	Acts 9:17
Paul	Acts 17:30	Acts 19:3-5	Acts 19:2, 6
Author of Hebrews	Hebrews 6:1	Hebrews 6:1; 10:22	Hebrews 6:1; 10:15
John the Apostle		I John 5:8-10	I John 5:8-10

Passages Teaching Water and Spirit Baptism

Passage	Comments
Matthew 3:11	Words of John the Baptist.
Mark 1:8	Words of John the Baptist.
Mark 16:15-17	Words of Jesus. Spirit baptism implied by Acts 1:8; 2:4.
Luke 3:16	Words of John the Baptist.
Luke 24:46-49	Words of Jesus. Water baptism implied by Acts 2:38.
John 3:5	Words of Jesus. See Chapter 4 for full discussion.
Acts 1:4-8	Words of Jesus.
Acts 2:38	Words of Peter.
Acts 3:19	Words of Peter. Baptisms implied by Isaiah 28:11-12 and Acts 2:38.
Acts 8:15-17	Conversion of the Samaritans.
Acts 8:36-39	Conversion of the Ethiopian eunuch. Spirit baptism implied by Romans 14:17.
Acts 9:17-18	Conversion of Paul. See also Acts 22:16.
Acts 10:44-48	Conversion of Cornelius and other Gentiles.
Acts 11:15-18	Peter's report of Cornelius' conversion.
Acts 16:31-34	Conversion of the Philippian jailer. Spirit baptism implied by Acts 11:17 and Romans 14:17.
Acts 19:1-6	Conversion of John the Baptist's disciples.
Romans 6:3-4	Spirit baptism implied by Romans 7:6 and 8:9-11.
I Corinthians 6:11	Water baptism implied by Acts 22:16.
I Corinthians 10:1-2	Typology from the wilderness wanderings.
Titus 3:5	See Chapter 4 for full discussion.
Hebrews 6:1-2	Fundamental doctrines.
Hebrews 10:15-23	Spirit, sprinkling of heart (blood), water.
I John 5:8-10	Blood, water, and Spirit are inseparable.

The Gospel in Typology

Since we are living under the new covenant, we have

established the gospel message from Ne
passages. However, the Old Testament is a
to bring us to Christ (Galatians 3:24), and it con
types, shadows, and figures of our salvation (Colossians 2:17; Hebrews 10:1). Let us briefly mention some Old Testament foreshadowings of the New Testament gospel.

(1) The Israelites' deliverance from Egypt typifies our deliverance from the bondage of sin. We find three key elements in their deliverance: the blood of the Passover lamb, the water of the Red Sea, and the cloud of the Lord's presence that guided them (Exodus 12-14). God used blood to save them from the plague that persuaded Pharaoh to release the Israelites, just as Christ's blood saves us. God used water to destroy Pharaoh's armies but deliver the Israelites, just as He uses water baptism to destroy the power of sin but to deliver us. God used the cloud to represent His presence and guidance, which the baptism of the Spirit imparts to us today. Paul taught this typology, saying the Israelites "were all baptized unto Moses in the cloud and in the sea" (I Corinthians 10:1-2).

(2) Just before God gave Israel the Ten Commandments at Mount Sinai, He required them to sanctify themselves (set themselves apart to Him) and wash their clothes with water, after which He promised to come down and visit them (Exodus 19:10-11). Immediately after God gave the law, Moses ratified the covenant by sprinkling the people with blood and water (Hebrews 9:18-20). The old covenant was inaugurated by separation, blood, water, and the manifestation of God's presence.

(3) The Tabernacle in the Wilderness also typifies our salvation (Hebrews 9:8-9). The first piece of
the courtyard was an altar made of brass, us

sacrifices (Exodus 27:1-8; 40:6). The altar was a place of bloodshed and death. It points to the death of Jesus Christ, who became our supreme sacrifice for sin, and to our repentance, in which we die to sin and apply Christ's death to our lives.

The next piece of furniture in the courtyard was a laver or basin of brass, which contained water (Exodus 30:17-21; 40:7). This was a place of self-examination and washing. After the priest sacrificed on the altar, he washed himself clean of blood, ashes, and any other impurities. This points to water baptism, for after we die at repentance we proceed to water baptism to wash away our sins. Titus 3:5 speaks of "the washing of regeneration" or "the laver of regeneration" (Conybeare). Many see this as a typological reference to the Tabernacle laver.[3] Since many commentators agree that Titus 3:5 describes water baptism (Chapter 4), we can safely assume a linking of the laver as type and baptism as antitype.

The Tabernacle itself consisted of two rooms separated by a veil (Exodus 26:33-35), and no priest could enter therein until he had sacrificed at the altar and washed at the laver. The first room, or holy place, contained a golden lampstand, a table of holy bread ("bread of the presence" *NIV*), and an altar of incense (Exodus 25:23-40; 30:1-10). The lampstand signifies God's light in this world, which today comes by Christ through His people (John 8:12; Matthew 5:14). The holy bread signifies spiritual nourishment, which we find in Christ, who is the Bread of life, and in the Word of God (John 6:51; Luke 4:4). The altar of incense represents the prayers of God's people (Revelation 5:8; 8:3). The whole room, therefore, emphasized communication between God and His people.

The room behind the veil, the most holy place, contained the ark of the covenant, which in turn contained the Ten Commandments, a pot of manna, and the rod of Aaron (Exodus 25:10-22; Hebrews 9:1-5). The ark was the witness of the mutual agreement between God and Israel, with its contents symbolizing Israel's duty to God, God's provision for Israel, and God's power and delegated authority. The high priest came into this room once a year to sprinkle blood on the mercy seat (the lid of the ark) as an atonement for the sins of the nation (Hebrews 9:7). This room, then, represented the highest possible fellowship and communion with God under the Law (Exodus 25:22).

When Moses erected the Tabernacle, the priests offered blood sacrifices at the brazen altar and washed at the laver, after which a cloud covered the Tabernacle and the glory of God filled it (Exodus 40:17-35). Thereafter, God made known His abiding presence and guidance through a cloud by day and a pillar of fire by night that rested over the Tabernacle (Exodus 40:36-38).

The Tabernacle building, and especially the most holy place, points to the baptism of the Spirit. In our day God's abiding presence, His guidance, communication with Him, and communion with Him come through the Spirit (Romans 8). The Spirit is the seal, guarantee, and witness of the new covenant (Ephesians 1:13-14; Hebrews 10:15-16).

(4) The consecration of the priests required a blood sacrifice, the washing with water, and the anointing with oil (Exodus 29:1-7). Anointing with oil is symbolic of the anointing of the Spirit today. (Compare I John 2:20, 27 with John 14:16-17, 26.)

(5) When the Israelites sacrificed a bullock, sheep, or goat, the priest killed the animal, sprinkled its blood on the altar, washed it with water, and then burned it with fire (Leviticus 1:1-13). On Mt. Carmel Elijah saturated the blood sacrifice with twelve barrels of water, and God consumed it with fire from heaven (I Kings 18:33-39). Fire is another symbol of God's presence (Hebrews 12:29), particularly the work of the Holy Ghost (Matthew 3:11; Acts 2:3-4).

(6) One who was healed of leprosy was purified by a ceremony involving blood, water, and oil before he could join the congregation (Leviticus 14). After the priest sprinkled him seven times with the blood of a bird mixed with water, he (the healed leper) washed with water, and then the priest applied blood and oil to him and offered sacrifices. Before this, the leper was physically cut off from all contact with society including his own family. His existence was a kind of living death. Likewise, the sinner is cut off from God and His people; he is alive physically but dead spiritually until blood, water, and Spirit bring him into spiritual communion with God and the church.

(7) One who became ceremonially unclean (typifying sin) under the law of Moses went through a purification ceremony involving blood, water, and fire (Numbers 19). The priest killed a red heifer, sprinkled some of its blood before the Tabernacle, and burned the sacrifice with fire. Then someone mixed the ashes with water and applied this water of purification to the unclean person.

(8) God commanded the Israelites to war against the Midianites because they had caused many Israelites to sin (Numbers 31:1-18). Afterwards, He ordained this purification ceremony for the spoils of war and the warriors'

clothing: everything was to be washed with water and everything that could pass through fire was to be purged with fire as well (Numbers 31:21-24).

(9) In Noah's day God used water to destroy sin on earth and at the same time He saved His people. Peter taught this was a type of baptism (I Peter 3:20-21). God will purge the earth a second time before the creation of a new earth, but this time He will do it by fire (II Peter 3:5-7). Likewise, we are purged at the waters of baptism and by the fire of the Spirit before we become new creatures in Christ.

Saving Faith and the Gospel

Chapter 2 defined saving faith to mean acceptance of the gospel of Jesus as the sole means of our salvation and appropriation of that gospel to our lives. In this chapter we have learned that the gospel is Christ's death, burial, and resurrection. We appropriate or apply that gospel to our lives by repentance (death to sin), water baptism (burial), and the Spirit baptism (new life in Christ), thereby identifying personally with the redemptive work of Christ. We obey the gospel by fulfilling these commands. The Old Testament foreshadowed and all New Testament preachers proclaimed this one message.

As we study each component of this message in subsequent chapters, we will find that the gospel presents a comprehensive remedy for every consequence of man's sin. We can say with the Apostle Paul, "I am not ashamed of the gospel of Christ: for it is the power of God unto salvation to every one that believeth" (Romans 1:16).

FOOTNOTES

[1]Vine, p. 507.

[2]*Ibid.*

[3]Robert Laurin, "Typological Interpretation of the Old Testament," in Bernard Ramm et al, *Hermeneutics* (Grand Rapids: Baker, 1967).

4

BIRTH OF WATER AND SPIRIT

"Jesus answered, Verily, verily, I say unto thee, Except a man be born of water and of the Spirit, he cannot enter into the kingdom of God" (John 3:5).

The New Birth Doctrine

Jesus introduced the doctrine of the new birth in John 3:5. Many subsequent passages build on this teaching when they mention regeneration or new life in Christ. As discussed in Chapter 1, the new birth is the same as the past tense experience of salvation. In this New Testament church age, the new birth is an indispensible part of receiving eternal salvation.

When Nicodemus came to Jesus, the Lord told him, "Except a man be born again, he cannot see the kingdom of God" (John 3:3). The words Christ used here can also mean "born from above," but in this case the primary meaning is "born anew."[1] As W. E. Vine noted, "Nicodemus was not puzzled about birth from Heaven; what perplexed him was that a person must be born a second time."[2] Nicodemus asked Jesus how a man could enter into his mother's womb a second time and be born again. Jesus then explained that He meant the birth of water and Spirit, that is, not a second physical birth but an experience that would impart new life spiritually. Nicodemus did not understand this statement either, for he asked, "How can these things be?" (John 3:9). Jesus in turn expressed amazement that a religious scholar and leader like Nicodemus did not understand what He meant.

Christ's doctrine of the new birth should not have been totally strange to the Jews. He built upon the promise of Ezekiel 36:25-26: "Then will I sprinkle clean water upon you, and ye shall be clean: from all your filthiness, and from all your idols, will I cleanse you. A new heart also will I give you, and a new spirit will I put within you: and I will take away the stony heart out of your flesh, and I will give you an heart of flesh."

Since Jesus divided the new birth into two components in order to explain it, we will do the same here. We must bear in mind, however, that the new birth is a single experience consisting of two parts; one part is incomplete without the other. There is only one birth, not two.

Birth of Water

Theologians have propagated many theories about the meaning of this phrase, the most prominent interpretations being: (1) it refers to the natural birth, which is accompanied by a flow of watery amniotic fluid; (2) it is identical to the birth of the Spirit; (3) it refers to spiritual cleansing performed by the Word of God; (4) it is water baptism; not merely the human ceremony, but the work God performs when He remits sin at water baptism. Let us analyze each of these views.

Natural Birth?

This interpretation is extremely unlikely for several reasons: (1) It would be a very strange way to describe the natural birth, especially since this usage does not appear elsewhere in Scripture or in ordinary speech; (2) Jesus specifically informed Nicodemus that the new birth was a birth of water and Spirit, not a natural birth. A comparison of verses 3 and 5 shows that "born again" is equivalent to "born of water and of the Spirit"; (3) If birth of water means natural birth, then Jesus either told Nicodemus to do something he had already done or to do a physical impossibility. If this were the case, Nicodemus' questioning was valid, and Jesus would not have rebuked him; (4) It seems unnecessary to say we must be born into this world since everyone obviously has been; (5) If the birth of water is actually the natural birth, why did Jesus indicate that the new birth has two components? There may be a parallel between water in the natural birth and the new birth, but the context of John 3 establishes that the birth of water itself is not the natural birth.

Identical to Birth of Spirit?

According to this view, Jesus actually meant, "You

must be born of water, which is the Spirit." Of course, a few passages do liken the Spirit to water (John 4:14; 7:38). However, there are several difficulties if we try to apply this symbolism to John 3:5: (1) The natural, ordinary reading of the verse makes a distinction between water and Spirit, and all major translations preserve this distinction; (2) Many other passages indicate that water and Spirit are two separate aspects of the gospel message. (See Chapter 3.); (3) In his later writings, John preserved the distinction between water and Spirit as they relate to salvation. "And there are three that bear witness in earth, the Spirit, and the water, and the blood: and these three agree in one" (I John 5:8); If John 3:5 actually equates water and Spirit, John would not have separated the two so sharply in I John 5:8, especially since both verses deal with the same subject (salvation).

Cleansing by the Word?

This view depends heavily upon Ephesians 5:26, which says the church is sanctified and cleansed "with the washing of water by the word." However, this verse can cut both ways. If John 3:5 refers to baptism, then Ephesians 5:26 could refer to water baptism administered in accordance with the Word of God. At any rate, there is no necessary connection between the two passages; one does not necessarily provide an interpretation for the other.

F. F. Bruce stated that the phrase from Ephesians 5:26 could be rendered "cleansing it by water and word" or, as he further amplified it, "cleansing her by the washing of water accompanied by the spoken word."[3] He continued: "[T]he accompanying 'word' (Gk. *rhema*) is probably not here Holy Scripture but the word of confession or invocation spoken by the convert, as in Ananias' words to Paul: 'Rise and be baptized, and wash away your sins, *calling on his name'* (Acts 22:16)."[4]

There are several serious objections to the view that the water of John 3:5 is actually the Word. (1) It ignores the literal meaning of *water* and chooses a symbolic meaning with no support from the context. This in turn raises further issues. Why would Jesus choose such an obscure symbol when explaining such a vital subject? Why would He not explain this symbolism to Nicodemus upon further questioning? Why did He not symbolize the Spirit as well? Why would He describe one aspect of the new birth literally and another aspect symbolically?

(2) This symbolism occurs nowhere in the Old Testament or in the teachings of Jesus, so how could Jesus expect Nicodemus to understand it? Since the Word of God had never been symbolized by water in Nicodemus' day or before, why would Jesus reproach him for lack of understanding? As Dwight Pentecost observed, "To interpret water as only a symbol of the Word of God. . . would be to render our Lord's answer unintelligible to Nicodemus."[5]

(3) We should not resort to a symbolic interpretation when the context does not indicate one. This is especially true here, where context, grammar, and later usage all offer a good literal reading. (See next section.)

(4) Theologically speaking, it is more appropriate to describe the Word of God as the agent of conception rather than part of the new birth itself. "Being born again, not of corruptible seed, but of incorruptible, by the word

of God, which liveth and abideth for ever" (I Peter 1:23). "You have been regenerated—born again—not from a mortal origin (seed, sperm) but from one that is immortal by the ever living and lasting Word of God" (*TAB*). In one of Christ's parables, a farmer sowed seed on four types of ground, only one of which bore fruit (Luke 8:4-15). When Jesus interpreted the parable, He said, "The seed is the word of God" (Luke 8:11). The four types of ground represented four types of people. Although God tried to plant His Word in all four, only three had initial results and only one had lasting results. In short, the Word of God is the origin of salvation; it is the seed that will cause conception. However, the new birth itself consists of water and Spirit and occurs when we believe, obey, and apply the Word.

Water Baptism

We believe this last view is correct, namely, that the birth of water occurs when God remits sins at water baptism. Many theologians throughout church history have supported this interpretation, particularly the early church fathers and the early Lutherans.[6] There are many good reasons why we accept this view.

(1) This results from a straightforward, literal reading of the text. Baptism is the only significant use of water in the New Testament church, so if we interpret *water* literally it indicates water baptism. The Early Church commonly used *water* to mean water baptism. For example, Peter asked with respect to Cornelius and his household, "Can any man forbid water, that these should not be baptized?" (Acts 10:47). John himself later

used *water* in a literal way when he spoke of Spirit, water, and blood agreeing in the one purpose of salvation (I John 5:8); if the Spirit and blood are literal then water is literal. *The Pulpit Commentary* agrees that I John 5:6-8 refers to water baptism.[7] Baptist theologian Beasley-Murray has remarked that John 3:5 refers to water baptism: "At a time when the employment of water for cleansing in view of the last day had taken the specific form of baptism, it is difficult to take seriously any other reference than baptism."[8]

(2) The context of John 3:5 strongly suggests water baptism. John 1:25-34 and 3:23 speak of John the Baptist's ministry of baptism. John 3:22 and John 4:1-2 describe baptism administered by Christ's disciples on His authority. In this context, the most natural understanding of *water* is water baptism. This view is supported by *The Tyndale New Testament Commentaries:* "In light of the reference to the practice by Jesus of water baptism in verse 22, it is difficult to avoid construing the words *of water and of the Spirit* conjunctively, and regarding them as a description of Christian baptism, in which cleansing and endowment are both essential elements."[9]

(3) This is the one meaning Nicodemus could have been expected to understand. As a Jewish religious leader, Nicodemus was familiar with the ceremonial cleansings of the Old Testament as well as Jewish proselyte baptism. More importantly, he had the witness of John the Baptist, for all the Jewish religious leaders of the day were well acquainted with John's baptism (Luke 20:1-7). Both Jewish proselyte baptism and John's baptism were part of conversion and repentance, so Nicodemus should not have been puzzled when Jesus spoke of water as part of

making a new start for God. In fact, by this time Jesus may have already authorized His disciples to baptize, as recorded only a few verses later (John 3:22; 4:1-2).

(4) The birth of the Spirit means Spirit baptism (see later section); so grammatically speaking the birth of water must mean water baptism.

(5) There is only one baptism (Ephesians 4:5), yet the Bible clearly teaches both water baptism and Spirit baptism. We can reconcile this apparent contradiction by recognizing that water baptism and Spirit baptism are two parts of one whole, with one being incomplete without the other. Doctrinally speaking, if one is part of the new birth, the other must be also.

(6) God remits sins at water baptism. (See Chapter 6). Therefore, baptism must be part of the new birth, for how could there be a new, spiritual life until the old life of sin is erased? Until sin and its punishment are washed away there can be no eternal life in God's kingdom.

(7) Titus 3:5 is a companion verse to John 3:5, and it apparently refers to water baptism. "Not by works of righteousness which we have done, but according to his mercy he saved us, by the washing of regeneration, and renewing of the Holy Ghost." Regeneration simply means new birth, so here is a second passage linking water and Spirit with the new birth. The wording of this verse points strongly to water baptism rather than to the other alternatives. It describes a specific act of washing, distinct from the work of the Spirit.

Many translations emphasize the connotation of a specific act: "the laver of regeneration" (Conybeare), "the bathing of the new birth" (Rotherham), "the bath of regeneration" (Weymouth), and "the water of rebirth"

(*New English Bible*). This act of washing is a cleansing from sin, which brings to mind Ananias' instructions to Paul: "Arise, and be baptized, and wash away thy sins, calling on the name of the Lord" (Acts 22:16). Paul recounted the story in Acts 22 and wrote the words in Titus 3, so presumably he was aware of the parallel thought.

The conclusion is inescapable: "the washing of regeneration," which means "the new birth of water," is the washing away of sins at water baptism. Indeed, according to Bloesch, "Biblical scholars generally agree that the washing of regeneration refers to the rite of baptism."[10]

(8) Many other passages link water and Spirit baptism together in the salvation message (see Chapter 3) and emphasize the important role baptism plays in salvation (see Chapter 6).

Opponents of this view usually protest that it makes salvation dependent on water baptism, thereby negating salvation by grace and faith alone. Of course, without repentance from sin and faith in Christ's sacrifice, water baptism is valueless. There is no saving power in the water itself or in man's actions at water baptism. The birth of water is not the human act but God's act in remitting sin. Water baptism in and of itself is not a saving act, and the birth of water is totally dependent upon God's grace. Titus 3:5 demonstrates that one can give God all the credit for salvation and still emphasize the role of water baptism in the new birth.

Throughout salvation history God has always required obedience to His Word as a part of faith, and this does not contradict His plan of salvation by grace through faith. (See Chapter 2.) By identifying the birth of water as God's work in water baptism, we do not detract from His grace or His position as our only Savior.

A second objection is that the Old Testament saints were not baptized in water as we are today. However, neither did they receive the Spirit as we do (John 7:38-39). (See also Chapter 8). The Old Testament saints were not born again in the sense Jesus described and established for the New Testament church. (See later section.)

Birth of the Spirit

The birth of the Spirit is the operation of the Holy Spirit in man's salvation. This is the literal reading of John 3:5-8, and no one seriously disputes this. While there is agreement that the birth of the Spirit means receiving the Spirit of God to dwell in one's life, there is some difference of opinion as to whether this is identical to the baptism of the Spirit. Most Protestants equate receiving the Holy Spirit with the baptism of the Holy Spirit, although they usually reject the sign of speaking in tongues. Thus Bloesch stated, "We insist that the baptism of the Spirit must not be distinguished from the new birth."[11] Likewise, Adam Clarke equated the birth of the Spirit with the baptism of the Spirit.[12] In the New Testament church, the birth of the Spirit, the gift of the Spirit, receiving the Spirit, and the baptism of the Spirit are all one and the same, as we explain below.

(1) Jesus expected Nicodemus to understand what He meant about birth of the Spirit, undoubtedly on the basis of Old Testament prophecies concerning the Spirit's outpouring. (See Chapter 8.) In particular, Nicodemus should

have known about Joel's prophecy, which Peter applied to the baptism of the Spirit on the Day of Pentecost (Acts 2:16-18).

(2) John the Baptist explicitly promised the baptism of the Spirit (Mark 1:8). No doubt Nicodemus was acquainted with John's ministry and should have been expecting its fulfillment.

(3) The Book of Acts teaches that we receive the Spirit when we are baptized with the Spirit. Jesus told the disciples to wait for the promise of the Father, which He described as being "baptized with the Holy Ghost" (Acts 1:4-8). The disciples received this promise on the Day of Pentecost when they were "filled with the Holy Ghost" (Acts 2:4). Peter promised this same experience, which he called "the gift of the Holy Ghost," to the repentant onlookers that day (Acts 2:38-39). When Cornelius and his household received the very same experience, the Bible describes it in several ways: "the Holy Ghost fell on all them," on them "was poured out the gift of the Holy Ghost," and they "received the Holy Ghost" (Acts 10:44-48). Peter identified it as both the gift and the baptism of the Holy Ghost (Acts 11:15-17). In short, Acts equates all the descriptions of the Spirit's saving work with the baptism of the Holy Ghost. (See Chapter 8 for a table summarizing these findings.)

(4) Some say the birth of the Spirit refers to the indwelling of the Spirit without the Spirit baptism. However, it is a contradiction in terms to say the Spirit dwells in someone even though he has not received the Spirit. If the words mean anything, the indwelling of the Spirit must begin with receiving, being filled with, or being baptized with the Spirit.

(5) First Corinthians 12:13 demonstrates that the work of the Spirit in salvation is the baptism of the Spirit: "For by one Spirit are we all baptized into one body."

(6) Many other passages emphasize the need for the Spirit baptism and link it with water baptism as part of the salvation message. (See Chapter 3.)

The New Birth as a Whole

We must stress that the new birth is a single whole. One is either born again or not; there is no such thing as being half born. Although Jesus identified two components—water and Spirit—He nevertheless spoke of one new birth. The Spirit, water, and blood all agree in one (I John 5:8). There is only one baptism (Ephesians 4:5), comprised of both water and Spirit. The Scripture encompasses both water baptism and Spirit baptism when it teaches that we are buried with Christ in baptism to rise in newness of life (Romans 6:3-4), that we are baptized into Christ (Galatians 3:27), and that we receive spiritual circumcision by baptism (Colossians 2:11-13). Whatever repentance, water baptism, and the Spirit baptism accomplish individually, we must always remember that the total work of salvation is completed at the union of the three. We should never attach so much importance to one element that we deem the others to be unnecessary.

The Bible pattern is to experience all three—repentance, water baptism, and the gift of the Spirit (Acts 2:38). Even though the Samaritans had been baptized in Jesus' name, they still needed to receive the Spirit (Acts 8:15-17). Even though Cornelius had already received the

Spirit, Peter commanded him to be baptized in Jesus' name (Acts 10:44-48).

Ideally, all three should occur practically simultaneously or in rapid succession. Acts 2:38 promises that when people repent and are baptized they will receive the Holy Ghost without any wait between the three components.

In particular, if people will exercise faith they will receive the Holy Ghost as soon as they repent and are baptized. This is exactly what happened to the disciples of John at Ephesus (Acts 19:1-6). The Ethiopian eunuch and the Philippian jailer both received a joyous experience after they were baptized, which apparently was the baptism of the Spirit (Acts 8:36-39; 16:31-34). God has designed it so that the entire new birth process can occur at one time.

Comparison of First and Second Births

A comparison to the natural birth will illustrate the unity of the new birth. We can view each as a single event, but each is also a process consisting of several components. One writer has compared the two as follows:[13]

Natural Birth	New Birth
1. Conception.	1. Hearing of gospel; beginning of faith.
2. Baby leaves womb.	2. Water baptism.
3. Baby takes first breath.	3. Baptism of the Holy Ghost.

When Is the Blood Applied?

Since the new birth is a single, indivisible whole, we believe that the blood of Christ applies throughout the process. The blood is not a magical substance to be daubed on our souls. When the Bible speaks of the blood of Jesus, it simply means Christ's substitutionary death that satisfied God's justice and made God's mercy available to us. The blood of Jesus purchases our salvation. Without Christ's atonement we could not seek God, could not repent effectively, could not receive remission of sins at water baptism, nor could we receive the Holy Ghost. In other words, the substitutionary death of Jesus makes repentance, water baptism, and the Spirit baptism both available and effective.

Using the terminology of the blood, the blood is applied to our hearts at the first hearing of the gospel to enable us to seek God, at repentance to enable us to turn from sin to God, at water baptism to remit sin, and at the Spirit baptism to enable us to receive God's Spirit. After the new birth, we continue to live an overcoming, holy life by the power of the blood. Thus, the blood is applied not just at one point in time, but throughout the salvation process, from the first hearing of the Word until the return of Christ for His church.

Characteristics of Born-Again Believers

First John discusses the new birth from the point of view of those who have already experienced it. John did not write his epistle to teach sinners how to be saved but to teach baptized, Spirit-filled believers how to have present assurance in their born-again status and how to live as born-again Christians. Nothing in John's epistle revokes the need for birth of water and Spirit as recorded in John's gospel. First John gives us the following characteristics that the born-again person will exhibit if he obeys the leading of his regenerated nature.

The Born Again Believer...	Verses in I John
1. Confesses that Jesus came in the flesh.	4:2
2. Has love.	4:7
3. Confesses that Jesus is the Son of God.	4:15
4. Believes that Jesus is the Christ.	5:1
5. Overcomes the world.	5:4
6. Does not continue to commit sin.	3:9; 5:18
7. Keeps God's commandments.	3:24
8. Has the Holy Spirit.	3:24; 4:13
9. Has the witness of Spirit, water, blood.	5:8-10

Thus, the believer has been baptized in water and Spirit and applied Christ's blood. He has assurance of salvation as long as he continues to confess, love, believe, overcome sin and the world, and submit to God.

Old Testament Saints Were Not Born Again As We Are

The saints under the old covenant were not regenerated in the sense Jesus taught, for regeneration is a new covenant experience. As part of the new covenant God promised to write His law in the hearts of His people (Jeremiah 31:31-34) and give them a new spirit (Ezekiel 11:19). The old covenant revealed God's moral law but gave no spiritual power to rise above the sinful nature and fulfill the law (Romans 7:7-25; 8:3). Under the new covenant, however, God's people receive a new nature—the Spirit of God—which supercedes the law and imparts power over sin on a daily basis (Romans 8:2-4; Galatians 5:16-18). As a result, we now serve God in "newness of spirit" rather than in "oldness of the letter" (Romans 7:6).

Likewise, there was no permanent forgiveness of sin under the law, but only a deferral of sin to the future, ultimately to the death of Christ (Romans 3:25). Blood sacrifices had to be offered continually in order to roll the penalty of sin forward for a season, but Christ's sacrifice made remission of sin an eternal reality in the new covenant (Hebrews 10:1-18). Only under the new covenant can we receive permanent remission of sins immediately (Jeremiah 31:31-34; Hebrews 10:14-18).

To summarize, Old Testament saints were not born again in the New Testament sense because neither (1) permanent remission of sin nor (2) the new nature in the form of the permanently indwelling Spirit was available to them. This corresponds to the fact that neither (1) baptism in Jesus' name for the remission of sins nor (2) the baptism of the Holy Spirit existed in the Old Testament.

Conclusion

From our discussion in this chapter we conclude that to be born again means to be baptized with water and with the Holy Spirit. This exactly parallels our conclusion in the first three chapters of this book. Chapter 1 asked, "How can I be saved?" Chapter 2 asked, "What is saving faith?" Chapter 3 asked, "What is the gospel of Jesus Christ and how can I apply it to myself?" Chapter 4 asked, "What is the new birth?" In each case the answer has been the same.

From our study of four great concepts of Christianity—salvation, faith, the gospel, and the new birth—we find that the full gospel is repentance, water baptism in the name of Jesus, and receiving the baptism of the Holy Spirit.

FOOTNOTES

[1]Vine, p. 43.

[2]*Ibid.*

[3]F. F. Bruce, *Answers to Questions* (Exeter, U. K.: Paternoster Press, 1972), p. 108.

[4]*Ibid.* Emphasis in original.

[5]J. Dwight Pentecost. *The Words and Works of Jesus Christ* (Grand Rapids: Zondervan, 1981), p. 125.

[6]John Peter Lange, *Commentary on the Holy Scriptures* (Grand Rapids: Zondervan, 1960), IX, 126-27; *The Interpreter's Bible* (Nashville: Abingdon, 1956), VIII, 505.

[7]*The Pulpit Commentary,* XXII (I John), 140.

[8]Beasley-Murray, p. 228.

[9]R. V. G. Tasker, *The Gospel According to St. John,* Vol. IV of *The Tyndale New Testament Commentaries* (Grand Rapids: Eerdmans, 1960), p. 71.

[10]Bloesch, II, 12.

[11]*Ibid,* p. 22.

[12]Adam Clarke, *Commentary on the Bible,* abr. by Ralph Earle (Grand Rapids: Baker Book House, 1967), p. 904.

[13]Ralph Reynolds, *Truth Shall Triumph* (Hazelwood, Mo.: Word Aflame Press, 1965), p. 40.

5
REPENTANCE

"I tell you, Nay: but, except ye repent, ye shall all likewise perish" (Luke 13:3).

"Then Peter said unto them, Repent. . ." (Acts 2:38).

In Chapter 3 we described repentance as death to sin and the old nature. In Chapter 4 we explained that repentance is necessary for the new birth and that it must accompany the baptism of water and the gift of the Spirit (Acts 2:38). There must be a death before there can be a new birth. This confirms both our identification of repentance with death and our identification of the new birth with water and Spirit.

Repentance Defined

According to the *Webster's Dictionary,* to repent means "to turn from sin and dedicate oneself to the amendment of one's life; to feel regret or contrition; to change one's mind."[1] The Greek word is *metanoeo,* which literally means "to perceive afterwards" and "hence signifies to change one's mind or purpose."[2] In the New Testament, this word always indicates a change for the better.

Many theologians list three necessary aspects of repentance: an intellectual change (change of views), an emotional change (change of feelings), and a volitional change (voluntary change of purpose).[3] This corresponds with the Bible's injunction to love God with all the heart, soul, mind, and strength (Mark 12:30). Basically, then, repentance is a change of mind, heart, and direction.

Many Bible references affirm this. God chose Paul as a preacher to the Gentiles "to open their eyes, and to turn them from darkness to light, and from the power of Satan unto God" (Acts 26:18). Paul fulfilled this by preaching that everyone "should repent and turn to God, and do works meet for repentance" (Acts 26:20). One of the fundamental doctrines of the church is "repentance from dead works" (Hebrews 6:1). In the context of biblical preaching, then, repentance is a turn from sin and a turn to God.

In a broad sense, repentance can mean everything that occurs when man turns from sin and to God, including the baptism of water and the gift of the Spirit. For example, upon hearing that Cornelius and his household had received the Holy Ghost and been baptized in Jesus' name, the Jewish Christians "glorified God, saying, Then hath God also to the Gentiles granted repentance unto life" (Acts 11:18). Most passages, however, use the word in a more restricted way to mean the first step away from sin and to God, prior to baptism of water and the gift of the Spirit (Acts 2:38). This is the meaning we will use in this chapter.

In this sense, repentance is a radical transformation of mind, attitude, conviction and direction. It is a voluntary act of man in response to the call of God. It denotes an active turn, not just a feeling of regret or an apology. It is more than a moral resolution or reformation; it is a spiritual decision and a spiritual change.

Repentance is the first act of faith, and it includes several important elements: recognition of sin, confession of sin, contrition for sin, and a decision to forsake sin.

Of course, the word *repent* can have usages that do not pertain to salvation. Here are some examples. (1) God repented that He made man (Genesis 6:6). Here the word means sorrow, grief, or regret. (See *NIV* and *TAB*.) (2) God repented of the judgment He had planned for Nineveh (Jonah 3:10). God changed His plan because the Ninevites changed their wicked ways and turned to Him. (3) God promised never to repent of His decision to make the man Christ a priest after the order of Melchizedek (Psalm 110:4). He promised not to change His mind. (4) Esau carefully sought a place of repentance, but in vain (Hebrews 12:16-17). He unsuccessfully sought to change his father's mind about the birthright and the blessing given to Jacob (Genesis 27:34-38). None of these passages refer to salvation, but they demonstrate that repentance has application to other situations as well.

Recognition of Sin

Before someone can repent from sin he must first

realize he is a sinner. Jesus said, "I came not to call the righteous, but sinners to repentance" (Mark 2:17; Luke 5:32). All men have sinned, so Jesus actually came for the whole world. However, His statement points out that He will save only those who recognize their sins.

"Blessed are the poor in spirit: for theirs is the kingdom of heaven" (Matthew 5:3). All of us are spiritual paupers without God, but only those who recognize their poverty will seek God and find heavenly riches. Many morally good people and devoutly religious people find it difficult to repent and receive the Holy Spirit, because they do not recognize their great need and do not develop a sense of urgency. Repentance can take place only when man recognizes his sins and acknowledges his need of God.

Confession of Sin

Once someone realizes he is indeed a sinner he must confess it to God. God already knows everything, but He requires honest confession to self and to Him. "He that covereth his sins shall not prosper: but whoso confesseth and forsaketh them shall have mercy" (Proverbs 28:13). When people received John's "baptism of repentance," they went into the water "confessing their sins" (Mark 1:4-5). If one sins after conversion, confession is still part of repentance (I John 1:9).

We confess sins directly to God, for He is the only One who can forgive us of our sins (Isaiah 43:25; Mark 2:7). We do not need an earthly mediator because the man Jesus is our mediator and high priest (I Timothy 2:5; Hebrews 4:15-16). It is appropriate for someone to confess his repentance openly (Acts 19:18). Moreover, there are times to confess to one another, such as when we seek prayer on our behalf or when we have wronged someone and seek his forgiveness (Luke 17:3-4; James 5:16).

Confession should be as public as the sin. Confession does not necessarily mean listing every sin committed throughout life, although one should ask God to forgive all the sins he recalls. The essence of confession, however, is acknowledging to self and to God that one is a sinner, asking God for forgiveness, and asking God for help to overcome sin in the future.

Contrition for Sin

With confession, there must be contrition, which is a genuine sorrow for sins committed. The sinner must feel regret for wrongs done, and his heart must be broken over his sins. "The sacrifices of God are a broken spirit: a broken and a contrite heart, O God, thou wilt not despise" (Psalm 51:17). The sinner must feel in himself a taste of God's displeasure, not just a human sorrow or regret. "For godly sorrow worketh repentance to salvation not to be repented of: but the sorrow of the world worketh death" (II Corinthians 7:10).

Many people are sorry for their sins but have not genuinely repented. They regret sin's consequences but they fail to turn from sin. Sometimes sin places them in terrible situations and they are sorry they got caught in them. However, when given a chance to escape those situations, they will continue to live in sin.

Sometimes people cry at the altar because they feel

sorry for themselves and are upset about their predicament, but they are not willing to give their lives totally to God. These are examples of worldly sorrow, which cannot bring repentance. True repentance stems from godly sorrow, which will cause a person to be sorry for his sins, decide to change his sinful lifestyle, and have no regrets about making the change.

Decision to Forsake Sin

Proverbs 28:13 says we must both confess and forsake sin in order to obtain mercy. There must be an actual turning from sin and to God. Repentance is more than sorrow for sins; it also includes a determination to do something about those sins. Repentance is more than confession of sins; it also includes forsaking sins by the help of God.

John the Baptist emphasized this element of repentance. When the multitudes came to be baptized he said, "O generation of vipers, who hath warned you to flee from the wrath to come? Bring forth therefore fruits worthy of repentance" (Luke 3:7-8). He refused to baptize many who came to him until they first showed evidence of repentance. For him, repentance was much more than a mental decision; it was a spiritual decision that brought about a change of life. Like John, Paul preached that men should "repent and turn to God, and do works meet for repentance" (Acts 26:20). True repentance causes an actual change in one's actions.

This does not mean repentance requires a certain length of time in which to prove oneself to God. God knows instantly whether or not someone has made a genuine commitment to forsake sin, so repentance and receiving the Spirit can happen in a moment. Unfortunately, some later renege on this commitment, but at the time they received the Spirit they had truly decided to forsake sin.

Restitution

As part of forsaking sin, the truly repentant person will seek to correct the impact of his past sins upon others to the extent possible. This is called restitution. For example, if he has stolen money, he will repay it (Luke 19:8). If he has wronged others he will seek their forgiveness. If he has harmed someone by lying or gossiping, he will seek to repair the damage done and set the record straight.

Jesus taught, "If thou bring thy gift to the altar, and there rememberest that thy brother hath ought against thee; Leave there thy gift before the altar, and go thy way; first be reconciled to thy brother, and then come and offer thy gift" (Matthew 5:23-24). God's plan of forgiveness does not let man continue to enjoy the earthly benefits of his sin without restitution, nor does it eliminate the need to seek forgiveness from someone he has wronged.

Repentance and Emotion

Repentance will affect the emotional side of man, since it includes godly sorrow and remorse. It will usually bring tears and other physical demonstrations of this emotion. However, a show of emotion cannot substitute for repentance. Some people shed tears of self pity but not godly sorrow. Some respond to God's presence but stop short of full repentance. God often lets them feel His presence as a means of drawing them to repentance, but we must not mistake this feeling for repentance itself.

When someone repents, he will feel joy because he is being restored to fellowship with God. He will also find relief because he has made his decision and he no longer has to face sin alone. However, he should not let this joy and relief hinder him from going further, for God has much more for him. God wants to deal with his past sins permanently through water baptism, and God wants to give him the Holy Spirit. Some people stop when they feel the joy of repentance, but they are to proceed to water baptism, another joyful experience. Then in praising God, they will receive the Spirit.

Examples of Repentance

The parable of the prodigal son illustrates all the elements of repentance (Luke 15:11-32). In the story, the errant son came to a realization of his sin and his desperate condition: "He came to himself" (Luke 15:17). Then he made a decision to return home and seek forgiveness: "I will arise and go to my father, and will say unto him, Father, I have sinned against heaven, and before thee, and am no more worthy to be called thy son: make me as one of thy hired servants" (Luke 15:18-19). Finally, he actually left the place where he was, returned to his father's house, and confessed his sin with contrition (Luke 15:20-21).

Another parable shows the proper attitude in repenting (Luke 18:9-14). A Pharisee stood and prayed in the Temple, thanking God that he did not commit sins and boasting to God of his good works. A tax collector also came to pray. He approached God with humility, beating his breast in an emotional, heart-felt expression of contrition. He prayed, "God be merciful to me a sinner." Jesus condemned the self-righteous Pharisee but commended the honest, repentant tax collector.

David's prayer after his adultery with Bathsheba is a beautiful example for a child of God who has sinned, and the spirit of his prayer is characteristic of all true repentance. "Have mercy upon me, O God, according to thy lovingkindness: according unto the multitude of thy tender mercies blot out my transgressions. Wash me thoroughly from mine iniquity, and cleanse me from my sin. For I acknowledge my transgressions: and my sin is ever before me. Against thee, thee only, have I sinned, and done this evil in thy sight. . .Purge me with hyssop, and I shall be clean: wash me, and I shall be whiter than snow. . .Hide thy face from my sins, and blot out all mine iniquities. Create in me a clean heart, O God; and renew a right spirit within me. Cast me not away from thy presence; and take not thy holy spirit from me. Restore unto me the joy of thy salvation; and uphold me with thy free spirit" (Psalm 51:1-4, 7, 9-12).

The Source of Repentance

Repentance is part of salvation, so the opportunity

and ability to repent come from God's grace. The goodness of God leads men to repentance (Romans 2:4). Repentance unto life is a gift God provides (Acts 11:18; II Timothy 2:25). God alone can give the sorrow that brings repentance (II Corinthians 7:10). When someone repents, he simply responds to God's universal call and voluntarily accepts God's saving work.

Repentance does not earn salvation, but it qualifies one for, and begins the work of, salvation. Repentance, then, comes by God's grace through man's faith. Men come to repentance in situations that emphasize God's presence, His Word, and faith in Him.

The Spirit of God is absolutely necessary to lead men to repentance. Jesus said, "When he [the Holy Spirit] is come, he will reprove the world of sin, and of righteousness, and of judgment" (John 16:8). Psychological tricks and gimmicks will not produce true repentance; it takes the convicting power of God's Spirit.

Rather than emphasizing oratory, persuasive techniques, or scare tactics, we should concentrate on preparing a spiritual atmosphere. Verbal persuasion and warning have their place, but our foremost concern should be to let the Spirit have perfect liberty, for only God can draw men to Him (John 6:44).

The Word of God has power to bring men to repentance as the Spirit applies it to hearts. The preached Word brings men to a realization of their sins and their need for God. Peter's sermon on the Day of Pentecost brought conviction and a desire to repent: "Now when they heard this they were pricked in their heart, and said unto Peter and to the rest of the apostles, Men and brethren, what shall we do?" (Acts 2:37). Jonah's preaching brought the entire city of Nineveh to repentance. Again, our emphasis should not be on man-made ideas or techniques but upon the pure Word of God.

Ministers must preach against sin and define it so that the sinner will realize his sin. Nathan explicitly named David's sin, and John the Baptist named Herod's sin. John told the tax collectors, "Exact no more than that which is appointed you" and told the soldiers, "Do violence to no man, neither accuse any falsely; and be content with your wages" (Luke 3:12-14).

In our day there is too much generality in proclaiming the Word of God. Where the Word reveals sin, we must be specific. If we will preach the Word, God will apply it to individual hearts. The hearing of God's Word brings faith (Romans 10:17), and faith will cause man to obey the command to repent.

Repentance comes as a response to the drawing, convicting power of God's Spirit, to the hearing of God's Word, and to the impulse of an awakening faith in God. From God's point of view it is a gift to enable man to be saved; from man's point of view it is his first voluntary act of faith in God.

The Command to Repent

Repentance is absolutely necessary for salvation; the Bible commands everyone to repent. When Adam sinned, God questioned him and expected a confession (Genesis 3:9-13). In Noah's day, God destroyed all but eight souls because mankind would not repent. He spared the wicked city of Nineveh only because its inhabitants repented in response to Jonah's preaching. In Ezekiel, God entreated Israel to repent: "Therefore I will judge you, O house of Israel, every one according to his ways, saith the Lord GOD. Repent, and turn yourselves from all your transgressions; so iniquity shall not be your ruin. Cast away from you all your transgressions, whereby ye have transgressed and make you a new heart and a new spirit: for why will ye die, O house of Israel? For I have no pleasure in the death of him that dieth, saith the Lord GOD: wherefore turn yourselves, and live ye" (Ezekiel 18:30-32). "As I live, saith the Lord GOD, I have no pleasure in the death of the wicked; but that the wicked turn from his way and live: turn ye, turn ye from your evil ways; for why will ye die, O house of Israel?" (Ezekiel 33:11). These passages portray the compassion of God, the necessity of repentance, and the definition of repentance as a turn from sin to God.

John the Baptist preached repentance strongly (Matthew 3:1-11; Mark 1:4-5; Luke 3:3-9), and so did Jesus. Jesus proclaimed, "Repent: for the kingdom of heaven is at hand" (Matthew 4:17). "Repent ye, and believe the gospel" (Mark 1:15). "I tell you, Nay: but, except ye repent, ye shall all likewise perish" (Luke 13:3, 5). While Christ was on earth He sent His disciples to preach repentance Mark 6:12), and just before His ascension He again commissioned them to preach repentance (Luke 24:47). Peter preached repentance (Acts 2:38; 3:19), and so did Paul (Acts 26:20).

Paul told the Athenians, "And the times of this ignorance God winked at; but now commandeth all men every where to repent" (Acts 17:30). In Old Testament times, God did not hold the Gentiles accountable to every command in the Mosaic law because they were ignorant of it. However, God did judge them by the standard of conscience and natural law and found them guilty even on that basis (Romans 2:12-16). In New Testament times, Jews and Gentiles are on an equal basis; all hear the same call to repent. God is "not willing that any should perish, but that all should come to repentance" (II Peter 3:9).

What Happens at Repentance?

At the moment of repentance, man begins to let God work in his life. Man decides to turn away from sin to God, and he allows God to turn him. As part of the turn from sin, God enables man to break away from sinful habits and desires. As part of the turn to God, God allows man to start a personal relationship with Him.

From the time of Adam and Eve's sin, sin has separated man from God, for sinful man cannot have fellowship with a holy God. When man repents from sin, he can begin to have communion with God on the basis of Christ's substitutionary death. Repentance removes the barrier that sin erected and allows man and God to begin a personal relationship. Thus repentance qualifies a person for water baptism and the infilling of the Holy Spirit.

Relationship to Water and Spirit Baptism

As a first step toward God, repentance alone does not bring the full power of salvation, although it does bring positive emotional feelings and a limited, temporary strength to break away from sin. Both water baptism and Spirit baptism are necessary to complete the work that repentance begins.

Repentance and water baptism together complete the full work of forgiveness. At baptism God washes away sin by removing the eternal record and penalty of sin. (See Chapter 6.)

Some like to say that God forgives sin at repentance and remits sin at water baptism. This is a fairly good description based on the English wording in the *KJV*. However, the original text does not support a clear-cut distinction, for these two words, *forgive* and *remit,* come from only one Greek word, *aphesis.* (See Chapter 6.) Theologically speaking, then, forgiveness and remission are equivalent terms, and forgiveness (or remission) comes with the combination of repentance and water baptism. We should not separate the two experiences.

For purposes of study only, perhaps we can make the following distinction: at repentance, God destroys sin's present dominion in a person's life, and He removes the barrier preventing a personal relationship with Him. At water baptism, God removes the legal record of sin and erases the penalty for that sin, namely death. God deals with the present consequences of sin at repentance and with the future consequences of sin at water baptism. Both are necessary for forgiveness. Thus Peter said, "Repent, and be baptized every one of you in the name of Jesus Christ for the remission of sins" (Acts 2:38). (The *New International Version* is more emphatic: "Repent and be baptized, every one of you, in the name of Jesus Christ so that your sins may be forgiven.")

Repentance is also insufficient without the baptism

of the Holy Spirit. Repentance alone brings temporary, limited power over sin; permanent, unlimited power comes only after the baptism of the Spirit (Acts 1:8). Old Testament saints repented, but this did not give them a regenerated nature with permanent overcoming power. (See Chapter 8.) Neither the Law of Moses nor the human mind can give power over sin (Romans 7:15-25). Only the Spirit imparts power over sin and power to fulfill the righteousness that the Law taught but could not give (Romans 8:2-4). At repentance God gives the initial ability to break away from sin's hold, but the indwelling Spirit makes new life in Christ a daily reality (Romans 8:10, 13).

Jesus taught that when an unclean spirit leaves a man he goes elsewhere seeking rest (Luke 11:24-26). When he finds no other place to go, he returns to his former house (the man). If he finds it empty, swept, and garnished (put in order), he brings seven other devils with him and reenters the house. This story contains a principle relevant to our discussion. Namely, merely expelling evil is not enough; one must replace evil with good. Merely cleaning up one's life and putting it in order at one point in time is not enough; one must receive power to keep it that way.

The man who repents and goes no further will fall victim to an endless, frustrating cycle of repentance and failure, and eventually he will be worse off than ever before. This is a great problem in Christendom today. Many groups proclaim the need for repentance and morality but do not preach the baptism of the Spirit, which provides the power to make Christianity a success instead of a failure. The Spirit will fill the empty life, keep it clean, and resist the devil when he returns.

Guidelines for Altar Work

It is important that those who pray with seekers at the altar have a correct understanding of repentance. Below are some practical guidelines based on our discussion.

(1) We should emphasize the moving of God's Spirit, not gimmicks or techniques. Special phrases or motions cannot substitute for repentance.

(2) We should attempt to discern where the seeker is spiritually. If he has not fully repented, we should not prematurely force him to express joy and expect the Spirit. Once he has repented, then we can encourage him to praise God and believe for the Spirit.

(3) We can put ourselves in the seeker's position and pray with him. This will show him how to pray and will help us pray with a burden.

(4) If the seeker does not seem to be making progress, there may be several problems, each of which requires a different approach. The problem may be a failure to understand what repentance is, a refusal to surrender everything to God, a lack of desire (hunger, desperation, sense of urgency), a lack of godly sorrow, or a lack of faith.

(5) We must not try to teach him how to speak in tongues. This sign will come as the Spirit gives utterance. Instead of stressing only that he should yield his tongue to God, we should stress that he should surrender his whole mind and life to God. When the seeker yields everything to God, concentrates totally on Him, and exercises faith, he will be able to yield his tongue to God.

(6) Let us avoid distracting practices such as shaking the seeker, pounding him, forcing him to do certain

things, giving conflicting advice, or otherwise annoying him. People often repent and receive the Spirit in spite of, not because of, the altar workers.

If the seeker is sincere and ready to repent, he will receive the Spirit in a short time. If he does not, there is something lacking in his repentance or in his faith. In such a case, altar workers need to be spiritually sensitive and knowledgeable so they can help him overcome these difficulties.

Repentance and the Christian

If we sin after the new birth, we still have an avenue of forgiveness by confession of sin to Christ (I John 1:9; 2:1). There is no need to be baptized again, because there is only one baptism and it is effective for all sins repented of, whether committed before or after baptism. There is no limit to God's forgiveness in this life as long as we genuinely repent. God expects us to forgive the truly repentant without limit, and He will do no less for us (Matthew 18:21-22; Luke 17:3-4). The important thing is that we sincerely regret our sin and honestly determine to do better with God's help.

Of course, the first principle for a born-again believer is, "Do not sin" (I John 2:1). If we do sin, we should confess it, obtain forgiveness, and accept no condemnation (Romans 8:1). However, we should not always need to repent of the same things since the Spirit gives strength to overcome. Repentance is a fundamental doctrine, but we should not have to stay in this foundational stage all the time. "Therefore let us leave the elementary teachings about Christ and go on to maturity, not laying again the foundation of repentance from acts that lead to death. . ." (Hebrews 6:1, *NIV*). Repentance is always available to a Christian, but at some point he should mature to where the need to repent from sin becomes the exception rather than the rule.

The Need to Emphasize Repentance

Many churches have neglected the doctrine and practice of repentance today. If we expect the lost to be saved, we must preach and teach repentance with the anointing of the Spirit. Preachers must name sin and be specific in explaining repentance. Ministers must counsel those who wish to be baptized to make certain they have actually repented, for without repentance baptism becomes an empty symbol. Altar workers must first guide a seeker to repentance, for without true repentance there will never be a Spirit baptism.

Unscriptural methods do not bring the Spirit baptism. Old-fashioned repentance must take place first! Certainly, someone can and should receive the Holy Spirit quickly, without tarrying, but he must repent first. The Holy Spirit will not enter or dwell in a spiritually unclean temple (II Corinthians 6:17-7:1). It is impossible to turn to God without first turning away from sin.

Could it be that Christendom is filled with people who profess Christ but yet fail to repent? Could it be that many people seek blessings, miracles, and sensational experiences without repentance? Many public figures and celebrities claim to be born again, yet they continue to pate in unclean, unholy activities. But their claims and confessions are not valid. Somehow we must realize that without repentance and holiness all spiritual experiences are worthless.

Those who bypass repentance are substituting their plan for God's plan, just as Cain did when he offered vegetables instead of a blood sacrifice. They may enjoy temporary blessings, but like the man at the wedding feast who did not have his wedding garment, they will be cast out when the king comes (Matthew 22:11-14).

Some people seem to enjoy the blessings of God and yet live ungodly, unholy, worldly lives. Because God does not execute judgment speedily they think they have escaped (Ecclesiastes 8:11), not realizing that God extends goodness, longsuffering, and patience so they will have space to repent (Romans 2:4; II Peter 3:9). It is imperative to repent and live a repented life.

Conclusion

Repentance is a turn from sin and to God. It is the first response of faith to the call of God. Repentance includes recognition of sin, confession of sin, contrition for sin, and a decision to forsake sin. It is death to sin, and it opens up the possibility of a permanent relationship with God.

Repentance alone is not the complete work of salvation. Water baptism makes the turn from sin permanent by burying the old man, and the Spirit baptism makes the turn to God permanent by imparting a new nature with power to overcome sin daily. Without repentance water baptism is of no value, and without repentance one cannot receive the baptism of the Spirit.

If we desire to retain the Spirit of God in our lives, we must live a repented life. If we desire to see others saved, we must preach and teach true repentance.

FOOTNOTES

[1]*Webster's,* p. 1924.

[2]Vine, pp. 961-62.

[3]Henry Thiessen, *Lectures in Systematic Theology* (Grand Rapids: Eerdmans, 1979), p. 265.

6

WATER BAPTISM

"He that believeth and is baptized shall be saved" (Mark 16:16).

"Then Peter said unto them, Repent, and be baptized every one of you in the name of Jesus Christ for the remission of sins. . ." (Acts 2:38).

Water Baptism Defined

Christian water baptism is a ceremony in which one who has repented of his sins is immersed in water in the name of Jesus for the remission of those sins. It is an act of faith in Jesus Christ.

In this chapter we will study baptisms in the Bible, establish that God commands all followers of Christ to be baptized, and analyze each part of the definition given above.

John's Baptism

John the Baptist, whom God sent to prepare the way of the Lord, preached and administered the baptism of repentance for the remission of sins (Mark 1:2-4; Luke 3:3-4). He came baptizing in order to manifest Christ to Israel (John 1:31). His baptism was a transitory one designed to prepare the Jewish people for Christ's message and Christian baptism. John made no attempt to abolish the Jewish law, but he supplemented it, expecting his converts to live a repented, moral life as defined by the law and to wait for the One who would baptize them with the Holy Ghost. John's baptism was pre-Christian, for the New Testament church was not yet founded. (See Chapter 8.) In fact, John's disciples were rebaptized in Jesus' name after the Day of Pentecost (Acts 19:1-5).

John's baptism was for, of, or unto repentance. Apparently he used no baptismal formula, but he told the people, "I indeed baptize you with water unto repentance" (Matthew 3:11). His baptism both motivated and displayed repentance; his converts repented and confessed their sins at baptism (Matthew 3:6; Mark 1:5).

Since John's baptism was "for the remission of sins," did it confer remission? It could not confer absolute remission of sins, nor could it deal with future sins, for before Christ's atoning death all remission was conditioned upon that future event. Some people contend that John's baptism did confer conditional remission, but conditional remission was already available through the sacrificial system, which John made no attempt to replace. It seems that his baptism simply pointed to future remission that would come through Christ and Christian baptism. It was "unto" remission, a valid translation of the Greek word *eis*, which is usually rendered "for." Hastings' *Dictionary of the Bible* concurs in this view.[1]

The Baptism of Christ

Jesus Himself was baptized by John. Since Christ was without sin (Hebrews 4:15), we know He was not baptized to show repentance or in anticipation of remission of sins. Instead, He was baptized to manifest Himself to Israel as Messiah, the Baptizer with the Spirit, and the Son of God (John 1:31-34); and He submitted to baptism in order "to fulfill all righteousness" (Matthew 3:15). We can subdivide these purposes into several points:

(1) Christ was baptized to introduce Himself publicly and to inaugurate His ministry. Significantly, both water (baptism) and Spirit (in the form of a dove) were present on this occasion, foreshadowing the gospel message He was to teach in John 3:5.

(2) By this act, Christ sanctioned John's baptism and his message of repentance, water baptism, and Spirit baptism.

(3) Christ provided an example for us to follow. He did not need baptism for Himself, but He submitted to it for our benefit. If the sinless Christ was baptized, how much more should we? If we are to conform ourselves to Christ (Romans 8:29), we must follow His footsteps in baptism.

(4) Since Christ was baptized to fulfill all righteousness, He did not regard it as a mere ceremony or ritual. Throughout His ministry Christ emphasized moral purity rather than ceremonial purity and described

the many traditional washings of the Pharisees as unnecessary (Matthew 15:1-20; Mark 7:1-23). By contrast, He recognized baptism as having moral significance and as being necessary for us.

Early Baptism by the Disciples

During Christ's early ministry, His disciples baptized many converts upon His authority (John 3:22; 4:1-3). The Bible says very little about this and does not explain its purpose. Some writers state that this was baptism in Jesus' name while others believe that it was basically a continuation of John's baptism.[2] Proponents of the first theory often say it was a latent form of Christian baptism that became effective to remit sin after Christ's atonement. However, the latter view is probably correct, as Hastings' *Dictionary of the Bible* holds.[3] The following four reasons support this view: (1) This baptism is mentioned in conjunction with John's; (2) The disciples did not yet have a full understanding of the gospel message; (3) Christ was preaching John's message of repentance, the coming kingdom, and the coming Spirit baptism; (4) It is doubtful whether Christian baptism could have existed even in latent form before Christ died since it is an identification with His burial. However a person interprets these pre-Christian baptisms, it should be recognized that both John's baptism and the disciples' baptism were preparatory to Christian baptism and did not confer absolute remission of sins.

Christ's Command

Just before Jesus ascended into heaven He commanded His disciples to go into all the world, to preach the gospel, to make disciples, and to baptize them (Matthew 28:19). He expected all believers to be baptized, and He promised salvation to those who believed and were baptized (Mark 16:16). The Pharisees "rejected the counsel of God" by refusing John's baptism (Luke 7:30), and we will be guilty of the same if we refuse the Lord's baptism.

Early Christian Baptism

The church in the Book of Acts carried out the Lord's expectation and command regarding baptism. In the first sermon of the church, Peter commanded everyone to be baptized in the name of Jesus (Acts 2:38): "Then they that gladly received his word were baptized" (Acts 2:41). When the Samaritans believed the preaching of Philip they too were baptized in the name of Jesus (Acts 8:12, 16). The Ethiopian eunuch, Saul of Tarsus, Cornelius, Lydia of Thyatira, the Philippian jailer, the Corinthians, and John's disciples at Ephesus were all baptized when they heard and believed the preaching of the gospel (Acts 8:35-38; 9:18; 10:47-48; 16:15; 16:33; 18:8; 19:5). Even though Cornelius and his household had received the Holy Ghost, Peter "commanded them to be baptized in the name of the Lord" (Acts 10:47-48). Ananias commanded Paul to be baptized in the name of the Lord (Acts 22:16).

Baptismal Mode: Immersion

Baptism requires the literal use of water (John 3:23;

Acts 8:36; 10:47-48). The word *baptism* comes from the Greek word *bapto,* which means "to dip."[4] W. E. Vine defines baptism as "the processes of immersion, submersion and emergence."[5] Other words existed to indicate sprinkling, but God chose a word to indicate immersion.

Immersion is the only mode of baptism the Bible records. John baptized in the Jordan River (Mark 1:5, 9) and "in Aenon near to Salim, because there was much water there" (John 3:23). He needed springs and rivers large enough for immersion, not just the few drops of water sprinkling would have required. John immersed Jesus: "And Jesus, when he was baptized, went up straightway out of the water" (Matthew 3:16). "And straightway coming up out of the water, he saw the heavens opened" (Mark 1:10). Philip immersed the Ethiopian eunuch: "They went down both into the water, both Philip and the eunuch; and he baptized him. And when they were come up out of the water, the Spirit of the Lord caught away Philip" (Acts 8:38-39).

Paul described baptism as a burial with Christ (Romans 6:4; Colossians 2:12). These passages presume that baptism is by immersion and only make sense if the reader understands this. No one is buried by sprinkling or pouring a little dirt over the body, but only by complete submergence. Relative to Romans 6:4, *The Pulpit Commentary* states: "The reference. . .is to the form of baptism, viz. by immersion, which was understood to signify burial, and therefore death."[6]

Since Bible days, other modes of water baptism have arisen, notably sprinkling (aspersion) and pouring (affusion). However, the Bible itself never describes these methods. Some Old Testament purification ceremonies involved the sprinkling of water, but while they may foreshadow Christian baptism we cannot expect them to teach a precise mode of baptism. Several verses mention the sprinkling of the blood of Jesus, but these verses simply describe Christ's sacrifice in a metaphoric way to connect it with Old Testament blood sacrifices (Hebrews 9:13; 10:22; 11:28; 12:24). These verses do not literally refer to the mode of baptism, but they do show that the Bible could have used another word for baptism that definitely meant "to sprinkle" rather than "to immerse."

Historically, sprinkling and pouring arose as a matter of convenience. Immersion became especially inconvenient after the emergence of three nonbiblical baptismal practices: (1) infant baptism, (2) triple baptism by some trinitarians, and (3) postponement of baptism until the deathbed (in an attempt to live one's whole life in sin and still be saved).

Does the Baptismal Mode Matter?

A person should follow the biblical mode for many reasons.

(1) Baptism is a biblical command, so we should follow the biblical mode. In view of the importance the Bible places on water baptism, we should perform it exactly as the Bible describes it.

(2) Jesus was immersed as an example for us to follow. If He, who did not need baptism, submitted to immersion, how much more should we? If baptism is worth doing, it is worth doing the way Jesus and His apostles did it.

(3) Other modes of baptism come from nonbiblical tradition, and tradition is a poor substitute for biblical teaching. Jesus condemned tradition quite strongly when it caused a deviation from God's Word. He told the Pharisees, "Laying aside the commandment of God, ye hold the tradition of men" (Mark 7:8), and "Thus have ye made the commandment of God of none effect by your tradition" (Matthew 15:6).

(4) The only advantage sprinkling has is convenience, which is also a poor excuse for not following the Bible. What right have we to insist on a more convenient method than Jesus and the Early Church used? Certainly it would have been more convenient for John to have sprinkled the multitudes, for the apostles to have sprinkled 3000 at Pentecost, for Philip to have sprinkled the eunuch in the wilderness, and for Paul to have sprinkled the jailer at midnight; yet they chose to immerse. Why should we deviate from this pattern on grounds of convenience, especially since the baptismal practices which made sprinkling so popular are themselves nonbiblical?

(5) Immersion demonstrates obedience to God and respect for His Word. Why invent an arbitrary mode and try to justify it? Why debate whether various man-made alternatives would be acceptable? True respect for God and His Word will cause us to be content with the biblical mode; instead of ignoring or refusing it we will obey it.

(6) Only by immersion do we retain the significance of baptism as a burial with Christ.

Remission of Sins at Baptism

John preached "the baptism of repentance for the

remission of sins'' (Mark 1:4; Luke 3:3), pointing to the time when God would remit sins at Christian water baptism. Just prior to the first Christian baptismal service, Peter said, ''Repent, and be baptized every one of you in the name of Jesus Christ for the remission of sins'' (Acts 2:38). Remission denotes a release, wiping out, cancellation, or dismissal. At baptism, God releases, wipes out, cancels, and dismisses our sins.

Some disagree with this understanding, holding that baptism is performed because one has already obtained remission of sins. To them the word *for* in Acts 2:38 means ''because of'' or ''with a view towards.'' It seems clear, however, that *for* actually means ''to receive'' or ''in order to obtain.''

(1) This is the literal meaning one gathers from reading both the Greek and English texts. The *NIV* translates Acts 2:38 as, ''Peter replied, Repent and be baptized, every one of you, in the name of Jesus Christ so that your sins may be forgiven. . . .''

(2) The context leads to this interpretation. Guilty sinners asked, ''What shall we do?'' (Acts 2:37). Peter answered them by explaining what they needed to do to receive remission of sins, not by describing optional conduct. He did not mean, ''Repent and be baptized because you already have received remission of sins.''

(3) Matthew 26:28 records exactly the same Greek wording when Jesus said, ''For this is my blood of the new testament, which is shed for many for the remission of sins.'' Christ shed His blood so that we might obtain remission of sins, not because we already have it. The phrase can point to future remission of sins (as John and Jesus used it), but it never points back to remission

already obtained.

(4) Many other verses of Scripture describe the role of baptism in remitting sins.

Baptismal Regeneration?

At this point, we must emphasize that the Bible does not teach "baptismal regeneration," for the water and the ceremony do not have saving power in themselves. Water baptism is not a magical act; it is without spiritual value unless accompanied by conscious faith and repentance. Baptism is important only because God has ordained it to be so. God could have chosen to remit sin without baptism, but in the New Testament church He has chosen to do so at the moment of baptism. Our actions at baptism do not provide salvation or earn it from God; God alone remits sins based on Christ's atoning death. When we submit to water baptism according to God's plan, God honors our obedient faith and remits our sin.

Baptism—Part of the New Birth

Jesus said we must be born of water and the Spirit in order to enter the kingdom of God (John 3:5). We are saved by "the washing of regeneration, and renewing of the Holy Ghost" (Titus 3:5). (Chapter 4 explained that both verses refer to water baptism.) These verses place water baptism within the process of the new birth, but they do not teach baptismal regeneration. Jesus mentioned one new birth that includes both water and the Spirit.

Belief and Baptism Bring Salvation

Jesus said, "He that believeth and is baptized shall be saved; but he that believeth not shall be damned" (Mark 16:16). Jesus linked both belief and baptism together in the promise of salvation, showing that both are necessary. If we say baptism is not necessary, we amend the Lord's statement to say, "He that believeth and is [not] baptized shall be saved."

Jesus did not discuss the situation of one who "believed" but refused baptism, for that is a contradiction in terms. He knew that if someone did not believe he would not be baptized or that if he were baptized, his baptism without belief would be worthless. He knew a true believer would be baptized. By saying "He that believeth not shall be damned," Jesus implicitly covered the case of one who would refuse baptism.

Washing of Sins

Acts 22:16 says, "And now why tarriest thou? arise, and be baptized, and wash away thy sins, calling on the name of the Lord." God washes away sins at baptism when we call on His name. "But ye are washed, but ye are sanctified, but ye are justified in the name of the Lord Jesus, and by the Spirit of our God" (I Corinthians 6:11). Many commentators see this verse as another reference to the washing of sins that occurs when one is baptized in the name of the Lord Jesus.

Part of Salvation

Peter recalled that in Noah's day "eight souls were

saved by water" (I Peter 3:20). He continued, "The like figure whereunto even baptism doth also now save us (not the putting away of the filth of the flesh, but the answer of a good conscience toward God,) by the resurrection of Jesus Christ" (I Peter 3:21). Another translation may help to explain the meaning of this verse: "Eight in all, were saved through water, and this water symbolizes baptism that now saves you also—not the removal of dirt from the body but the pledge of a good conscience toward God. It saves you by the resurrection of Jesus Christ" (*NIV*). The Greek word translated as *answer* (*KJV*) or *pledge* (*NIV*) also means "inquiry" (*Strong's Exhaustive Concordance*) or "appeal" (W. E. Vine, *An Expository Dictionary*). Other versions of the Bible reflect the various meanings of *answer*: "an appeal to God for a clear conscience" (*RSV*); "the prayer for a clean conscience before God" (Moffat); and "the request unto God for a good conscience" (Rotherham).

The same flood waters that killed the people of Noah's day actually served as the instrument of salvation for the eight in the ark, for the ark floated on the water. They were saved through the water, which symbolizes the role of baptism today. Baptism has become a means of salvation for us, not because it washes dirt from our physical bodies but because it provides us with a good conscience before God. Since God washes away sins at baptism, it is a request or an appeal to Him to give us a conscience free from condemnation.

We should not suppose, however, that the waters of baptism possess saving virtue in themselves; water alone does not save a person just as the flood water alone did not save the eight. Salvation was found in the ark, and only those who obeyed God's plan to enter the ark were saved. In the same manner, obedience to God in water baptism places a person in a place of safety. In other words, baptism is the water through which we receive salvation, but Jesus Himself is the ark of salvation.

The Pulpit Commentary supports this explanation of I Peter 3:21: "The literal translation will be, 'Which (as) antitype is saving you also, (namely) baptism'; that is, the water which is saving you is the antitype of the water of the Flood."[7] It concludes, "Baptism doth save us, but not the mere outward ceremony. . . .The outward and visible sign doth not save if separated from the inward and spiritual grace. The first is necessary, for it is an outward sign appointed by Christ; but it will not save without the second."[8]

Burial with Christ

Paul taught that baptism was a burial with Christ (Romans 6:3-4; Colossians 2:12). The old man is buried at baptism. The old man is the unregenerate lifestyle, the record of past sins, and the dominion of sin. After baptism, we never have to face the record of our past sins again. With respect to Romans 6:3, F. F. Bruce stated in *The Tyndale New Testament Commentaries,* "From this and other references to baptism in Paul's writings, it is certain that he did not regard baptism as an 'optional extra' in the Christian life, and that he would not have contemplated the phenomenon of an 'unbaptized believer.' "[9]

Baptism into Christ

Paul also taught that we are baptized into Christ:

"For as many of you as have been baptized into Christ have put on Christ" (Galatians 3:27). We understand this to mean the one baptism of water and Spirit that places us into the body of Christ. Water baptism is necessary to identify us with Christ and to place us in His spiritual family.

Spiritual Circumcision

Paul compared baptism to circumcision in the Old Testament: "In whom [Christ] also ye are circumcised with the circumcision made without hands, in putting off the body of the sins of the flesh by the circumcision of Christ: Buried with him in baptism, wherein also ye are risen with him through the faith of the operation of God, who hath raised him from the dead. And you, being dead in your sins and the uncircumcision of your flesh, hath he quickened together with him, having forgiven you all trespasses" (Colossians 2:11-13).

This verse refers to water and Spirit baptism, which includes both burial of the old man and the resurrection of the new man in Christ. Water baptism is a spiritual circumcision that separates from sins, cuts away the control of the sinful nature, and results in forgiveness of sins. The Spirit baptism completes the circumcision process by imparting new spiritual life.

Old Testament circumcision was the means by which a male Jew became part of the Jewish religion and heir to God's promises to Abraham. God told Abraham, "This is my covenant, which ye shall keep, between me and you and thy seed after thee; Every man child among you shall be circumcised. . .And the uncircumcised man child. . .shall be cut off from his people; he hath broken my covenant" (Genesis 17:10, 14). Circumcision alone was valueless without a corresponding faith in God and obedience to His Word (Romans 2:25; 4:12). But God demanded that the Jews practice literal circumcision (Exodus 4:24-26; Joshua 5:2-9). An uncircumcised man could not participate in the Passover supper (Exodus 12:43-44). Likewise, at Christian baptism God cuts away a person's old sins and joins him to God's people. Without circumcision an Israelite male was not part of God's people; he was subject to the penalty of death and could not participate in God's salvation plan.

Baptism in Typology

In Chapter 3 and this chapter we have discussed the following typological references to water baptism: (1) the Red Sea crossing; (2) washing and sprinkling of Israel at the giving of the Law; (3) the laver in the Tabernacle courtyard; (4) washing of priests at their consecration; (5) washing of animal sacrifices; (6) washing and sprinkling of lepers who were healed; (7) washing of the ceremonially unclean; (8) washing of spoils of war and warriors' clothing; (9) Noah's flood; and (10) circumcision. Some additional examples are: (11) the Levites, who ministered before God, were consecrated by the sprinkling of the water of purification (Numbers 8:7); (12) on the Day of Atonement the high priest had to wash twice (Leviticus 16:4, 24); (13) Naaman the leper received healing after he dipped seven times in the Jordan River in obedience to Elisha's command (II Kings 5:10-14).

Naaman thought it beneath his dignity to dip in the

muddy Jordan, yet he did not receive his healing until he obeyed. His servants asked him, "If the prophet had bid thee do some great thing, wouldest thou not have done it? how much rather then, when he saith to thee, Wash, and be clean?" This principle applies to any of God's commands, including baptism. We should not question His plan or despise it, but obediently submit to water baptism and receive the spiritual cleansing God provides there.

A close look at some of these types indicates the role of baptism as a cleansing from sin. Before the priest could enter the Tabernacle he had to wash at the laver; otherwise God would strike him dead. God commanded, "They shall wash with water, that they die not" (Exodus 30:20). A ceremonially unclean person had to wash with water before he could become clean (Leviticus 15; 17:15-16; Numbers 19; compare Ezekiel 36:25). This was "the water of separation. . .a purification for sin" (Numbers 19:9) or the "water of cleansing. . .for purification from sin" (*NIV*). If the unclean person refused to wash in this manner, he continued to bear his iniquity (Leviticus 17:16). "That soul shall be cut off from Israel: because the water of separation was not sprinkled upon him, he shall be unclean; his uncleanness is yet upon him" (Numbers 19:13). "But the man that shall be unclean, and shall not purify himself, that soul shall be cut off from among the congregation, because he hath defiled the sanctuary of the LORD: the water of separation hath not been sprinkled upon him; he is unclean" (Numbers 19:20).

A close look at some of the types shows that blood was applied by means of water. This indicates that in water baptism, the blood of Christ is applied for remission of sins. After the giving of the Law at Mt. Sinai, Moses mixed blood and water and sprinkled it on the people (Hebrews 9:19). When cleansing an ex-leper, the priest mixed a bird's blood with water and sprinkled it on the person (Leviticus 14:1-7). In order to prepare the water of purification for an unclean person, the priest killed a red heifer and burned it as a sacrifice, with much of its blood still in it (Numbers 19:1-5). The ashes became equivalent to blood as a purifying agent (Hebrews 9:13) and were mixed with water to make the water of purification (Numbers 19:9). In all these cases, water was the means by which the atoning blood was applied.

More than a Public Confession

Those who do not believe sins are remitted at baptism hold that it is merely a public confession of faith, an announcement that sins have already been remitted, or a declaration of joining the visible church. However, many Bible accounts indicate that it is not primarily a public confession or a sign of a previous spiritual event.

The Ethiopian eunuch was baptized in the middle of the desert with no one to observe his baptism (Acts 8:26-39). The Philippian jailer was baptized around midnight by Paul and Silas who had just received a brutal scourging (Acts 16:25-33). If baptism was merely a public ceremony of no immediate necessity, surely they would have waited until Paul and Silas had recovered somewhat from their wounds, or at least until daylight. John's disciples had already been baptized once and had made a public confession, but Christian baptism was so important that Paul rebaptized them in the name of Jesus (Acts 19:1-5). Cornelius and his household had already received the Holy Ghost and had spoken in tongues as public evidence to all, yet Peter still commanded water baptism (Acts 10:47-48).

"Christ Sent Me Not to Baptize"

In an attempt to denigrate the importance of baptism, some quote Paul's statement, "Christ sent me not to baptize, but to preach the gospel" (I Corinthians 1:17). Just prior to this verse Paul reproved the Corinthians because they had formed factions, some claiming to follow Paul, some Apollos, some Cephas, and some Christ (I Corinthians 1:11-13). Paul expressed relief that he had personally baptized only a few of them. No one could accuse him of trying to start his own following or to baptize in his own name (I Corinthians 1:14-16). As far as Paul was concerned, others could have the honor of baptizing, but he had a special calling to preach. It did not matter who performed the ceremony, but only that the gospel be preached.

In this way, Paul emphasized to the Corinthians that salvation comes solely through Christ, not through great leaders. Instead of looking to the personalities who had preached and administered baptism to them, they needed to look to Jesus and His gospel. As Bruce noted in *The Tyndale New Testament Commentaries,* Paul's "references to baptism in I Cor. i. 14-17 do not mean that he regarded the sacrament itself as unimportant, but that the identity of the baptizer was unimportant. He takes it for granted that all the members of the Corinthian church were baptized."[10] Paul's correction of the Corinthians in no way detracted from the importance of baptism as part of the gospel, which he taught in many other passages.

The Human Element in Baptism

Some contend that baptism cannot be necessary because this would mean salvation by human works. We must understand that baptism is an act of faith; it is the occasion at which God has chosen to remit the sin of the repentant believer. With Martin Luther, we affirm both justification by faith and the essentiality of water baptism.

God frequently requires an observable faith response on man's part before He performs a spiritual work. The Old Testament requirements of circumcision, blood sacrifice, and purification ceremonies were consistent with justification by faith. Before Jesus turned water into wine He required the servants to fill the water pots (John 2:7). Before Jesus raised Lazarus from the dead He required the onlookers to roll the stone away (John 11:39). He could have performed these miracles without assistance, but He required a manifestation of faith and obedience.

Just because one man baptizes another does not mean man saves man. Man does not remit sin; God just uses him as an instrument to transmit the gospel. By the same principle God uses man's preaching to bring salvation (I Corinthians 1:18, 21), and no one will hear the salvation message without a preacher (Romans 10:13-17). When God arrested Paul on the road to Damascus, He did not reveal the plan of salvation to him, but He directed him to a preacher named Ananias (Acts 9). The angel of God did not preach to Cornelius but directed him to Peter for the salvation message (Acts 10). God uses humans to bring the message of salvation to others, and water baptism is simply another example of this fact.

If we can ignore the command to be baptized because it is a "work," then we can ignore the command to repent also. This would lead to the absurd view that one can be saved without repentance.

Forgiveness and Remission

Some people teach that forgiveness and remission are two distinct events, the former occurring at repentance and the latter at water baptism. According to this teaching, at repentance God accepts man's apology and restores him to a personal relationship, and at baptism God removes the record and penalty of past sins. This distinction has some basis in the definitions and *KJV* usage of the English words. For example, *Webster's Dictionary* defines *forgive* as "to cease to feel resentment against (an offender): Pardon" and it defines *remit* as "to release from the guilt or penalty of. . .to refrain from exacting. . .to cancel or refrain from inflicting."[11] Forgiveness conveys the idea of personal reconciliation, while remission connotes a legal settlement.

However, even in English, *forgive* and *remit* are often used interchangeably. *Webster's Dictionary* defines *pardon* as "to free from penalty. . .to remit the penalty or forgive."[12] More importantly, there is no distinction between *forgiveness* and *remission* in the Greek. There is only one Greek word, *aphesis,* which the *KJV* sometimes translates as "forgiveness" (Acts 5:31) and sometimes as "remission" (Acts 2:38). Most later translations, such as the *RSV* and *NIV,* use only *forgiveness* and not *remission. Strong's Exhaustive Concordance* defines *aphesis* as "freedom; (fig.) pardon." Vine's *Expository Dictionary* says it "denotes a dismissal, release" and defines the verb form, *aphiemi,* as "primarily, to send forth, send away. . .denotes besides its other meanings, to remit or forgive."[13]

The Old Testament associated forgiveness with an atoning sacrifice. Not only did the Israelite have to confess his sin to God and ask for pardon, but he also had to offer a blood sacrifice in order to receive forgiveness. The following passages explicitly define the condition that forgiveness depends upon a blood sacrifice: Leviticus 4:13-35; 5:7-18; 6:1-7; 19:22, Numbers 15:22-28, and Deuteronomy 21:1-8. At the dedication of the Temple, Solomon prayed that God would hear prayers offered there and forgive (I Kings 8:30-50; II Chronicles 6:21-39). He did not mean prayer instead of sacrifice, but prayer associated with the Temple sacrifices.

In other Old Testament passages God promised forgiveness if His people would repent (II Chronicles 7:14; Jeremiah 36:3), and His people often asked for forgiveness (Psalm 25:18; Daniel 9:19; Amos 7:2), but no verse repudiates the necessity of blood sacrifices offered sincerely and without hypocrisy. We can assume that the penitent cry was associated with the Temple sacrifices whenever possible. Hebrews 9:22 states, "Without shedding of blood is no remission." Although animal sacrifices did not provide forgiveness in themselves, they pointed to Christ; the Old Testament saints demonstrated faith by obedience to God's plan of blood sacrifices.

Many New Testament passages speak in general terms of the forgiveness one can obtain from God (Matthew 12:31-32; Mark 4:12; Luke 23:34; Romans 4:7), while others speak of forgiveness that man gives to man (Matthew 18:21; II Corinthians 2:10; 12:13). Many speak of forgiveness that believers can receive for sins committed after conversion (Matthew 6:12-15; Acts 8:22; James 5:15; I John 1:9; 2:1), in which case prior water baptism is assumed.

In the New Testament two individuals expressly received forgiveness apart from water baptism—the man with palsy and the woman who washed Christ's feet (Matthew 9:2-6; Luke 7:47-49). Both cases occurred during the transition from the old covenant to the new, before the founding of the New Testament church and before Christian baptism. Jesus expected those whom He forgave to follow the Law and wait for further revelation, but in no case did God grant forgiveness apart from obedience to His plan for that day. Even the repentant thief on the cross was saved under the old covenant, with Christ being both his high priest and his sacrifice.

The following table summarizes every occurrence of the Greek word *aphesis* in the New Testament:

Aphesis (Forgiveness/Remission) in the New Testament

Scripture	KJV wording	NIV wording	Context
Matthew 26:28	remission	forgiveness	through blood of Jesus
Mark 1:4	remission	forgiveness	baptism of repentance for *aphesis*
Mark 3:29	forgiveness	forgiveness	for blasphemy
Luke 1:77	remission	forgiveness	through Jesus
Luke 3:3	remission	forgiveness	baptism of repentance for *aphesis*
Luke 4:18a	deliverance	freedom	through Jesus
Luke 4:18b	liberty	release	through Jesus
Luke 24:47	remission	forgiveness	disciples to preach repentance and *aphesis*
Acts 2:38	remission	forgiveness	repentance and baptism for *aphesis*
Acts 5:31	forgiveness	forgiveness	Jesus gives repentance and *aphesis*
Acts 10:43	remission	forgiveness	believers receive *aphesis* through name of Jesus
Acts 13:38	forgiveness	forgiveness	through Jesus
Acts 26:18	forgiveness	forgiveness	after turning to God
Ephesians 1:7	forgiveness	forgiveness	through blood of Jesus
Colossians 1:14	forgiveness	forgiveness	through blood of Jesus
Hebrews 9:22	remission	forgiveness	blood necessary
Hebrews 10:18	remission	forgiveness	no other sacrifice needed

The table demonstrates that the following elements are part of New Testament forgiveness: the blood of

Jesus, faith, repentance, the name of Jesus, and water baptism. In the New Testament church we receive forgiveness by repentance and water baptism in the name of Jesus, both of which are made possible and effective by the blood of Jesus.

This explains an otherwise very difficult passage of Scripture. Jesus told His disciples, "Whose soever sins ye remit, they are remitted unto them; and whose soever sins ye retain, they are retained" (John 20:23). If forgiveness comes by confession alone, how could the apostles forgive sin? They could not take God's place as the forgiver, nor could they assume Christ's place as mediator, but those whom they baptized received remission of sins. The apostles could not arbitrarily refuse to baptize believers (Acts 10:47); all who accepted the apostles' baptism received remission of sins while those who rejected it did not.

Faith Is Necessary at Baptism

True faith in God and His Word will lead to water baptism. Without faith in God, baptism is meaningless. Without faith it is impossible to please God, and baptism is no exception (Hebrews 11:6). Baptism in Jesus' name is ineffective unless the candidate actually has faith in Jesus and the power represented by His name (Acts 10:43). Philip told the Ethiopian he had to believe in Jesus before he could be baptized (Acts 8:37). For God to remit sins at baptism, one must have faith in Jesus as Savior, looking to Him for forgiveness and not to the ceremony, the water, the works of the candidate, or the goodness of the administrator.

Repentance and Baptism Are Both Necessary

According to Acts 2:38 and other verses of Scripture, it takes both repentance and water baptism to receive the gift of forgiveness or remission: "Repent, and be baptized every one of you in the name of Jesus Christ for the remission of sins. . ." (Acts 2:38). We can say that God deals with the present consequences of sin at repentance and with the eternal consequences at baptism. (See Chapter 5.) Repentance does play a crucial role in receiving forgiveness, but rather than saying we receive complete forgiveness at repentance alone it is more biblical to speak of forgiveness after repentance and water baptism together.

Repentance should precede baptism. John preached repentance first, and his converts confessed their sins to God at baptism (Matthew 3:6; Mark 1:5). When people came to be baptized, he demanded that they first repent and show evidence of repentance (Matthew 3:8; Luke 3:8). Baptism is a burial of past sins, but for this burial to have meaning there must be a death to sin by repentance. For sins to be remitted at baptism there must be repentance from those sins.

Baptism without Prior Repentance

Since the Bible teaches repentance should precede baptism, a minister should carefully explain repentance to the baptismal candidate. If the candidate manifests a failure to repent, the minister could refuse baptism even as John did. Of course, he cannot demand a high level of spiritual maturity; that will take time and teaching to develop. Ultimately, each person must answer to God for himself, so the minister should usually respect a knowledgeable person's sincere statement that he has repented.

It is scriptural, however, for the minister to question the candidate as to his faith in Jesus Christ. Philip elicited a statement of faith from the Ethiopian eunuch before agreeing to baptize him (Acts 8:37), and the minister has the responsibility to receive such a confession prior to the baptismal act.

The Bible does not specifically state what to do when a person confesses that he did not repent until after his baptism. One option would be to rebaptize him, but the Bible does not teach this or record any rebaptisms for this reason. Since baptism is essentially an act of faith, it would appear that rebaptism is not necessary if the original baptism was motivated by faith in God and a sincere desire to live for Him. Faith and a desire for God indicate a measure of repentance. The validity of baptism depends upon faith, which involves an acknowledgement of sins and an acceptance of the Cross, not upon a complete list of sins a person has committed.

Here are some examples to demonstrate this position: (1) Infant baptism is not valid since the infant cannot exercise faith. The person should be rebaptized when he is older and after demonstrating understanding, faith, and repentance. (2) If an adult is baptized for social rather than spiritual reasons, he should be rebaptized after he possesses personal faith and after he experiences repentance. (3) When an adult sees his need of God and feels a desire to live for God, and is baptized, but he realizes later that he had not completely repented of his sinful lifestyle, there is no need for him to be rebaptized. Later he must repent of these sins and receive the Holy Ghost. He does not need to be rebaptized because his baptism was an act of faith in Christ. Although his baptism did not remit unrepented sins at the time, it became effective later as he repented. (4) A man repents, is baptized, and receives the Holy Ghost, but later he returns to a life of sin. When he repents of his backsliding, he does not need to be rebaptized because his baptism covers his subsequent sins when he repents.

In conclusion, one baptism is sufficient if done in the name of Jesus with faith in Him, but no sins (either before or after baptism) are remitted without repentance from those sins. Baptism's validity does not depend upon the faith, morality, or lack of either on the part of family, friends, or administrator, but rather on the candidate's repentance and faith in Christ.

Infant Baptism

As this discussion suggests, infant baptism is not valid and can never become valid later in life since infants do not have conscious faith. Some people suggest that God gives faith to infants to validate baptism. However, while God is the ultimate source of faith, man is responsible for using that faith and has the choice to do so or not. Saving faith is a conscious, voluntary response to God. The

Bible teaches baptism for believers only (Mark 16:16; Acts 8:37) and for the repentant only (Luke 3:8; Acts 2:38). Infants can neither believe nor repent, and the Bible records no examples of infant baptism.

Some people point to household conversions as evidence for infant baptism. For example, Lydia's household and the Philippian jailer's household were baptized (Acts 16:15; 31-33). However, Cornelius' household received the Holy Ghost and spoke in tongues (Acts 10:24, 44-46; 11:14-17), yet it is evident that infants did not speak in tongues. The household literally included domestic animals, but no one contends that animals were baptized. The Bible explicitly records that the jailer's whole house believed and that Crispus' whole house believed (Acts 16:34; 18:8), but any infants present did not have conscious faith. We must understand household baptism to include only those scripturally qualified for baptism—those old enough to repent, have faith, and be saved.

Some persons teach infant baptism on the grounds that infants were circumcised in the Old Testament. However, baptism is a spiritual and not physical circumcision and it involves a spiritual and not physical cleansing. Past sins and the old lifestyle are cut away, which necessitates conscious faith and repentance. Colossians 2:11-12, the passage that describes baptism as a spiritual circumcision, teaches that this spiritual work takes place through our faith in the working of God. Furthermore, circumcision typifies both water and Spirit baptism; the candidate for water baptism should be ready to receive the Spirit.

In the Old Testament God dealt in a special way with a nation that was physically identified and separated from the world. Today God deals on an individual basis rather than on a national basis; His chosen people are those who have been born again and spiritually separated from the world.

Baptism for the Dead

Baptism on behalf of dead people is not biblical. The dead cannot have saving faith, nor can they repent; it is too late for them: "It is appointed unto men once to die, but after this the judgment" (Hebrews 9:27). The Bible does not teach that souls can be saved after death, especially by actions taken by others on their behalf.

The practice of baptizing on behalf of dead people is based on a erroneous interpretation of I Corinthians 15:29. In I Corinthians 15, Paul taught the resurrection of Jesus and the future resurrection of the dead. As part of his argument, he asked, in essence, "If there is no resurrection why are some baptized for the dead?" There are several theories as to what Paul meant, but this verse does not teach or approve of baptism on behalf of the dead, especially since this would contradict the rest of Scripture.

Here are three possible explanations of the verse: (1) Paul referred to those who became converts as a result of the death of Christian loved ones. (2) He referred to baptism by proxy, not to condone it, but to use it as an example of belief in the resurrection. Perhaps some Corinthians taught against the resurrection, yet they baptized on behalf of the dead, and he pointed out their inconsistency. (3) He meant baptism into Christ's death. "The dead" probably does not mean Christ since the

Greek word is plural, but it may mean the old sinful selves that died in repentance. Baptism buries the dead ones with Christ so they can rise in newness of life as Christ did (Romans 6:3-5). Viewed this way, baptism is a confession of faith in Christ's resurrection, which is what Paul affirmed in this entire passage.

Sins after Baptism

As Christians, we can obtain forgiveness for sins committed after baptism (I John 2:1). God simply requires us to repent and confess our sins: "If we confess our sins, he is faithful and just to forgive us our sins, and to cleanse us from all unrighteousness" (I John 1:9). He does not require a second baptism; the original water baptism becomes effective with respect to subsequent sins when we confess those sins in repentance to God.

Why Did God Choose Baptism?

God is sovereign in His plans, and we have no right to question His choice of plans. Neither does our lack of understanding lessen our duty to obey. Nevertheless, we can understand some reasons why God designed water baptism and made it so important.

Water symbolizes death. Water causes great destruction and death through storms and floods, and a human being will drown after a few minutes of immersion in water. In Noah's day God used water to bring death to the entire unbelieving world.

Second, water is universally associated with washing and cleansing. For many reasons it is the most commonly used cleansing agent. It dissolves dirt, it is readily available, it can be used on almost anything without causing damage; as a liquid it is easy to use, and it can be applied with great force.

Finally, water symbolizes life itself. No plant, animal, or human life can exist without water. A man can survive for several weeks without food but for only several days without water. Water dissolves many substances, making it possible for the necessary chemical reactions to take place in the body. Approximately sixty percent of the human body is water, and about eighty percent of the blood is water.[14] Blood, which distributes oxygen and nutrients to every part of the body, could not flow without water in it; it would cease to be "the life of all flesh" (Leviticus 17:14). Even in the physical realm, water transports and applies life-giving blood to the body.

These three important truths about water make it uniquely suited to symbolize what happens at baptism. When we are submerged in the waters of baptism, God destroys, drowns, and buries the old man. During baptism, God applies Christ's life-giving blood to cleanse us from sin. When we emerge from the waters of baptism, we are ready for the new life in the Spirit.

Distinction Between Water and Spirit Baptism

Although water baptism and Spirit baptism combine to form one baptism, we must not equate the two events as some have done. Ideally, one will receive the Holy Spirit as he comes out of the water of baptism, but this does not always happen. There may be a lack of knowledge, faith, or repentance. The Samaritans are a good example (Acts 8:12-17). In other cases, people repent and receive the Holy Ghost before they are baptized in water. Cornelius is a good example of this (Acts 10:44-48). The Bible describes water and Spirit baptism as two distinct events even though they agree in one purpose.

Is Baptism Necessary?

Our answer to the necessity of baptism is in the affirmative. God could have chosen to remit sins apart from baptism, but His Word teaches that He has chosen to remit sins at baptism. The question is not what God could do but what He does. We do not question God's sovereignty, and we have no authority to teach remission of sins in this age apart from Christian baptism. The Bible does not discuss the possibility. We must avoid human speculation with respect to possible exceptions. Our task is to preach and practice baptism for the remission of sins. We know the Bible teaches us that God remits sins at baptism in the name of Jesus, and that is sufficient for our task.

The Significance of Water Baptism

Let us summarize what happens at water baptism.

(1) God remits sins at water baptism (Acts 2:38; 22:16). Sins are forgiven in the total sense of the word.

God's record of us as sinners is wiped out, and the penalty for sin—eternal spiritual death—is removed. Our sins are washed away—gone forever. Remission applies to all sins from which we repent, no matter when they are committed. Remission occurs only when the person baptized believes and repents, but the validity of baptism does not depend on the spiritual condition of anyone else (such as the administrator of baptism).

(2) Water baptism is part of the new birth. The baptized person is born of water, which simply refers to the spiritual work God performs in him (John 3:5; Titus 3:5).

(3) Baptism identifies us with the death and burial of Jesus (Romans 6:1-4; Colossians 2:12). It indicates that we died to sin by repentance and are burying not only our past sins, but also the "old man"—the dominion of sins and the sinful lifestyle.

(4) Water baptism is part of the one baptism of water and Spirit that places us into the body of Christ (Romans 6:3-4; Galatians 3:27). It is a personal identification with Jesus and part of our entrance into His family.

(5) Water baptism is part of our spiritual circumcision (Colossians 2:11-13). God performs spiritual surgery, cutting away the "old man" with its sins. Baptism denotes our new covenant relationship with Him.

This chapter has discussed the importance and necessity of water baptism. In the next chapter we will discuss the scriptural formula for water baptism, its significance, and its importance for us today.

FOOTNOTES

[1]"Baptism," *A Dictionary of the Bible* [hereinafter *ADB*], James Hastings, ed. (New York: Charles Scribner's Sons, 1898), I, 243.

[2]*Ibid,* pp. 240-41.
[3]*Ibid.*
[4]Vine, pp. 98-99.
[5]*Ibid,* p. 98.
[6]*The Pulpit Commentary,* XVIII (Romans), 156.
[7]*Ibid,* XXII (I Peter), 137.
[8]*Ibid.*
[9]F. F. Bruce, *The Tyndale New Testament Commentaries,* VI, 136.
[10]*Ibid,* n.1.
[11]*Webster's,* pp. 891, 1920.
[12]*Ibid,* p. 1640.
[13]Vine, pp. 462-63.
[14]Isaac Asimov, *The Human Body* (New York: The New American Library, Inc., 1963), pp. 180-81.

7

BAPTISMAL FORMULA: IN THE NAME OF JESUS

"Then Peter said unto them, Repent, and be baptized every one of you in the name of Jesus Christ for the remission of sins. . ." (Acts 2:38).

Christian baptism is to be administered "in the name of Jesus." This means to invoke the name Jesus orally at water baptism.

The Biblical Record

The Book of Acts contains five examples of baptism in the name of Jesus, while no biblical account mentions any other name or formula in connection with an actual baptism. Below are six indisputable references in the New

Testament to baptism in the name of Jesus.

(1) After the first sermon of the New Testament church, Peter commanded baptism "in the name of Jesus Christ" with the support of the rest of the apostles (Acts 2:14, 37-38). Those who accepted his message were baptized according to this commandment–that is, in the name of Jesus (Acts 2:41).

(2) After the Samaritans believed Philip's preaching concerning "the name of Jesus Christ," they were baptized "in the name of the Lord Jesus" (Acts 8:12, 16).

(3) After Cornelius and his fellow Gentiles received the Holy Ghost, Peter "commanded them to be baptized in the name of the Lord" (Acts 10:48). The most ancient Greek manuscripts contain the name "Jesus Christ" in this verse, as later translations indicate: "So he ordered that they be baptized in the name of Jesus Christ" (*NIV*); "And he ordered that they be baptized in the name of Jesus Christ, the Messiah" (*TAB*).

(4) When Paul met certain disciples of John the Baptist at Ephesus, he asked about their baptism. When he found out they had only received John's baptism, he baptized them again, this time "in the name of the Lord Jesus" (Acts 19:5).

(5) Paul himself was baptized in the name of Jesus, for Ananias told him, "Arise and be baptized, and wash away thy sins, calling on the name of the Lord" (Acts 22:16).

(6) In addition to these five accounts in Acts, I Corinthians shows that the Gentile believers in Corinth were baptized in Jesus' name. The church there was full of divisions, with various groups claiming to be followers of Paul, Peter, Apollos, or Christ. When Paul rebuked them for

their divisions, he asked, "Is Christ divided? was Paul crucified for you? or were ye baptized in the name of Paul?" (I Corinthians 1:13). The obvious answer to the last question is, "No, we were baptized in the name of Christ." Since the Corinthians were baptized in (literally, "into") the name of Christ, not Paul, they belonged to Christ, not Paul. Paul was saying this: Jesus died for the whole church and the whole church was baptized in His name, so the church should unite in following Him. If the Corinthians were not baptized in Jesus' name, Paul's argument makes no sense.

We conclude from these six passages that the apostolic church always baptized in Jesus' name. All believers—Jews, Samaritans, and Gentiles—received baptism in the name of Jesus.

Burial with Christ

Baptism is a burial with Christ, an identification with His death and burial (Romans 6:4; Colossians 2:12). Only Jesus died and was buried on our behalf, so baptism is administered in the name of Jesus.

Identification with Christ

Baptism is a personal identification with Jesus Christ, for we are baptized into Christ (Romans 6:3; Galatians 3:27). We are baptized in His name to identify ourselves personally with Him and to take on His name. To become part of the body of Christ, which is the church, we must take on Christ's name.

In the Old Testament God identified His Temple by investing His name in it (I Kings 8:29). In the New Testament the church is God's temple (I Corinthians 3:16-17), and it must bear His name. The saints of God in the Book of Revelation have His name written on them as a mark of identification (Revelation 3:12; 14:1; 22:4).

That the name serves to identify us with Jesus becomes even more apparent when we study the Greek word *eis*, which the *KJV* translates as "into" in Galatians 3:27. This word also appears in Acts 8:16, Acts 19:5, and I Corinthians 1:13. In these three verses the *KJV* translates the relevant phrase as "baptized in the name," but the *NIV* conveys its true meaning more strongly by translating it as "baptized into the name." W. E. Vine explained the significance of this phrase: It "would indicate that the baptized person was closely bound to, or became the property of, the one into whose Name he was baptized."[1] Another Protestant author wrote, "The Name stands for the person, authority, and power, so that baptism in the Name of the Lord Jesus is into citizenship or membership in His Person, authority, and power."[2] "To be baptized into the Name of Jesus means to be baptized into His Body, His Life, into citizenship and membership in His kingdom."[3]

Baptism identifies us with Jesus, and it is specifically baptism in His name that identifies us with Him, makes us His property, and places us into His body. We should not be reluctant to identify with the One who died for us, and to become His property by calling His name at baptism.

Taking on the Family Name

The Bible describes salvation both as a new birth and as an adoption. Viewed either way, we must take on the legal name of our new family. This occurs at baptism since it is part of the new birth and part of our identification with Christ.

A boy in the Old Testament officially received his name at circumcision (Luke 1:57-63; 2:21), and baptism is our spiritual circumcision (Colossians 2:11-12). Certain priests in the Old Testament were barred from the priesthood because they were not registered under their father's name and could not prove their geneology (Ezra 2:61-62). However, we can claim our priesthood and our spiritual inheritance when we become "registered" in our Father's name.

Jesus came in the Father's name, having received His name by inheritance (John 5:43; Hebrews 1:4), so Jesus is the name by which the Father has revealed Himself to us. The whole spiritual family of God has taken on the name of Jesus (Ephesians 3:14-15). Clearly, then, Jesus is the name we take at baptism. If we expect to become part of His family at baptism, we must take on His name.

Remission of Sins in the Name

Baptism is for the remission of sins (Acts 2:38), and the name of Jesus is vitally connected with remission of sins. Peter proclaimed this about the name of Jesus: "Neither is there salvation in any other: for there is none other name under heaven given among men, whereby we must be saved" (Acts 4:12). He also preached, "Through his name whosoever believeth in him shall receive remission of sins" (Acts 10:43) and "Whosoever shall call on the name of the Lord shall be saved" (Acts 2:21). Ananias specifically associated the name of Jesus with the washing of sins at baptism: "And now, why do you delay? Rise and be baptized and by calling upon His name wash away your sins" (Acts 22:16, *TAB*).

Power and Authority in the Name

One Protestant writer stated, "To invoke the Name. . .invoked aid and protection."[4] When we need a manifestation of God's power, we can invoke the name Jesus.

The invocation of a name also represents the authority behind that name; when a sheriff said, "Open, in the name of the law," he invoked the authority of the law as well as its power. When we call the name of Jesus we rely upon the power and authority of Jesus. Here are some examples: (1) Jesus said, "All power is given unto me in heaven and in earth. Go ye therefore, and teach all nations, baptizing them in the name. . ." (Matthew 28:18-19). (2) The Sanhedrin council asked Peter and John, in reference to the lame man's healing, "By what power, or by what name have ye done this?" (Acts 4:7). Peter answered, "By the name of Jesus Christ of Nazareth" (Acts 4:10). (3) The Lord promised, "If ye shall ask any thing in my name, I will do it" (John 14:14).

God makes all His power and authority available to us when we invoke His name in faith (Acts 3:6, 16). When we call the Lord's name at baptism we rely on His authority to perform the act and on His power for the spiritual work to be done.

Do All in the Name

"And whatsoever ye do in word or deed, do all in the name of the Lord Jesus, giving thanks to God and the Father by him" (Colossians 3:17). Baptism consists of both word and deed, so this verse applies. Of course, we do not orally utter the name Jesus before every statement or act in our lives. The verse primarily means to say or do everything with the power and authority of Jesus, as His representative, as His follower, and in dependence upon Him.

When it comes to specific spiritual acts that require the invocation of God's name, however, this verse applies literally. We pray, cast out devils, and lay hands on the sick in the name of Jesus, all by uttering His name, and water baptism should be no exception. One who lives by the spirit of Colossians 3:17 as Christ's representative and follower will certainly be baptized in His name.

Jesus Is the Highest Name

Baptism is an important spiritual act that requires the invocation of the Name of God. The highest, greatest, most powerful, and most self-revelatory name that God has ever made known to man is Jesus: "Wherefore God also hath highly exalted him, and given him a name which is above every name: That at the name of Jesus every knee should bow" (Philippians 2:9-10). For baptism we should certainly use the highest name. If we do not voluntarily accept the name of Jesus now, one day we will be forced to acknowledge the supremacy of this name anyway.

Acceptance of Jesus as Savior

One writer wrote, "The invocation of a Name was the invocation of one's lord. . . .To invoke the Name was to swear allegiance to one's king and Lord."[5] Baptism in the name of Jesus signifies acceptance of Him as Lord and Savior.

After Peter preached that Jesus was both Lord and Christ, he commanded baptism in His name (Acts 2:36-38). When his hearers accepted Christ's Lordship and Messianic role, they were baptized (Acts 2:41). When the Samaritans accepted Philip's preaching about Jesus, they were baptized in Jesus' name (Acts 8:12, 16).

The conversion of John's disciples is especially significant in this regard. Paul told them, "John verily baptized with the baptism of repentance, saying unto the people, that they should believe on him which should come after him, that is, on Christ Jesus. When they heard this, they were baptized in the name of the Lord Jesus" (Acts 19:4-5). By being rebaptized, this time in Jesus' name, they expressed faith in Jesus and recognized Him as Messiah, Lord, Savior, and the fulfillment of John's ministry.

Acceptance of Jesus as the Fulness of the Godhead

Baptism in Jesus' name also demonstrates faith that

all the fulness of the Godhead is in Jesus and that everything we need is in Him: "For in him dwelleth all the fulness of the Godhead bodily. And ye are complete in him" (Colossians 2:9-10). Paul associated this concept with water baptism, for only two verses later he said we are "buried with him in baptism" (Colossians 2:12). Not only do we recognize Jesus as our Savior, but we recognize Him as our God and our Savior (II Peter 1:1; Jude 25). We recognize Him as the only way of access to God (John 14:6-11). Baptism in the name of Jesus emphasizes the full deity of Jesus and His all-sufficient role in our salvation.

Not a Magic Formula

The name Jesus is not a magical formula; the sound waves reverberating from the spoken name do not remit sin or bring other special powers. However, when we call the name Jesus in faith, Jesus responds. The Name represents His presence and work. We must have personal faith in Jesus for the name to have any meaning and for anything to happen (Acts 3:16; 10:43).

The sons of Sceva could not cast out a devil even though they used the name Jesus, because they did not have a personal relationship with Him or faith in Him (Acts 19:14-17).

That the name of Jesus cannot be taken as a magical incantation does not detract from the need to invoke the name orally. Peter prayed for the lame man by saying, "In the name of Jesus Christ of Nazareth rise up and walk" (Acts 3:6). When the man walked, Peter explained, "And his name through faith in his name hath made this man strong" (Acts 3:16). It takes the name of Jesus called in faith. We cannot separate inner faith from obedience to God's Word. At baptism, when we invoke the name Jesus in faith as His Word commands, He comes and remits our sins.

Further Research

For further discussion of the significance of the name of Jesus, see Chapter 3 of *The Oneness of God* by David Bernard. For further discussion of the full deity of Jesus Christ, see Chapter 4 of the same book.

For All People

Numerous arguments have been put forth in an attempt to avoid the teaching of Scripture relative to baptism in the name of Jesus. For example, some argue that only Jewish Christians were baptized in the name of Jesus in order to emphasize their acceptance of Jesus as the Messiah. However, this ignores the plain teaching of Scripture. The Samaritans, who were of mixed Jewish and Gentile descent, received baptism in the name of Jesus. Cornelius, his kinsmen, and his friends, who were all Gentiles, were also baptized in the name of Jesus.

Cornelius was obviously not a Jewish proselyte (Acts 10:28, 45; 11:1-3, 18). Proselytes were present at Pentecost (Acts 2:10), and one of the seven deacons was a proselyte (Acts 6:5). The controversy surrounding Peter's visit to Cornelius would not have existed had Cornelius been a Jewish convert.

In any event, other Gentiles, such as the Corinthians, were baptized in Jesus' name. In short, every conceivable class of believers was baptized in the name of Jesus.

All such attempts to explain the use of two separate formulas for baptism are doomed to failure. There can be only one biblical form of Christian baptism. There cannot be one way to baptize certain groups of people and another way to baptize other groups, for God is no respecter of persons (Acts 10:34). There cannot be one way to baptize at one time in New Testament church history and another way for another time in church history. Nor can there be several different types of baptism at one time. There is only one baptism for the New Testament church.

Oral Invocation of the Name

Some contend that "baptism in the name of Jesus" means only in the authority and power of Jesus, and does not mean the name should be uttered orally as part of the baptismal formula. However, the following evidence shows that "in the name of Jesus" is the actual formula:

(1) Baptism in the name of Jesus does mean baptism with His power and authority, but the way to invoke His power and authority is to invoke His name in faith. The authority represented by a name is always invoked by actually using the proper name. All the discussion of power and authority cannot obscure one point: when we actually use a name at baptism it should be the name Jesus.

(2) The Bible reveals that the name Jesus was orally invoked at baptism. Acts 22:16 says, "And now why tar-

riest thou? arise, and be baptized, and wash away thy sins, calling on the name of the Lord." Here is a biblical command to call the Lord's name (Jesus) at baptism.

Some argue that in this verse only the baptismal candidate called the name of Jesus, not the administrator. This is debatable, but even so the name Jesus was orally invoked. In general, the baptizer normally invokes the name, but the candidate may also call on the name of Jesus as well, for baptism's validity depends on the candidate's faith, not on the baptizer's faith.

An oral calling did occur, for the Greek word rendered "calling" is *epikaleomai,* which means "to call over" or "to invoke."[6] This is the same word that describes Stephen's oral prayer to God: "And they stoned Stephen, calling upon God, and saying, Lord Jesus, receive my spirit" (Acts 7:59).

The same verb also appears in Acts 15:17: "the Gentiles, upon whom my name is called, saith the Lord," and in James 2:7: "Do not they blaspheme that worthy name by the which ye are called?" Both passages imply a specific time when the name of Jesus was invoked over believers, which occurred at water baptism. Other translations of James 2:7 are as follows: "[Do] not they blaspheme the good name called on you?" (*Interlinear Greek-English New Testament*); "Do not they defame the noble name which hath been invoked upon you?" (Rotherham); "Is it not they who slander and blaspheme that precious name by which you are distinguished and called [the name of Christ invoked in baptism]?" (*TAB*). Thus the Bible states in one verse and indicates in several others that the name of Jesus is to be orally invoked at baptism.

(3) The clear, common sense reading of the baptismal

passages leads one to believe that "in the name of Jesus" is the baptismal formula. That is the natural, literal reading, and a person must use questionable and twisted methods of biblical interpretation to deny that the words mean what they appear to mean. If this is not a formula, it is strange that it appears so many times as if it were a formula without any explanation to the contrary.

(4) In other situations, "in the name of Jesus" means orally uttering the name Jesus. Jesus told His disciples they would pray for the sick in His name (Mark 16:17-18), and James said we should pray for the sick "in the name of the Lord" (James 5:14). When Peter prayed for a lame man, he actually used the name, for he said, "In the name of Jesus Christ of Nazareth rise up and walk" (Acts 3:6). Then he explained that the man was healed "by the name of Jesus" (Acts 3:16; 4:10). In other words, when the Early Church prayed for the sick in the name of Jesus, they actually uttered the name Jesus. Likewise, when the Early Church baptized in the name of Jesus, they actually uttered the name Jesus as part of the baptismal formula.

(5) If "in the name of Jesus" does not represent a formula, then the Bible gives no formula for Christian baptism. The only other candidate for a baptismal formula would be the wording of Matthew 28:19. However, if "in the name of Jesus" does not teach a formula, then neither does "in the name of the Father, and of the Son, and of the Holy Ghost," for the grammatical structure is identical in both verses. If "in the name" means "by the authority of" without literally invoking a name, then neither verse gives a formula.

However, we do not believe Jesus left us without guidance on such an important subject. In Chapter 6, we demonstrated that water baptism is very important, so it is inconceivable that the Bible would not give adequate instructions as to its administration. If we do not have a formula, what distinguishes Christian baptism from heathen baptisms, Jewish proselyte baptism, or John's baptism? If there is no formula, or if the formula does not matter, why did Paul rebaptize John's disciples in the name of Jesus? No reputable scholar holds that baptismal formula is irrelevant or that the Bible gives no direction regarding a baptismal formula. Yet, if "in the name of" does not describe a formula, we have none.

(6) Theologians and church historians recognize that the Book of Acts does give the baptismal formula of the Early Church. The *Encyclopedia of Religion and Ethics* says with respect to baptism in the New Testament, "The formula used was 'in the name of the Lord Jesus Christ' or some synonymous phrase: there is no evidence for the use of the trine name."[7] The *Interpreter's Dictionary of the Bible* states, "The evidence of Acts 2:38; 10:48 (cf. 8:16; 19:5), supported by Galatians 3:27, Romans 6:3, suggests that baptism in early Christianity was administered, not in the three-fold name, but 'in the name of Jesus Christ' or 'in the name of the Lord Jesus.' "[8]

Some argue that "in the name of Jesus" is not a formula since the various baptismal accounts use different descriptive phrases, such as "in the name of Jesus Christ," "in the name of the Lord Jesus," and "in the name of the Lord." However, all these phrases are equivalent, for they all describe the same name, which is Jesus. *Lord* and *Christ* are simply titles that distinguish the Lord Jesus Christ from any others who might have the name Jesus, but the unique name of the Son of God is Jesus. Even Matthew 28:19 describes the baptismal formula as being in the name of Jesus.

Matthew 28:19

This verse records the words of Jesus just before His ascension: "Go ye therefore, and teach all nations, baptizing them in the name of the Father, and of the Son, and of the Holy Ghost." How do we reconcile this verse with all the later references to baptism in the name of Jesus, such as Acts 2:38? There are several views one could take.

First, one could say the two verses describe two different baptismal formulas. If so, they are contradictory. One must be right and the other wrong, for there can be only one form of Christian baptism. Since God's plan of salvation in the New Testament church age is the same for all people, there cannot be two contradictory baptismal formulas. Since the Bible is the inerrant Word of God, it does not contradict itself. If the Bible gives two formulas, which is correct? Which do we trust?

Matthew recorded Matthew 28:19 and also stood with Peter when he preached at Pentecost (Acts 2:14). The question, "Men and brethren, what shall we do?" was addressed to all the apostles (Acts 2:37). If Peter had given an incorrect answer, Matthew would have corrected him.

Some people say, "I would rather obey the words of Jesus than the words of Peter." However, they must not realize that Peter heard Jesus speak Matthew 28:19, that Matthew heard Peter speak Acts 2:38, and that only seven to ten days separated the two events. If Acts 2:38 contradicts Matthew 28:19, then the first spokesman of the church (Peter) was in doctrinal error, the other apostles (including Matthew) followed him in error, and we cannot trust anything the apostles preached or recorded. If that be the case, we might as well discard all the teachings of the New Testament.

A second solution is to say that Matthew 28:19 describes a formula while Acts 2:38 does not, or vice versa. This is unsatisfactory because the same words "in the name of" appear in both verses. If one does not describe a formula, neither does the other. We have already seen many reasons why Acts 2:38 does describe a formula.

A third answer is that neither Matthew 28:19 nor Acts 2:38 describes a formula, leaving us without any formula at all. This is very unlikely in light of the importance of baptism, the need to distinguish Christian baptism from other types of baptism, and the common sense reading of the passages in question.

This leaves only one remaining possibility: namely, that Matthew 28:19 and Acts 2:38 both describe the same baptismal formula. If true, this solution is very attractive because it will both give a formula and preserve the harmony of Scripture.

A basic biblical principle is that truth must be established by more than one witness (II Corinthians 13:1). Matthew 28:19 is the only verse in the Bible to use the baptismal phrase "in the name of the Father, and of the Son, and of the Holy Ghost," while many verses reiterate the baptismal phrase in Acts 2:38, "in the name of Jesus Christ." Apparently, Matthew 28:19 is the more indirect passage that we should harmonize and interpret in light of the others.

Comparison of the Great Commission Accounts

Matthew was not the only one who recorded the last words of Jesus to His disciples. Both Mark and Luke recorded the Lord's last instructions, albeit in somewhat different language. Below is a comparison of their accounts (Matthew 28:19-20; Mark 16:15-18; Luke 24:47-49; Acts 1:4-8).

The Great Commission

	Matthew	Mark	Luke
1.	Go, teach all nations	Go to whole world preach to everyone	Preach among all nations
2.	Baptize	Belief and baptism	Repentance and remission of sins
3.	In name of Father, Son, Holy Ghost	In my name	In his name
4.	I am with you always	Signs will follow	Wait for power from on high (the Spirit)

Matthew and Mark explicitly mention baptism. Since baptism is closely associated with remission of sin (Acts 2:38), Luke indirectly refers to it as well. Significantly, all three accounts describe a name. In each case, including Matthew, the name is singular. Mark and Luke both unquestionably describe the name Jesus. Apparently, Matthew 28:19 also describes the name Jesus.

The Singular Name

Matthew 28:19 describes only one name, for *name* is singular and not plural. (If one thinks this distinction is not significant, he should read Galatians 3:16 where Paul placed utmost importance on the singular in Genesis 22:18.) Matthew Henry recognized the significance of the singular here, for he wrote, "We are baptized not into the 'names' but into the name, of the Father, Son, and Spirit, which plainly intimates that these are one, and their name one."[9] Father, Son, and Holy Ghost are not proper names but descriptive titles. Even if they were proper names, this verse specifically describes only one name, not three. We must still ask what is the one proper name of the Father, Son, and Holy Ghost.

The Name of the Son

Without doubt the name of the Son is Jesus, for the angel told Joseph, "And she shall bring forth a son and thou shalt call his name JESUS" (Matthew 1:21).

The Name of the Father

Jesus said, "I am come in my Father's name" (John 5:43). He said to the Father, "I have manifested thy name. . .I have declared unto them thy name" (John 17:6, 26). The Old Testament predicted that the Messiah would declare God's name (Psalm 22:22; Hebrews 2:12). Jesus received His name by inheritance (Hebrews 1:4). What name did Jesus come in, manifest, declare, and receive by inheritance? Jesus. Therefore, the Father has revealed Himself to man through the name Jesus.

The Name of the Holy Ghost

Jesus said, "But the Comforter, which is the Holy Ghost, whom the Father will send in my name, he shall teach you all things" (John 14:26). The Spirit is given and revealed through the name Jesus.

The Context of Matthew 28:19

The context of Matthew 28:19 gives further confirmation that the singular name of the verse is Jesus. In verse 18 Jesus said, "All power is given unto me in heaven and in earth." Verse 19 continues, "Go ye therefore. . . ." Jesus did not mean, "I have all power; therefore, baptize in three different names (or in another name)." Rather, He was saying, "I have all power, so baptize in my name." A Baptist scholar has said, "A whole group of exegetes and critics have recognized that the opening declaration of Mt. 28:18 demands a Christological statement to follow it: 'All authority in heaven and on earth has been given to Me' leads us to expect as a consequence, 'Go and make disciples *unto Me* among all the nations, baptizing them in *My* name, teaching them to observe all *I* commanded you.' "[10]

Because of this, many scholars have even thought that there must have been an earlier Christological formula in verse 19 that was changed to a trinitarian one by early Christianity.[11] In support, they note that the church historian Eusebius, who lived in the 300's, often quoted verse 19 using the phrase "in my name."[12] (He did this many times before the Council of Nicea but never afterwards.) Some say Matthew or an early copyist paraphrased Christ's words or borrowed words from another context. Others hold that verse 19 describes the nature of baptism and was not originally interpreted as a baptismal formula.

The textual debate over Matthew 28:19 is interesting but not crucial, for by applying accepted principles of interpretation we find that the verse refers to baptism in the name of Jesus. While some scholars see that the context demands a Christological formula, due to their trinitarian preconceptions they fail to see that the existing wording does in fact describe the formula of baptism in the name of Jesus.

The explanation of Matthew 28:19 in *The Tyndale New Testament Commentaries* is very interesting in this regard: "It is often affirmed, that the words *in the name of the Father, and of the Son, and of the Holy Ghost* are not the *ipsissima verba* [exact words] of Jesus, but either the evangelist's words put into His mouth, or a later liturgical addition. . . .It may well be that the true explanation why the early Church did not at once administer baptism in the threefold name, is that the words of xxviii. 19 were not originally meant by our Lord as a baptismal formula. He was not giving instructions about the actual words to be used in the service of baptism, but, as has already been suggested, was indicating that the baptized person would by baptism pass into the possession of the Father, the Son, and the Holy Ghost."[13]

Jesus Is the New Testament Name of God

The meaning of Matthew 28:19 is very plain. The

singular name of the Father, Son, and Holy Ghost is Jesus. Father, Son, and Spirit are different titles for God. The one God is Father of all creation, has come in flesh in the Son, and abides in our hearts as the Holy Ghost. The one name that reveals all of these roles is Jesus.

The Old Testament predicted that God would be revealed by one name: "Therefore my people shall know my name" (Isaiah 52:6); "In that day shall there be one LORD, and his name one" (Zechariah 14:9). The name of Jesus is above every other name (Philippians 2:9-10), so it is not surprising that Matthew 28:19 refers to the name of Jesus.

One can analyze the verse as follows. Who is the Father, Son, and Holy Ghost? Of course, this describes God. What is God's name? In the Old Testament, Jehovah (or Yahweh) was the unique name by which God distinguished Himself from all other gods (Isaiah 42:8). This analysis led a Presbyterian professor to say, "The 'name' not 'names' of the Father and of the Son and of the Holy Spirit in which we are to be baptized, is to be understood as Jahweh, the name of the Triune God."[14] However, the supreme name of God in the New Testament is not Jehovah but Jesus. Jesus supercedes all other names and specifically includes Jehovah within its meaning, since Jesus literally means "Jehovah-Savior" or "Jehovah is Salvation."

In the Book of Revelation the servants of "God and the Lamb" shall have "his name" (singular) in their foreheads (Revelation 22:3-4). The name of the Lamb is Jesus, so the name of God is Jesus.

Many twentieth-century evangelicals have recognized at least partially the significance of Jesus' name. Essex

Kenyon held that Jesus was the revealed name of God in the New Testament and the family name of God.[15] He taught that using the name gives the Christian legal power of attorney in prayer and applies Christ's redemptive benefits in the present.

William Phillips Hall, President of the American Tract Society of New York, undertook a study of the name of God. In 1929 he published a booklet entitled *Remarkable Biblical Discovery or "The Name of God" According to the Scriptures.*[16] His conclusion: The Name of the Lord Jesus Christ is the full revelation of God and the apostles correctly understood and obeyed Matthew 28:19 by invoking this Name. Furthermore, the words of Matthew 28:19 "were never used in baptism by the original apostles, or by the Church during the early days of its existence" and "all baptisms of those early days were commanded to be, or stated to have been, performed in, or with the invocation of, the Name of Lord Jesus Christ."[17]

Conclusion About the Baptismal Formula

All biblical references to the baptismal formula, including Matthew 28:19, describe the name Jesus. To be biblical, a formula must include the name Jesus, not merely recite the Lord's verbal instructions. "I baptize you in the name of the Father, and of the Son, and of the Holy Ghost" or "I baptize you in the name of the Lord" or "I baptize you in His name" are all insufficient, because none of them actually use the name Jesus Christ commanded us to use. A correct formula would be, "I baptize you in the name of Jesus." It is also appropriate to add titles such as *Lord* or *Christ* to distinguish the Lord Jesus Christ from any others who have borne the name Jesus.

The Doctrine of the Trinity

In the face of these powerful points, the only practical reason why some insist on a formula that repeats the words of Matthew 28:19 (rather than actually using the name it describes) is their attempt to confess the doctrine of the trinity. We should note, for their benefit, that many trinitarians see the correctness of baptism in the name of Jesus. For example, the first leader of the twentieth-century Pentecostal movement, Charles Parham, baptized in the name of Jesus although he never explicitly denied trinitarianism.

In recent years, a prominent independent pastor named James Beall wrote a book on baptism called *Rise to Newness of Life,* which advocates baptism in Jesus' name while retaining trinitarian doctrine. See Chapter 10 for a list of other trinitarians today who baptize in Jesus' name. As already noted, many trinitarian scholars such as W. E. Vine, Matthew Henry, and James Buswell have recognized the significance of the singular in Matthew 28:19 although apparently not associating it with baptism in the name of Jesus.

We should also note in passing that there is no reason to use a trinitarian baptismal formula to uphold the erroneous doctrine of the trinity. The word *trinity* never appears in Scripture, and the Bible always emphasizes that God is one, not three. Furthermore, Jesus is the

Father (Isaiah 9:6), the Son (Matthew 1:21), and the Holy Ghost (II Corinthians 3:17-18). All the fulness of the Godhead dwells in Christ bodily (Colossians 2:9). Father, Son, and Holy Ghost are simply three different manifestations of the one God who came in flesh as Jesus. There is no reason, then, to insist on a trinitarian baptismal formula when the Bible does not teach the modern doctrine of trinitarianism. (For a full discussion of the biblical doctrine of one God and the doctrine of the trinity, see *The Oneness of God* by David Bernard. Especially see Chapter 6 of that book for an explanation of the biblical meanings of the terms *Father, Son,* and *Holy Ghost.*)

Matthew 28:19 Teaches Baptism in the Name of Jesus

In summary, below are nine reasons why Matthew 28:19 refers to the name of Jesus in baptism.

(1) Its grammar designates one name (singular).

(2) Its context shows that Jesus described His power and therefore told the disciples to baptize in His name.

(3) Mark's and Luke's descriptions of the same instructions of Christ show that Jesus was the only name mentioned.

(4) The Early Church, including Matthew, carried out Christ's instructions by baptizing in the name of Jesus (Acts 2:38; 8:16; 10:48; 19:5; 22:16; I Corinthians 1:13).

(5) The name of the Father is Jesus; the Father is revealed through the name Jesus (John 5:43).

(6) The name of the Son is Jesus (Matthew 1:21).

(7) The name of the Holy Ghost is Jesus; the Holy

Ghost is revealed through the name Jesus (John 14:26).

(8) God has revealed Himself in the New Testament by one name (Zechariah 14:9) and that name is Jesus (Revelation 22:3-4).

(9) The Bible does not teach the doctrine of the trinity, so there is no theological justification for a trine formula.

The Witness in Church History

Not only did the apostles baptize in the name of Jesus, but the Christians of the early post-apostolic era did also. Most theologians agree that the Book of Acts describes the original formula. Church historians generally agree that Jesus' name was the older formula and that the trine formula was only gradually adopted. (See Chapter 10 for full discussion of this subject.)

Does the Baptismal Formula Really Matter?

Everyone should use the biblical formula. If the name Jesus was not called over someone at baptism, he should be rebaptized in the name of Jesus. Here are the reasons why:

(1) The Bible places so much importance on water baptism that we should practice it exactly as the Bible commands.

(2) We should follow the example of the apostolic church.

(3) Tradition is an inadequate substitute for biblical

teaching.

(4) Obedience to and respect for God's Word will cause us to follow it exactly. We should obey the clear teaching of Scripture instead of inventing another method and attempting to justify it. Refusal to use the biblical formula could signify disobedience, rebellion, or a casual approach to God's Word.

(5) John's disciples had already been immersed in water unto repentance, yet Paul baptized them again, this time in Jesus' name (Acts 19:1-5). The only physical difference between the two baptisms was the name, but this was significant enough to require rebaptism.

(6) The name of Jesus is uniquely associated with all the purposes of baptism, such as burial with Christ, identification with Christ, and remission of sins.

Even if one has already received the Holy Ghost, he needs to be baptized in the name of Jesus Christ. As the story of Cornelius indicates, God will give the Spirit to all who repent and believe, even to those who do not understand baptism in the name of Jesus. He specifically said that He gives His Spirit to guide people into all truth (John 16:13), but they may subsequently ignore or reject the leading of the Spirit and the teaching of the Word. God does not stamp His approval on their doctrine by filling them with His Spirit; rather, this exhibits His grace and strict adherence to the promises of His Word. Regardless of someone's spiritual experience, continual obedience to God's Word is always necessary.

Some say that if one has faith in Christ the baptismal formula is an irrelevant technicality. By this reasoning, however, one could justify celebrating the Lord's Supper with cake and punch, performing baptisms by sprinkling with milk, or even omitting the baptismal ceremony altogether. We do not believe any teaching of Scripture is irrelevant; in the case of baptism the Bible teaches it to be part of salvation and commands baptism in Jesus' name.

If the formula is irrelevant, baptism in any name would be valid Christian baptism, which is absurd. Obviously, the spiritual significance of baptism is expressed by the formula used and the name invoked. Using Jesus' name demonstrates faith in (1) the person of Christ (who He really is), (2) the work of Christ (His death, burial, and resurrection for our salvation), and (3) the power and authority of Christ (His ability to save us by Himself). This is the essence of saving faith.

A baptismal candidate does not need a fully developed understanding of the Godhead to be saved, for faith precedes complete knowledge. However, it is one thing to have limited knowledge but yet submit to the biblical formula out of faith and obedience; it is quite another thing to disregard the teaching of Scripture and use a man-made formula that confesses a false doctrinal system. Interestingly, Roman Catholics have traditionally taught that baptism is essential to salvation and that pronouncement of the words "in the name of the Father, Son, and Holy Ghost" is necessary to its validity.[18]

Simply put, the Bible teaches no baptismal formula other than one using the name Jesus. If any other formula will suffice, the Bible does not tell us. If we limit ourselves to the scriptural record, we must draw two conclusions: (1) Christian baptism should be performed in the name of Jesus, which means by His power and authority, by faith in Him, and by orally invoking His name; (2)

No other baptismal formula has biblical validity.

Conclusion

In conclusion, below are the biblical reasons for baptism in the name of Jesus.

(1) The Bible gives this formula and no other.

(a) Matthew 28:19 describes this formula.

(b) The apostolic church adhered to this formula (Acts 2:38; 8:16; 10:48; 19:5; 22:16; I Corinthians 1:13).

(2) Baptism is a burial with Christ and no one else (Romans 6:4; Colossians 2:12).

(3) Baptism is a personal identification with Christ (Romans 6:3; Galatians 3:27), and His name identifies us as His possession.

(4) At baptism we take on our new family name, as part of our new birth, adoption, and spiritual circumcision. The name God's spiritual family bears is Jesus (Ephesians 3:14-15).

(5) Baptism is for the remission of sins (Acts 2:38), and Jesus is the only name that remits sin (Acts 10:43).

(6) The name of Jesus represents all the power and authority of God (Matthew 28:18; Acts 4:7, 10). When we invoke His name in faith, that power and authority become available to us (Acts 3:6, 16).

(7) Everything we do in word or deed should be done in the name of Jesus (Colossians 3:17), and baptism is both word and deed.

(8) The name of Jesus is the highest name known to man, and everyone must bow to that name (Philippians 2:9-11).

(9) Baptism is part of our salvation, and Jesus is the only saving name (Acts 4:12).

(10) Baptism in Jesus' name manifests complete faith in Jesus as our only Savior and our only access to God (John 14:6-11).

(11) It signifies belief that the fulness of the Godhead is manifested in Jesus (Colossians 2:9).

(12) Jesus is the name by which God has revealed Himself in the New Testament (Matthew 1:21; John 5:43; 14:26).

(13) Baptism in the name of Jesus demonstrates reverence for and obedience to the Word of God over and above human tradition.

In view of all the important things baptism in Jesus' name signifies, why would anyone refuse to use the name? Why would anyone hesitate to take on the name of the One who died for them and be identified publicly with Him? Why would anyone reject the only saving name—the name that is above every name?

FOOTNOTES

[1]Vine, p. 99.

[2]Rousas John Rushdoony, "Baptism and Citizenship," *Chalcedon Position Paper No. 37* (Vallecito, Ca.: Chalcedon, n.d.), p. 1.

[3]*Ibid*, pp. 1-2.

[4]*Ibid*, p. 2.

[5]*Ibid.*

[6]James Strong, *Exhaustive Concordance of the Bible* (Nashville: Abingdon, 1890).

[7]"Baptism (Early Christian)," *Encyclopedia of Religion and Ethics* [hereinafter *ERE*], James Hastings, ed. (New York: Charles Scribner's Sons, 1951), II, 384.

[8]"Baptism," *The Interpreter's Dictionary of the Bible* (Nashville: Abingdon, 1962), I, 351.

[9]Matthew Henry, *Commentary* (Old Tappan, N.J.: Fleming H. Revell, n.d.), V, 443.

[10]Beasley-Murray, p. 83. Emphasis in original.

[11]*Ibid,* pp. 83-84.

[12]*Ibid,* p. 81.

[13]R. V. G. Tasker, *The Gospel According to St. Matthew,* Vol. I of *The Tyndale New Testament Commentaries* (Grand Rapids: Eerdmans, 1961), p. 275.

[14]James Buswell, Jr., *A Systematic Theology of the Christian Religion* (Grand Rapids: Zondervan, 1980), I, 23.

[15]David Arthur Reed, *Origins and Development of the Theology of Oneness Pentecostalism in the United States* (Ann Arbor, Mich.: University Microfilms International, 1978), pp. 47, 66-67, citing Essex Kenyon, *The Wonderful Name of Jesus* (Los Angeles: West Coast Publishing Co., 1927).

[16]Reed, pp. 46, 49, 68.

[17]William Phillips Hall, *Remarkable Biblical Discovery or "The Name" of God According to the Scriptures* (1929; Rpt. by St. Louis: Pentecostal Publishing House, 1951), p. 10. However, Hall placed primary emphasis on *Lord* rather than on *Jesus.*

[18]Elmer Clark, *The Small Sects in America* (Nashville: Cokesbury Press, 1937), p. 200.

8

THE BAPTISM OF THE HOLY SPIRIT

"Ye shall be baptized with the Holy Ghost not many days hence" (Acts 1:5).

"And they were all filled with the Holy Ghost, and began to speak with other tongues, as the Spirit gave them utterance" (Acts 2:4).

The Holy Spirit

God is holy (I Peter 1:16). In fact, God alone is holy in Himself. Furthermore, God is a Spirit (John 4:24), and there is only one Spirit of God (Ephesians 4:4). The Holy Spirit is God (Acts 5:3-4; I Corinthians 3:16-17 with 6:19-20). One of the titles of the Holy Spirit is "Spirit of God" (Romans 8:9).

The titles "Holy Ghost" and "Holy Spirit" are interchangeable, with the *KJV* ordinarily using the former but sometimes the latter (Luke 11:13; Ephesians 1:13; 4:30). The original Greek text, however, uses only one phrase, *pneuma hagion*. All major translations since the *KJV* have uniformly chosen "Holy Spirit" since it is more understandable for modern English readers.

This title for God emphasizes His holiness and His spiritual nature. The Bible uses it most frequently in reference to the part of God's activity among and in mankind that only a Spirit can perform. The New Testament particularly associates the Holy Spirit with God's work of regeneration and His dwelling in man (John 3:5; 14:16-17).

The Baptism of the Spirit

This is a vital New Testament experience with God. The *KJV* speaks of being "baptized with the Holy Ghost" (Acts 1:5). *With* in this phrase comes from the Greek word *en*, which can also be rendered *in*, as both *TAB* and *NIV* note.

The word *baptism* means plunging, dipping, or immersing. By using this terminology, the Bible depicts the experience as a complete immersion in the Spirit of God. At the same time, the Bible describes a person who receives this experience as being filled with the Spirit. These are complementary (not contradictory) illustrations, for when an empty container is completely submerged into liquid it is not only surrounded but also completely filled with the liquid. These descriptions communicate the idea that a person who receives the Holy Spirit achieves a close personal union with God. He lives in constant contact with God, and God becomes a part of his life. He becomes a temple in which God dwells, and the Spirit of God affects his every thought and action.

Biblical Terminology

The Book of Acts describes the baptism of the Spirit in many ways: "filled with the Holy Ghost" (2:4); "the promise of the Holy Ghost" (2:33); "the gift of the Holy Ghost" (2:38); "the Holy Ghost fell on all them" (10:44); "poured out the gift of the Holy Ghost" (10:45); "received the Holy Ghost" (10:47); and "the Holy Ghost came on them" (19:6). The epistles explain that the Holy Spirit dwells in us (Romans 8:9).

All these phrases simply identify the same New Testament experience in different ways. When empty human vessels are baptized in the Spirit, they are filled with the Spirit. When God pours out His Spirit on people, the Spirit comes on them, they receive the Spirit, and they are filled with the Spirit. When God gives the Spirit, He fulfills His promise and men receive the Spirit. The following chart demonstrates the equivalence of all these phrases.

Biblical Terminology for the Spirit Baptism*

	Baptized	Came on	Fell on	Filled	Gift	Received	Poured
Came on (upon)	1:5, 8						
Fell on	11:15-16	10:44-47 19:2, 6					
Filled with	1:5 2:4	1:5, 8 2:4	2:4 11:15				
Gift	11:15-17	2:38 19:2, 6	10:44-45	2:4 11:17			
Received	1:5 2:33	19:2 19:6	10:44 10:47	2:4 2:33	2:38		
Poured out	10:45 11:15-16	1:8 2:16-18	10:44-45	2:4 2:16-17	10:45	10:45 10:47	
Promise	1:4-5	1:4 1:8	1:4-5 11:15-16	2:4 2:33	2:38-39	2:33	1:4 2:16-17

*All scriptural references are from the Book of Acts.

Some of these descriptions compare the Holy Spirit to water, and Jesus described the Spirit as living water that would quench spiritual thirst (John 4:14; 7:38). However, the Holy Spirit is not actually a fluid but is God Himself. The Bible also associates the Spirit with fire (Matthew 3:11) and wind (John 3:8), but the Spirit is not literally fire, wind, or water.

Filled with the Spirit

This phrase appears in Acts as the equivalent of "baptized with the Holy Ghost," with both describing the initial experience of receiving the Spirit of God to dwell in one's life.

Some time after Pentecost a number of Spirit-baptized believers came together for a prayer meeting and were "filled with the Holy Ghost" (Acts 4:31). God met with these believers in a mighty way and renewed their original experience. When Peter spoke to the Jewish religious council he was "filled with the Holy Ghost" (Acts 4:8). Paul, "filled with the Holy Ghost," prophesied that the sorcerer Barjesus would be blind for a time (Acts 13:9). From these instances we see that *filled* may mean a special, momentary endowment of power to one who has already been baptized in the Spirit. Today, many speak of this endowment as being anointed by the Spirit.

Other verses use the term "filled" to describe the continual dwelling of the Spirit in one who has been baptized in the Spirit. The seven men chosen to assist the apostles were "full of the Holy Ghost" (Acts 6:3, 5). Paul exhorted the Ephesian church to "be filled with the Spirit" (Ephesians 5:18). The latter verse is an exhortation to Spirit-baptized believers to let the Spirit continually control them. In this sense, to be "filled with the Spirit" is basically the same as to "walk after the Spirit" (Romans 8:4), meaning to receive daily guidance and power from the Spirit.

Even when a backslider repents, he is not "baptized" with the Spirit again, but refilled. Due to the backslider's faithlessness and disobedience, he is disinherited, but he is not "unborn." The historic fact of his regeneration and justification is still a reality. When he repents he does not need to be "born again" another time. He does not experience a second baptism of water or a second baptism of the Spirit, for the original baptism of water and Spirit becomes effective again when he repents. Instead, he is simply restored to a justified status and entitled once again to inherit eternal life as an obedient son of God.

In sum, the phrase "filled with the Spirit" can convey any one of these three meanings in apostolic church usage: (1) the initial Spirit baptism; (2) the daily guidance and power that the Spirit grants to Spirit-baptized believers who continue to yield to Him, and (3) subsequent experiences that renew the initial experience.

We must distinguish the baptism of the Spirit from all Old Testament experiences with God. The filling of the Spirit in Acts is different from the filling of the Spirit that John the Baptist had. It is a new experience for a new church. (See later section.)

Part of Salvation

As the chart indicates, every description of the work of the Spirit in the initial experience of salvation can be equated with the baptism of the Spirit. The baptism of the Spirit is the same as the birth of the Spirit (John 3:5; Chapter 4.) The Spirit first begins to "dwell" in a person's life when he is baptized with the Spirit. Any other alternative would not be logical. For example, how can the Spirit dwell in a person if he has not received the Spirit, if he has not been filled with the Spirit, if the Spirit has not come upon him, or if the Spirit has not fallen upon him?

First Corinthians 12:13 settles any doubt in this matter: "For by one Spirit are we all baptized into one body." The Greek preposition translated *by* is *en*—the same preposition used in Acts 1:5. We could translate the sentence as, "With one Spirit we are all baptized into one body" or "In one Spirit we are all baptized into one body," as the *NIV* indicates in a footnote. The Greek phrasing demonstrates that Paul referred to the same experience Jesus had promised in Acts 1:5. Thus, the baptism of the Spirit is part of salvation and not an experience subsequent to salvation.

Most theologians recognize the essentiality of being filled with the Holy Spirit, that the baptism of the Holy Ghost is part of the new birth. Bloesch said, "We insist that the baptism of the Spirit must not be distinguished from the new birth."[1] Another non-Pentecostal theologian, Anthony Hoekema stated, "If we have been born again, we have the Spirit, since only the Spirit can regenerate us."[2] He also wrote, "Baptism in the Spirit . . .is not an experience distinct from and usually subsequent to conversion. . .but is simultaneous with conversion and an integral aspect of conversion. . . .All Christians have been Spirit-baptized. Spirit-baptism is. . .identical with regeneration."[3]

The baptism of the Spirit is the means by which we receive Christ into our lives. There is no separation between Jesus Christ and the Holy Spirit, for the Holy Spirit is the Spirit of Christ (Romans 8:9). Christ dwells in us by the indwelling of the Spirit (Ephesians 3:16-17). "The Lord is the Spirit," and the Holy Spirit is "the Spirit of the Lord" (II Corinthians 3:17-18, *NIV*). It is impossible to receive Christ on one occasion and receive the Spirit on another, for there is only one Spirit (Ephesians 4:4; I Corinthians 12:13). When we are baptized in the Spirit we receive Christ into our lives.

The baptism of the Holy Spirit is just the beginning of a continual life of being filled with the Spirit. It is not an experience only for the select few, nor is it a post-conversional experience received only after long tarrying and agonizing. Rather, it is part of conversion and it comes with repentance and faith. A person who receives the Spirit has not reached a point of perfection, but has simply begun to live a Christian life. After being baptized in the Spirit, he must seek to be renewed continually by submitting to the leading of the Spirit, letting Him have full control, and bearing the fruit of the Spirit.

Some people teach that the Spirit baptism is a second or third "work of grace," meaning an instantaneous experience subsequent to saving conversion. Most Protestant denominations regard the baptism of the Spirit as part of conversion and deny the existence of instantaneous works of grace thereafter. The Holiness movement of the 1800's taught that there was a second work of grace after conversion, called sanctification, in which a person is completely purified of indwelling sin.

In the early 1900's, many Holiness people received the baptism of the Holy Ghost with tongues and classified that experience as a third work of grace. Others who received the Spirit baptism held that sanctification is a continual process throughout a person's Christian life, and so classified the Spirit baptism either as a second work of grace or as part of conversion itself. In light of our analysis of biblical teaching and terminology, we conclude that the baptism of the Spirit is neither a second work nor a third work but part of conversion and regeneration.

The Founding of the New Testament Church

The New Testament church began on the Day of Pentecost after Christ's ascension. John the Baptist did not start the church but only prepared the way for Jesus. Jesus declared John to be as great as any prophet, but then He said, "He that is least in the kingdom of God is greater than he" (Luke 7:28).

Everyone who participates in God's rule today, which is accomplished by His indwelling Spirit, has greater spiritual privileges, blessings, and power than John had. John preached that the kingdom of heaven was at hand (Matthew 3:1-2); the message of the kingdom began with him (Matthew 11:11-13; Luke 16:16). However, he did not participate in the fulness of that kingdom, for the fulness of grace came only through Christ (John 1:16-17). He did not have the baptism of the Spirit, but he preached that Jesus would baptize with the Spirit (Matthew 3:11).

Jesus did not found the New Testament church during His earthly ministry, but He spoke of the church in the future tense: "Upon this rock I will build my church" (Matthew 16:18). He told the disciples shortly before His ascension that "repentance and remission of sins should be preached in his name among all nations, beginning at Jerusalem" (Luke 24:47). He told them to wait in Jerusalem until they received the baptism of the Holy Ghost. The Spirit would give them power, and then they would become witnesses (Luke 24:49; Acts 1:4-8).

The New Testament church dates from the Day of

Pentecost rather than from John's preaching or the Lord's earthly ministry. God had designed a new covenant with man, and this covenant required Christ's death and resurrection before it would come into effect. This new covenant or new testament (both *covenant* and *testament* in the *KJV* come from the single Greek word *diatheke*) includes the promise of the Holy Spirit (Jeremiah 31:31-33; II Corinthians 3:3-6).

Before the new covenant could come into effect, Jesus had to die: "And for this cause he is the mediator of the new testament, that by means of death, for the redemption of the transgressions that were under the first testament, they which are called might receive the promise of eternal inheritance. For where a testament is, there must also of necessity be the death of the testator" (Hebrews 9:15-16). Jesus became the mediator of the new covenant by His death, and His resurrection made the death effective (Romans 4:24-25). Therefore, the Holy Spirit was given only after Christ's death and resurrection: "But this spake he of the Spirit, which they that believe on him should receive: for the Holy Ghost was not yet given; because that Jesus was not yet glorified" (John 7:39); "It is expedient for you that I go away: for if I go not away, the Comforter will not come unto you; but if I depart, I will send him unto you" (John 16:7). The New Testament church began on the Day of Pentecost, after Christ's death, burial, and resurrection made the new covenant (testament) available.

A New Experience for the New Church

The baptism of the Holy Spirit is a new experience

given to the New Testament church after Christ's death, resurrection, and ascension (John 7:39; 16:7). Just before Christ's ascension He promised the Spirit as a new, future experience to be received by His disciples while they tarried in Jerusalem (Luke 24:47-49; Acts 1:4-8). This promise was fulfilled on the Day of Pentecost (Acts 2:1-4, 33).

No one before Acts 2:1-4 received this experience. The new covenant is a "better covenant, which was established upon better promises" (Hebrews 8:6), one of which is the promise of the Holy Ghost. After Hebrews 11 lists many great men of faith in the Old Testament, it closes by stating that they had not received the promise: "And these all, having obtained a good report through faith, received not the promise: God having provided some better thing for us, that they without us should not be made perfect" (Hebrews 11:39-40).

The prophets predicted the gift of the Spirit and desired to participate in its glory, but God reserved the Holy Spirit baptism for the New Testament church: "Of which salvation the prophets have enquired and searched diligently, who prophesied of the grace that should come unto you. . .Unto whom it was revealed, that not unto themselves, but unto us they did minister the things, which are now reported unto you by them that have preached the gospel unto you with the Holy Ghost sent down from heaven" (I Peter 1:10, 12).

That the Spirit of God dealt with men in many different ways in the Old Testament is clearly stated in Scripture. Men of God were moved by the Holy Ghost (II Peter 1:21). The Spirit of God anointed chosen vessels for specific purposes. However, beginning with Pentecost, God made a new experience and a greater dimension of His Spirit available. Today we can have His abiding presence in our lives, imparting power to overcome sins in a way unknown under the law (Romans 8:3-4). This inner power of the Spirit is a key factor that distinguishes the new covenant from the old (Jeremiah 31:31-33; Ezekiel 11:19). Before Pentecost, men were not regenerated (born again) in the New Testament sense; they did not have the Spirit baptism described in the Book of Acts.

Before Pentecost, John the Baptist, his mother Elisabeth, and his father Zacharias were "filled with the Holy Ghost" at specific times (Luke 1:15, 41, 67). Their experience, however, was not the experience of the New Testament church, for the Holy Ghost was not yet given. John did not have the baptism of the Holy Ghost, nor did his disciples (Luke 3:16, 7:28; Acts 19:1-6). In Luke 1, the phrase, "filled with the Holy Ghost," describes an Old Testament experience in which God's Spirit moved on people at a particular time for a particular purpose. In John's case, the Spirit anointed him and separated him from his mother's womb for a special ministry just as He had done with Jeremiah (Jeremiah 1:5). John's parents were temporarily endued with power of the Spirit to give prophetic utterances. Only after Pentecost does "filled with the Holy Ghost" specifically refer to the New Testament Spirit baptism, which first became available at that time.

Old Testament Prophecy

Although the Old Testament prophets did not receive the Spirit baptism, they did record God's promises concerning the coming of the Spirit (I Peter 1:10-12): "And it shall come to pass afterward, that I will pour out my spirit upon all flesh; and your sons and your daughters shall prophesy, your old men shall dream dreams, your young men shall see visions: And also upon the servants and upon the handmaids in those days will I pour out my spirit" (Joel 2:28-29). Peter quoted this prophecy and applied it to the baptism of the Spirit at Pentecost (Acts 2:16-18).

God promised a new covenant in which He would write His laws upon the hearts of His people (Jeremiah 31:31-33). This promise is fulfilled by the outpouring of the Spirit, who writes the laws of God on our hearts (II Corinthians 3:3-6) and who gives us power to fulfill the righteousness of the law (Romans 8:3-4). God said, "And I will give them one heart, and I will put a new spirit within you; and I will take the stony heart out of their flesh, and will give them an heart of flesh" (Ezekiel 11:19; see 36:26). In another prophetic passage He stated, "Neither will I hide my face any more from them; for I have poured out my spirit upon the house of Israel" (Ezekiel 39:29).

New Testament Promise and Command

John the Baptist preached the promise of the Holy Spirit baptism: "I indeed baptize you with water unto repentance: but he that cometh after me is mightier than I, whose shoes I am not worthy to bear: he shall baptize you with the Holy Ghost, and with fire" (Matthew 3:11). John did not preach that the Spirit was only for a select few, but for everyone who repented and received his baptism. God gave John a sign whereby he would recognize the One who would fulfill the promise (Jesus): "Upon whom thou shalt see the Spirit descending, and remaining on him, the same is he which baptizeth with the Holy Ghost" (John 1:33).

Jesus both promised the Spirit baptism and commanded His disciples to receive the Spirit, as the following quotations demonstrate:

- "If ye then, being evil, know how to give good gifts unto your children: how much more shall your heavenly Father give the Holy Spirit to them that ask him?" (Luke 11:13).
- "Except a man be born of water and of the Spirit, he cannot enter into the kingdom of God" (John 3:5).
- "But whosoever drinketh of the water that I shall give him shall never thirst; but the water that I shall give him shall be in him a well of water springing up into everlasting life" (John 4:14). The next quotation indicates that Jesus spoke of the Spirit outpouring.
- "In the last day, that great day of the feast, Jesus stood and cried, saying, If any man thirst, let him come unto me, and drink. He that believeth on me, as the scripture hath said, out of his belly shall flow rivers of living water. (But this spake he of the Spirit, which they that believe on him should receive: for the Holy Ghost was not yet given; because that Jesus was not yet glorified)" (John 7:37-39).

This last passage teaches several very important things: (1) The Holy Spirit is promised to all who believe on Jesus. (2) Belief in Christ must be in accordance with the teaching of Scripture, not divorced from it. (3) To believe is not just mental assent at a certain point in time, but continual believing, as the use of the present tense indicates. (4) The gift of the Holy Ghost to which Jesus referred did not come until after His glorification, which was accomplished by His resurrection and ascension. He specifically meant the outpouring of the Spirit at Pentecost, and this is the experience all believers should receive.

Shortly before Christ's death He emphasized to His disciples that the Holy Ghost would come after He left them. Furthermore, He said the Holy Ghost would be Himself in another form—in Spirit rather than in flesh: "And I will pray the Father, and he shall give you another Comforter, that he may abide with you for ever; Even the Spirit of truth; whom the world cannot receive, because it seeth him not, neither knoweth him: but ye know him; for he dwelleth with you, and shall be in you. I will not leave you comfortless: I will come to you" (John 14:16-18).

- "But the Comforter, which is the Holy Ghost, whom the Father will send in my name, he shall teach you all things, and bring all things to your remembrance, whatsoever I have said unto you" (John 14:26).
- "But when the Comforter is come, whom I will send unto you from the Father, even the Spirit of truth, which proceedeth from the Father, he shall testify of me" (John 15:26).
- "Nevertheless I tell you the truth; It is expedient for you that I go away: for if I go not away, the Comforter will not come unto you; but if I depart, I will send him unto you. . . .Howbeit when he, the Spirit of truth, is come, he will guide you into all truth: for he shall not speak of himself; but whatsoever he shall hear, that shall he speak: and he will shew

you things to come" (John 16:7, 13).

Jesus reiterated the promise of the Spirit after His resurrection and turned it into a command. He commanded His disciples, "Receive ye the Holy Ghost" (John 20:22). They did not receive the Spirit at that time, as Luke's account makes clear. "And, behold, I send the promise of my Father upon you: but tarry ye in the city of Jerusalem, until ye be endued with power from on high" (Luke 24:49); "And being assembled together with them, commanded them that they should not depart from Jerusalem, but wait for the promise of the Father, which, saith he, ye have heard of me. For John truly baptized with water; but ye shall be baptized with the Holy Ghost not many days hence. . . .But ye shall receive power, after that the Holy Ghost is come upon you: and ye shall be witnesses unto me both in Jerusalem, and in all Judaea, and in Samaria, and unto the uttermost part of the earth" (Acts 1:4-5, 8).

Other accounts of the Great Commission record the Lord's promise to be with His disciples until the end of the age (Matthew 28:20) as well as His promise to give all believers power to cast out devils, speak with new tongues, be victorious over serpents, be protected against poison, and pray successfully for the healing of the sick (Mark 16:17-18). All these promises come to pass through the indwelling power of the Spirit.

Fulfillment in the Apostolic Church

The New Testament church continued to proclaim the baptism of the Holy Spirit as a promise and a command to all. Peter preached the promise on the Day of Pentecost with the support of all the apostles (Acts 2:38). Paul emphasized the need of the Spirit (Acts 19:1-6). He wrote, "But ye are not in the flesh, but in the Spirit, if so be that the Spirit of God dwell in you. Now if any man have not the Spirit of Christ, he is none of his" (Romans 8:9). Paul defined the kingdom of God as "righteousness, and peace, and joy in the Holy Ghost" (Romans 14:17).

The Significance of Acts

The New Testament consists of four divisions: (1) Gospels (Matthew, Mark, Luke, John), (2) Church History (Acts), (3) Epistles (Romans to Jude), and (4) Prophecy (Revelation). The Gospels are historical accounts of the life, teachings, ministry, death, resurrection, and ascension of Jesus Christ. None of them describes the establishing of a church; they describe the One who would establish the church upon His person, teaching, and work. The Book of Acts is a narrative history of the New Testament church, describing its beginning in Jerusalem and its spread to all Judea, Samaria, and the Gentile world. The Epistles are letters of instruction and admonition written to born-again believers to help them in Christian living. While the Epistles do contain references to the initial conversion experience, they assume the readers have already been born of water and the Spirit. The Book of Revelation is also addressed to established churches and believers, revealing God's plan for the future.

Acts is the only book in the Bible to contain historical accounts of people who received the new birth experience in the New Testament church, including all accounts of

Christian water baptism and Spirit baptism. Because of the nature and purpose of the book, it contains most of the direct evidence relative to the question, "How can I be saved?" The Book of Acts is the pattern and norm for the New Testament church, not the exception. If Acts is not the norm, then the Bible gives no example of what the church should be like. The five accounts of the Spirit baptism in Acts are not exhaustive, but representative of the way in which God poured out His Spirit across the entire spectrum of humanity.

The Day of Pentecost

In obedience to Christ's command, approximately 120 disciples returned to Jerusalem after His ascension to await the baptism of the Spirit. Included in this number were the twelve apostles (with Matthias replacing Judas), Mary the mother of Jesus, the brothers of Jesus, and several women (Acts 1:12-26). It appears that they were gathered in an upper room on the Day of Pentecost, a Jewish feast day that came fifty days after the Passover. (The Greek word *pentecoste* literally means "fiftieth day.") On this first Pentecost after Christ's ascension, the 120 received the Holy Ghost and spoke in tongues (Acts 2:1-4).

Some people contend that only the twelve apostles received the Spirit, but this is demonstrably incorrect: (1) Jesus gave the promise to all those at His ascension, not just to the Twelve. (2) All the 120 went to the upper room to await the fulfillment of the promise, and we find no record that any of them left. (3) In Joel's prophecy, which Peter applied to Pentecost, God said He would pour out

His Spirit on all flesh, including sons, daughters, young men, old men, servants, and handmaidens (Acts 2:16-18). This certainly describes more than the Twelve; all 120, including the women, received the Spirit.

We can assume that an additional 3000 received the Spirit in response to Peter's sermon, as shown by the following: (1) Peter promised the gift of the Holy Ghost to all who heard his word (Acts 2:38-39), and 3000 received his word gladly (Acts 2:41). Peter began his sermon by explaining what had just happened to him; he ended it by offering the same experience to his audience. (2) The 3000 believed his message and applied it to their lives, and he preached that the gift of the Holy Ghost was available to them. (3) The 3000 were baptized (Acts 2:41). Even if this means water baptism alone, the Spirit was promised to all who would repent and be baptized in water. (4) The 3000 were "added unto them," namely to the 120 who had just received the Spirit. We conclude, as does *The Pulpit Commentary,* that 3120 received the Holy Spirit on the Day of Pentecost.[4]

The 3120 were all Jews and Jewish proselytes, for much later Jewish Christians still were not certain that Gentiles could be saved (Acts 10-11). Some could have been proselytes—Gentiles by birth but Jews by conversion (Acts 2:10). The 120 were mostly Galileans, but the 3000 included Jews from many different countries who had come to Jerusalem to celebrate the feast of Pentecost (Acts 2:5-11).

The company of believers later came together to pray and were "all filled with the Holy Ghost" (Acts 4:31). This was not a first-time Spirit baptism but a renewal and an anointing of the Spirit-baptized Jewish believers.

In conclusion, the Day of Pentecost represents the first

occurrence of the baptism of the Holy Ghost, specifically, the first outpouring on the Jews.

Samaria

The second recorded Spirit baptism (i.e., outpouring of the Spirit on people for their first time) occurred in Samaria. Racially and religiously, the Samaritans were a mixture of Jew and Gentile and thus constituted a class of people distinct from either.

Philip the evangelist (one of the Seven, not one of the Twelve) took the gospel to Samaria. The Samaritans listened to him, saw miracles (including healing and casting out of evil spirits), had great joy, believed his message and were baptized in water in the name of Jesus. However, despite all this they had not received the Holy Ghost (Acts 8:6-16).

This incident reveals that the baptism of the Spirit is a definite experience not to be confused with and not necessarily accompanying miracles, great emotion, mental belief, repentance, or water baptism. When the apostles heard what was happening in Samaria, they sent Peter and John. When Peter and John prayed for the Samaritans and laid hands on them, they received the Holy Ghost (Acts 8:17).

The Samaritans did not receive the Holy Ghost until Peter and John laid hands on them. Apparently they were not fully prepared earlier. They had "believed Philip," but evidently they had not committed themselves totally to Christ. When Peter and John arrived, prayed for them, and laid hands on them, their faith increased to the point of receiving the Spirit.

This story does not teach that one of the twelve apostles had to bestow the Holy Ghost, for Paul was filled with the Spirit when Ananias prayed for him (Acts 9), and the Ephesians received the Holy Ghost when Paul prayed for them (Acts 19). Similarly, the laying on of hands is not an absolute requirement, for the 120 received the Spirit without this act (Acts 2), and so did Cornelius (Acts 10).

The laying on of hands has the following significance and purpose: (1) it demonstrates submission to God's plan and leadership; (2) it symbolizes the bestowal of God's blessing, promise, and calling; and (3) it helps instill faith in the seeker.

The experience of the Samaritans demonstrates that one can believe to a certain extent and even be baptized in water and yet not receive the Spirit. There is no salvation without the Spirit (Romans 8:9), so the Samaritans needed the baptism of the Spirit to complete their salvation, as the case of Simon the Magician exemplifies. Hoekema says, "The Samaritans were not true believers when Philip baptized them, and therefore did not receive the Spirit for salvation until the apostles laid hands on them. . . .Could it not be that the whole point of the narrative is to teach that salvation is impossible without the Holy Spirit?"[5] Most other Protestant commentators agree that the Samaritans were not saved until they received the Spirit.[6]

Paul's Conversion

God arrested Saul of Tarsus (Paul) by a light from heaven, but we find no indication that Paul was saved at this moment. Rather, the Lord told him, "Arise, and go into the city, and it shall be told thee what thou must do" (Acts 9:6). God sent Paul to Ananias in order for Paul to receive his sight and "be filled with the Holy Ghost" (Acts 9:17). When Ananias laid hands on Paul and prayed for him, Paul immediately received his sight, arose, and was baptized (Acts 9:18).

We can safely assume Paul received the Holy Ghost at this time although the Bible does not specifically describe Paul's Spirit baptism. But we know the Lord's stated purpose must have been accomplished. Paul's writings and ministry confirm that he indeed received the Spirit. Again Hoekema's analysis is useful: "We conclude that Saul's conversion was not an instantaneous happening but a three-day experience. Saul's being filled with the Spirit at the end of the three days, therefore, must not be understood as a 'Spirit-baptism' which occurred after his conversion, but as an integral aspect of his conversion."[7] Bloesch agrees that Paul's new birth occurred when he received the Spirit at his baptism by Ananias.[8]

The Gentiles in Caesarea

The next account of the Spirit baptism centers around Cornelius, a Roman centurion (captain over one hundred men) who lived in the city of Caesarea. He was devout, feared God, gave much alms, prayed to God often, and even had an angelic visitation. Despite all of these qualities and honorable activities, he was not saved. The angel told him to send for Peter, "who shall tell thee words, whereby thou and all thy house shall be saved" (Acts 11:14). Probably he had repented but had not received the Holy Spirit and so was not saved.

Cornelius was not a Jew, either by birth or conversion, but a Gentile. Upon God's direct command, Peter went to Caesarea and preached to Cornelius, his kinsmen, and his friends. While Peter was preaching, his Gentile listeners all received the Holy Ghost and began to speak in tongues (Acts 10:44-46). Peter identified this sign as the baptism of the Spirit—the same gift that the Jews received on the Day of Pentecost (Acts 11:15-17). This is a very significant account, because it marks the first time that Gentiles were baptized with the Spirit.

The Disciples of John at Ephesus

When Paul met about twelve disciples of John the Baptist in the city of Ephesus, he asked, "Have ye received the Holy Ghost since ye believed?" (Acts 19:2). They answered, "We have not so much as heard whether there be any Holy Ghost" (Acts 19:2).

Possibly these disciples had never heard John preach about the Spirit baptism, or more likely, they did not know the time had actually come to receive the promised experience. They were probably saying, "We have not heard whether the Holy Ghost is given yet." (See John 7:39, which literally says "The Holy Ghost was not yet" but which the *KJV* translates as "The Holy Ghost was not yet given.") At any rate, Paul next asked these men, "Then what baptism did you receive?" (Acts 19:3, *NIV*).

When he found that they had received only John's baptism, he rebaptized them in the name of Jesus. Then he prayed for them and laid hands on them, upon which they received the Holy Ghost, spoke in tongues, and prophesied (Acts 19:6).

It is enlightening to see Paul's approach to these "believers." He was not content until he asked two very important questions: (1) Have you received the Holy Ghost? and (2) How were you baptized? He taught them and worked with them until they were baptized in the name of Jesus and received the Holy Ghost with the sign of tongues.

This incident is extremely important to us today because it provides strong evidence that baptism in the name of Jesus and the baptism of the Spirit with tongues were the norm for the entire New Testament church. Not only is this evident from Paul's two questions for "believers," but it is also apparent from the very fact that God chose to record this incident. If it were not for Acts 19, the other accounts could possibly be explained away as unusual, one-time events. For example, Acts 2 records the birth of the church among the Jews, Acts 8 records the extension of the gospel to the Samaritans, and Acts 10 records its extension to the Gentiles. However, no such special circumstances existed in Acts 19; Acts 19 shows that the baptism of the Holy Ghost with tongues is for all who believe on Jesus.

Hoekema attempts to explain away Acts 2, 8, and 10 as described above and then admits that Acts 19 is "probably the most baffling of all the passages in Acts associated with glossolalia [speaking in tongues]."[9] Nevertheless, he attempts to explain why the Ephesians needed this experience while we supposedly do not: "(1) The faith which these Ephesian believers had when Paul first came to them was not full-orbed Christian faith but a faith which was quite incomplete. (2) There were special circumstances which made the bestowal of glossolalia on these Ephesian disciples necessary."[10] These "special circumstances," he contends, were: (1) They had not heard about the outpouring of the Spirit at Pentecost and thus needed tongues to convince them that it had in fact occurred. (2) They were a prominent group of believers who were to form the nucleus of the Ephesian church, yet they did not have an adequate understanding of Christianity. For the sake of the Ephesian church, this nucleus needed tongues to complete their understanding.

It should be noted that all of this reasoning applies with equal force today. The baptism of the Spirit is still necessary to complete Christian faith. Tongues are still needed as a sign of the outpouring of the Spirit. People still need to be convinced that the Spirit has been given. The Spirit is still necessary to transform a small group of believers into the nucleus of a local church. Whatever reasons God had for giving the Ephesians the baptism of the Spirit, those reasons are still valid for individuals and local congregations today. If anything, we have a greater need today for people to come to a complete Christian faith and to understand that the Spirit has indeed been poured out on the church.

Conclusion About the Spirit Baptism

Our study of these five cases demonstrates two important concepts this chapter has emphasized: (1) The baptism of the Holy Spirit is an essential part of salvation for the New Testament church age (the new birth) and not a separate experience subsequent to salvation. (2) The baptism of the Spirit is for all people in the New Testament church age (from Pentecost to the Second Coming of Christ), not just for a special group segregated from us by race, nationality, time, or position.

Those Saved in the Gospels

Some people object to the teaching that the baptism of the Spirit is essential on the basis of people in the Gospels who were saved without receiving the Spirit, such as Christ's disciples before Pentecost, the thief on the cross, and others whom Jesus forgave of sins. However, these examples occurred under the Law and in a unique transitional period in salvation history. The Holy Spirit was not given, and the New Testament church did not exist until the Day of Pentecost.

During the time of Jesus' earthly ministry, He upheld the old covenant as the path to eternal life (Luke 10:25-28) and commanded His followers to obey the Law of Moses (Matthew 19:16-19; 23:1-3, 23). He told an adulteress, "Go, and sin no more" (John 8:11), leaving her with the Law as a moral guide. He told one leper He healed, "Go thy way, show thyself to the priest, and offer the gift that Moses commanded" (Matthew 8:4), and He told ten other lepers, "Go shew yourselves unto the priests" (Luke 17:14).

Those who accepted Christ's message were saved under the old covenant while they waited for the new covenant and the promised Holy Spirit. They were saved in harmony with the Law, not in contradiction to it. For example, Jesus served as both sacrificial lamb and high priest for the thief on the cross. Before Pentecost, God expected people to follow the Law; after Pentecost God expects them to follow the gospel for the New Testament church age.

Only for the Apostolic Church?

A few people hold that the baptism of the Spirit was only for the apostles or the apostolic age. However, the Spirit was promised to and received by men, women, young, old, Jew, Samaritan, and Gentile. Joel promised this experience to all flesh in the latter days (Joel 2:28; Acts 2:16-18). If Pentecost was in the latter days, then all subsequent history is also. Peter told the crowd at Pentecost, "For the promise is unto you, and to your children, and to all that are afar off, even as many as the Lord our God shall call" (Acts 2:39). He expressly promised the gift to their children, which included some not yet born and also some who would live past the days of the twelve apostles.

"All that are afar off" included those distant from the Day of Pentecost both in space and in time. The call of the Lord extends to everyone—to "whosoever will" (Revelation 22:17). The example of the Ephesians shows that the baptism of the Spirit is for everyone and was not just given once to each national group as an unrepeatable experience. Indeed, the Bible promises the Spirit to all believers (John 7:38-39; Acts 11:15-17) and to all who ask (Luke 11:13).

Those who say the Book of Acts is not for today have the burden of proof. If Acts is not the pattern for the New Testament church, what is? Where in the Bible does God retract His promises relative to the baptism of the Spirit?

Where does the Bible say the experience of the Book of Acts is not for today? We must conclude that the promise of the Spirit is still ours today.

Salvation in Acts Without the Spirit?

Some claim that people in the Book of Acts were saved without receiving the Spirit. For example, the Bible does not explicitly record that the following received the Holy Spirit: the 5000 who believed after the healing of the lame man (Acts 4:4), the Ethiopian eunuch (Acts 8), Lydia (Acts 16), and the Philippian jailer (Acts 16). However, this is an argument from silence. No verse says they did not receive the Spirit. The Bible simply does not go into detail to describe all these conversions. Just as the Gospels record only representative miracles and events in Christ's ministry for lack of space (John 21:25), so Acts describes only a sampling of the important conversion experiences. God inspired Luke to choose five accounts of the Spirit baptism that would have great symbolic significance for later ages. Luke recorded enough to establish a precedent for every situation so that it was not necessary to record every other case or to describe other conversions in detail.

Even so, there is still evidence that all converts received the Spirit. The 5000 "believed" and Lydia "believed," and true belief leads to receiving the Spirit. The eunuch and the jailer both received an experience that caused rejoicing, which probably was the result of the baptism of the Spirit.

In sum, five key examples include the baptism of the Spirit as part of conversion, and these five cases represent all classes of people. A number of other conversion experiences are not told in detail, but the accounts of many of them imply the baptism of the Spirit while none specifically excludes it. We conclude that the five examples were meant to establish the pattern. The less specific cases should be read in light of the five examples given to us. Under no circumstances can mere silence or lack of a complete description overthrow the clear evidence of the five cases Acts records.

How to Receive the Holy Spirit

Since the baptism of the Holy Spirit is part of salvation and is available to us today, the Spirit is not difficult to receive. God promises His Spirit to all who ask (Luke 11:13), believe (John 7:38-39), and obey His Word (Acts 5:32). The seeker must have faith in God's promise, for without faith it is impossible to please God (Hebrews 11:6).

Peter promised the Spirit to all who would repent and be baptized in the name of Jesus (Acts 2:38). The example of the Samaritans shows that in the absence of complete faith, water baptism cannot automatically bring the Spirit. Moreover, the example of Cornelius shows that the Spirit can come before water baptism. The recipient must totally submit himself to God, willing to do anything God requires. At that point of complete submission and released faith, God pours out His Spirit. If the recipient has not been baptized in water in Jesus' name, he is commanded to do this as soon as possible.

Repentance is necessary. For the Holy Spirit to dwell in a life, that person must turn from sin and separate himself from spiritual uncleanliness (II Corinthians 6:16-7:1). Only God can make him righteous, but he must express a desire to turn from sin and receive pardon, ask for God's help in turning from sin, and surrender totally to God.

If someone will repent and have faith, God will give His Spirit, even though that person may have some false concepts in other areas, such as water baptism. In such cases, God grants His Spirit to lead the sincere person into further truth. God is not looking for reasons to deny the seeker, but He will give His Spirit to anyone who meets the conditions of repentance and faith as set forth in His Word.

If someone wants the baptism of the Holy Spirit, he should come to God with faith, believing His Word and expecting to receive the promise. He should repent from his sins by confessing them, asking pardon, pledging to do God's will (with His help), and totally surrendering to Him. He should determine in his mind that he wants God's Spirit that very day, regardless of what God may require of him in the future. After he repents and makes this total commitment, he should begin to praise God for hearing and answering prayer. Then, the Spirit will come in, take complete control, and inspire the seekers to speak in a language he has never learned. Often, the laying on of hands after repentance helps the seeker focus his faith at a point in time and receive the Spirit. This was a very common practice in the Early Church, although it was not a prerequisite for receiving the Spirit.

It is not wise to emphasize expectation and praise until the seeker has repented, for no matter how much he praises God he cannot receive the Spirit without repentance.

Receiving the Spirit is only as difficult as the seeker makes it. It takes only as much time as he needs to repent and surrender completely to God, which may be just a moment. Tarrying for long periods of time or seeking many times is not necessary. Those who do not receive the Spirit either lack faith to receive or have not fully repented and yielded every area of their lives to God. The 120 on the Day of Pentecost had to wait seven to ten days for the first outpouring, but since that time the Spirit has been freely available to all.

If people are taught how important it is to receive the Spirit baptism, how simple it really is to be filled with the Spirit, and how to prepare their hearts, they usually receive the Spirit easily. If the necessity of the Spirit baptism is taught many people will be filled. On the other hand, if the experience is merely presented as an optional blessing, most people will not. If repentance and faith are taught, most seekers will receive the Spirit in the water of baptism or when hands are laid upon them after repentance.

Young children, the elderly, the uneducated, the educated, the poor, and the rich all receive the Spirit. Buddhists and others from non-Christian backgrounds often receive the Spirit on their first visit to a Christian church. The accounts of Cornelius and the Ephesians both show that a person can receive the Spirit instantly, at the moment he repents and believes.

The Work of the Spirit

When a person is baptized in the Spirit, he receives

the Spirit of Christ in his life on a permanent basis (Romans 8:9; Ephesians 3:16-17). He becomes a part of God's spiritual family, and God's Spirit begins to guide him. The Bible describes this in several ways: (1) By the Spirit we are born into the kingdom of God (John 3:5); (2) the Spirit adopts us into the family of God (Romans 8:15-16; Galatians 4:5-6); (3) the Spirit baptizes us into the body of Christ (I Corinthians 12:13); (4) the Spirit sanctifies us (I Corinthians 6:11; I Peter 1:2); (5) the Spirit is the seal of our salvation (Ephesians 1:13); and (6) the Spirit is the earnest (pledge, guarantee, first installment) of our inheritance (Ephesians 1:14). In short, receiving the Spirit is part of our salvation. Of course, as Chapter 4 discussed, we should not sharply separate the baptism of the Spirit from water baptism since they join together to complete the new birth and bring all the benefits of salvation.

In addition to being part of salvation, the baptism of the Spirit brings power (II Timothy 1:7), which includes: (1) power to witness and be a living testimony that Christ saves from sin (Acts 1:8); (2) power to overcome sin, live righteously, and mortify the deeds of the flesh (Romans 8:4, 13); and (3) resurrection power when Christ comes for His church (Romans 8:11).

The Spirit brings rest and refreshing (Isaiah 28:11-12; Acts 3:19), and gives a sound mind (II Timothy 1:7). The Spirit becomes a teacher, a guide into all truth, and an illuminator of the Word of God (John 14:26; 16:13). He also becomes our intercessor and way of access to God (Romans 8:26-27; Ephesians 2:18). Finally, the Spirit works in our lives to give the ninefold fruit of the Spirit; namely, love, joy, peace, longsuffering, gentleness, goodness, faith, meekness, and temperance (Galatians 5:22-23; Romans 5:5;

14:17).

All these works of the Spirit reinforce the doctrine that receiving the Spirit is essential to salvation. Without all the above workings of the Spirit, we cannot successfully live a victorious Christian life that is pleasing to God. Anyone who tries to be saved without receiving God's Spirit is attempting to be saved by his own efforts and is doomed to failure.

Conclusion

The baptism of the Holy Spirit is the normal, basic New Testament experience with God. It is the birth of the Spirit. God has promised this experience to all who will believe Him and has commanded all to receive the Spirit. A person can receive the Spirit today by simply repenting of sin, having faith in God, and asking God for His gift. Once he receives the Holy Spirit, He will give him power to overcome sin and live a holy life. If a person lets the Spirit continually fill (control and guide) him, he will bear the fruit of the Spirit and truly live a Christ-like life.

FOOTNOTES

[1]Bloesch, II, 22.

[2]Anthony Hoekema, *What About Tongues Speaking?* (Grand Rapids: Eerdmans, 1966), p. 114.

[3]Anthony Hoekema, *Holy Spirit Baptism* (Grand Rapids: Eerdmans, 1972), pp. 20-21.

[4]*The Pulpit Commentary,* XVIII (Acts), 251.
[5]Hoekema, *Holy Spirit Baptism,* pp. 36-37.
[6]*The Pulpit Commentary,* XVIII (Acts), 279; Bloesch, II, 12.
[7]Hoekema, *Holy Spirit Baptism,* p. 39.
[8]Bloesch, II, 18.
[9]Hoekema, *What About Tongues Speaking?,* p. 73.
[10]*Ibid,* p. 77.

9

SPEAKING IN TONGUES

"And they were all filled with the Holy Ghost, and began to speak with other tongues, as the Spirit gave them utterance" (Acts 2:4).

Speaking in Tongues Defined

Speaking with (or in) tongues is "the supernatural gift of speaking in another language without its having been learnt."[1] The Greek word underlying this phrase is *glossa,* which means a tongue, either as the organ of the body or as a language. Hence, a modern theological term for speaking in tongues is *glossolalia.* Some modern translations render the *KJV* phrase "speak with other tongues" as "speak in foreign tongues" (Moffat), "speak in foreign languages" (Goodspeed), and "speak in different languages" (Phillips).

The New Testament contains four passages that indisputably describe speaking in tongues: Acts 2, Acts 10:44-47, Acts 19:6, and I Corinthians 12-14. In each case, those who spoke in tongues did so by the power of God's Spirit, "as the Spirit gave them utterance" (Acts 2:4).

Speaking in tongues is not gibberish or merely an unintelligible, ecstatic utterance without objective meaning. Those who speak in tongues speak in genuine languages, even though the speakers themselves do not understand what they say. Many times observers recognize these languages (Acts 2). The languages can be either human or angelic in nature (I Corinthians 13:1). Speaking in tongues is not an accidental, irrelevant, unimportant, or rare phenomenon; it is a gift from God and a significant part of God's plan for the New Testament church.

Isaiah 28:11-12

Isaiah foretold the role of tongues in the church: "For with stammering lips and another tongue will he speak to this people. To whom he said, This is the rest wherewith ye may cause the weary to rest; and this is the refreshing: yet they would not hear" (Isaiah 28:11-12). The rest and refreshing is the baptism of the Holy Spirit (Acts 2:38 with 3:19), and Isaiah predicted that stammering lips and foreign languages would accompany it.

Some assert that Isaiah referred merely to an invasion of Israel by foreigners, but this argument ignores several important points: (1) Isaiah associated tongues with rest and refreshing, not invasion. (2) Peter's words further link this refreshing with the Holy Spirit. (3) Paul applied Isaiah's words to speaking in tongues: "In the law it is written, With men of other tongues and other lips will I speak unto this people; and yet for all that will they not hear me, saith the Lord. Wherefore tongues are for a sign, not to them that believe, but to them that believe not" (I Corinthians 14:21-22). Paul used the passage in Isaiah to teach that God has chosen speaking in tongues as a sign in the New Testament church to encourage unbelievers to believe His Word.

If Isaiah 28:11-12 does refer to a foreign invasion of Israel, then it has an immediate fulfillment (Assyrian invasion) and a distant fulfillment (tongues in the New Testament church). Double fulfillment of prophecy or typology is such a common occurrence in the Bible that it is known as the "law of double reference." At any rate, on the authority of Peter and Paul Isaiah 28:11-12 does have a valid application to speaking in tongues in the New Testament church.

Mark 16:17

Just before Christ's ascension, He promised that speaking in tongues would follow believers as a sign: "And these signs shall follow them that believe; In my name shall they cast out devils; they shall speak with new tongues" (Mark 16:17). Some translations render "new tongues" as "new languages" (*TAB*) or "foreign tongues" (Goodspeed).

Opponents of speaking in tongues have attacked this verse by pointing to verse 18, which lists several other signs: "They shall take up serpents; and if they drink any deadly thing, it shall not hurt them; they shall lay hands on the sick, and they shall recover." Some small sects in the southeastern United States interpret this verse to mean Christians should prove their faith by handling poisonous snakes, and critics attempt to associate tongues with snake handling in order to discredit the former. In effect they say, "We do not understand verse 18, so we refuse to listen to verse 17." However, the proper approach is to understand both verses.

Verse 18 does not mean we should deliberately handle poisonous snakes as a test of faith. An example from Satan's temptation of Christ makes this clear. Satan quoted an Old Testament promise of protection and demanded that Jesus prove the truth of Scripture and His own righteousness by attempting to commit suicide (Matthew 4:6). Jesus answered, "It is written again, Thou shalt not tempt the Lord thy God" (Matthew 4:7). We should not try to force God to act in a certain way, and we should not deliberately ask for trouble to see what God will do. We cannot prove our faith or His Word by trying to harm ourselves, for that is contrary to His will.

Rightly understood, Mark 16:18 promises protection in case of accidents. If a child of God is accidentally bitten by a serpent, he can trust God for deliverance. This harmonizes well with the rest of verse 18, which tells us we can trust God in cases of sickness or accidental poisoning. As an example, when Paul was accidently bitten by a deadly viper, he calmly shook it off and was miraculously unharmed (Acts 28:1-6).

It is probable that Mark 16:18 also has a spiritual application, promising the believer power over demonic powers. From Genesis to Revelation the Bible characterizes the devil as a serpent. When Jesus gave seventy of His disciples power over evil spirits, He said, "Behold I give unto you power to tread on serpents and scorpions, and over all the power of the enemy: and nothing shall by any means hurt you" (Luke 10:19). It is logical to conclude that Mark 16:18 promises both protection against the effect of snake bites and victory in battle against spiritual foes. At the same time, the promise does not instruct us to tempt God by deliberately handling snakes as a test of faith. We should not try to discredit verse 18 in order to ignore verse 17, but we should seek to understand and apply both verses to our lives.

A second objection to Mark 16:17 is that two important Greek manuscripts of the Bible do not contain Mark 16:9-20. Critics thus imply that this passage is not the inspired Word of God. However, many conservative scholars believe that this passage is part of God's Word for the reasons stated below.[2]

(1) The argument against the passage is based primarily on the two oldest existing manuscripts, the Codex Sinaiticus and the Codex Vaticanus. However, both admittedly contain other incorrect additions and omissions. For example, both contain several apocryphal books, and the latter omits the New Testament after Hebrews 9:14. It also contains a blank column where Mark 16:9-20 should go. Their age does not necessarily mean greater reliability. Perhaps these manuscripts were not used very much because of their known unreliability, while more correct manuscripts wore out due to great use and were destroyed when new copies were made from them.

(2) A vast number of other important manuscripts

contain the passage, including the third oldest in existence, the Codex Alexandrinus.

(3) The passage appears in many early versions, including the Old Latin, Syriac Peshitta, Coptic, and Gothic.

(4) Many early church fathers quoted or alluded to the passage, including Irenaeus, Papias, Justin, Tertullian, Hippolytus, Ambrose, Chrysostom, Jerome, and Augustine.

(5) The passage is consistent with the other Gospel accounts.

(6) The doctrines taught in the passage are affirmed in other scriptural passages.

(7) It is extremely unlikely that someone would deliberately manufacture this passage with its teaching on tongues, power over demons, divine protection, and divine healing. If the church did not believe these doctrines (as critics of tongues maintain), why would someone add this passage and why would the ancient church accept it?

(8) Mark 16:8 reads, "And they went out quickly, and fled from the sepulchre; for they trembled and were amazed: neither said they any thing to any man; for they were afraid." This simply does not sound like a plausible ending for Mark's Gospel. We do not believe God would leave the account at this low point of fear and despair without mentioning the resurrection and the commissioning of the disciples.

(9) The passage was probably questioned because of the gradual disappearance of spiritual gifts as most of Christendom lost contact with the Holy Spirit. Indeed, some modern critics reject it primarily because of its content.

(10) If for some reason a few copies of Mark were circulated in an unfinished condition, it does not necessarily follow that other copies did not contain the passage.

In short, there is simply not enough evidence to discard Mark 16:9-20 from the Bible. We must take the words of Jesus in verse 17 at face value; speaking in tongues is a sign that will follow Christian believers everywhere.

The Day of Pentecost

The initial fulfillment of the prophecies concerning tongues occurred on the Day of Pentecost. On this occasion 120 Jewish disciples of Christ were baptized with the Spirit and spoke in tongues, including the apostles, the brothers of Jesus, Mary the mother of Jesus, and a number of women: "And when the day of Pentecost was fully come, they were all with one accord in one place. And suddenly there came a sound from heaven as of a rushing mighty wind, and it filled all the house where they were sitting. And there appeared unto them cloven tongues like as of fire, and it sat upon each of them. And they were all filled with the Holy Ghost, and began to speak with other tongues, as the Spirit gave them utterance" (Acts 2:1-4).

The supernatural sound filled the room, signifying that the Spirit had come to that place to manifest Himself in a special way and to do a special work. The tongues like fire settled on each individual, signifying that the Spirit was ready to baptize and fill each person. "They saw what seemed to be tongues of fire that separated and came to rest on each of them" (Acts 2:3, *NIV*). After this, they were all filled with the Spirit and began to speak in other tongues as the Spirit enabled them. Acts 2:4 teaches that the miracle took place as the Spirit moved on the speakers, not on the hearers. They began to speak in tongues only after the Spirit had entered, so speaking in tongues was the unique sign that each person had been baptized or filled with the Spirit.

The sound of wind and the tongues like fire never appear again in Scripture. Apparently they accompanied the founding of the New Testament church and the first outpouring of the Spirit much as lightning, thunder, and fire had accompanied the giving of the Law in the Old Testament (Exodus 19:16-19). Once God demonstrated that His Spirit was freely available to all, there was no need to emphasize it again in this fashion. Unlike the sound and the fire, however, speaking in tongues does reoccur a number of times in the Bible. Since it is the only sign particularly associated with an individual Spirit baptism (the others are signs of the availability of the Spirit), speaking in tongues has a lasting importance and function that the other signs do not.

Jews from many nations were in Jerusalem to celebrate the feast of Pentecost. When the 120 received the Spirit and began to speak in tongues, many of these visitors began to gather, with fourteen foreign lands being represented (Acts 2:5-11). These foreign Jews began to hear the various languages of their native countries and marvelled that uneducated Galileans could speak all these foreign tongues.

Some people assert that God performed this miracle so the foreigners could hear the gospel preached to them, but a short time later Peter delivered a sermon to all of them in one language. This was probably Aramaic, the native language of all Jews at that time, or possibly Greek, the international language of commerce. At any rate, the audience did not need the miracle of tongues to bring them the gospel message.

Instead, God used tongues as a miraculous sign to show them He had bestowed His Spirit. Peter used their questions and comments about tongues to open his sermon, and he immediately told them this was the fulfillment of Joel's prophecy concerning the outpouring of the Spirit (Acts 2:14-21). Later in his sermon, Peter said, "Exalted to the right hand of God, he [Jesus] has received from the Father the promised Holy Spirit and has poured out what you now see and hear" (Acts 2:33, *NIV*). The audience had just seen and heard people speaking in tongues, so Peter emphasized it as the evidence of the promised Holy Ghost.

Cornelius Spoke in Tongues

We find the next explicit record of speaking in tongues in the story of the first Gentiles to receive the Spirit: "While Peter yet spake these words, the Holy Ghost fell on all them which heard the word. And they of the circumcision which believed were astonished, as many as came with Peter, because that on the Gentiles also was poured out the gift of the Holy Ghost. For they heard them speak with tongues, and magnify God" (Acts 10:44-46).

The Jewish Christians with Peter did not expect these

Gentiles to receive the Holy Ghost immediately, because Jews traditionally believed one first had to convert to Judaism in order to be saved (Acts 15:1). Despite this strong preconception, the Jews with Peter were forced to admit that Cornelius and his household had indeed received the Spirit, for they heard them speak with tongues. As *The Pulpit Commentary* states, "This was the incontrovertible evidence of their reception of the Holy Ghost."[3] There is no mention of either a sound like wind or tongues like fire; speaking in tongues alone was the conclusive evidence.

The Spirit-filled Gentiles also "magnified God," meaning they praised God, either in tongues or in their own language. If the latter, it was a consequence of receiving the Spirit but certainly not the miraculous sign that convinced skeptical Jews.

Peter reported these events to the church in Jerusalem, saying, "And as I began to speak, the Holy Ghost fell on them, as on us at the beginning" (Acts 11:15). Speaking in tongues is the only sign that both Acts 2 and Acts 10 have in common, but it alone was enough to convince Peter that the Gentiles had received the Pentecostal experience.

The Ephesians Spoke in Tongues

The disciples of John the Baptist at Ephesus also spoke in tongues when they received the Spirit: "And when Paul had laid his hands upon them, the Holy Ghost came on them; and they spake with tongues, and prophesied" (Acts 19:6).

This account demonstrates that the baptism of the Spirit with tongues is for all believers. The tongues in Acts 2 and 10 perhaps could be explained away as one-time signs for the Jews and Gentiles respectively, but Acts 19 has no precedent-setting value other than to establish this experience as the norm for the New Testament church. The only purpose tongues accomplished in this setting was to be a sign to these individual believers that they had received the same experience already given to others. This use of tongues is just as valid and as needed today. Whatever reasons God had for giving the Ephesians the sign of tongues, those reasons still exist today.

These Ephesians also "prophesied" after they received the Spirit. Prophecy is "the speaking forth of the mind and counsel of God" or "the forth-telling of the will of God."[4] According to *Strong's Exhaustive Concordance,* one definition of the verb *to prophesy* is to "speak under inspiration." This can mean the gift of prophecy in which God speaks a direct message through human lips (I Corinthians 12:10), or it can mean any anointed preaching, praising, and testifying (I Corinthians 11:4-5; Revelation 19:10). Just as the 120 on Pentecost told of the wonderful works of God as they spoke in tongues (Acts 2:11), so these Ephesians apparently prophesied as they spoke in tongues. Possibly, the Spirit anointed these men to speak words in their own language after they had spoken in tongues. At any rate, prophecy resulted from the Spirit baptism but was not a sign such as tongues, because of these facts: (1) Tongues preceded prophecy, so tongues was the initial sign. (2) No other account of Spirit baptism mentions prophecy, so it is not a uniform sign. (3) Tongues is readily identifiable as a supernatural, miraculous sign while prophecy is not, especially with respect to a nonbelieving observer.

The Samaritans Spoke in Tongues

The account in Acts 8 of the Samaritans who received the Holy Ghost does not explicitly mention speaking in tongues; it gives no description of signs of their Spirit baptism. Despite the lack of detailed description, some tangible sign was present. The Spirit baptism was an objectively observable phenomenon that both believers and nonbelievers immediately recognized as supernatural. It is logical to assume that this sign was speaking in tongues.

(1) Despite the miracles, joy, belief, and water baptism, everyone knew the Samaritans had not yet received the Spirit. Philip, Peter, and John all expected a particular sign and knew the Samaritans did not have the Spirit due to the absence of the sign.

(2) Everyone knew the Samaritans received the Spirit at the moment Peter and John laid hands on them. There must have been a definite sign for everyone to perceive this with such certainty. Moreover, this sign was more than an emotional feeling, a confession of faith, or water baptism, since those had occurred earlier. Neither were they looking for a manifestation of any miracle or any spiritual gift, because healing and casting out of spirits had already occurred.

(3) There must have been a definite, supernatural sign for Simon the Magician to be impressed enough to desire it. Simon apparently wanted to buy and use this miracle in his magical shows; he desired the power to lay

hands on people and have the miraculous sign manifest itself. Again the sign was much more than an expression of joy, a confession of faith, or praise to God, all of which could be counterfeited with ease and none of which would impress a magician or his skeptical audience. Moreover, this sign impressed Simon in a way that all the other miracles had not.

The Pulpit Commentary acknowledges the existence of a sign: "There are signs of an impartation of the Spirit by the apostles which we do not appear to understand fully, because it differs from any impartation of the Spirit with which we have experience."[5] It continues, with respect to Acts 8: "These points assume that the indications of the Spirit's coming on the disciples were such as we find at Pentecost. There was some gift of tongues, or preaching, or praying—some outward sign which all could realize."[6] Of course, in the Pentecostal account only tongues served as the outward sign of the Spirit baptism itself. Neither preaching or praying is a possibility, since neither is a unique, miraculous sign and since the Samaritans had already observed both.

When we compare the Samaritans' experience with the other accounts, it is obvious that the accompanying miraculous sign was speaking in tongues. Indeed, Hoekema, who does not even believe speaking in tongues is available for the church today, comes to the same conclusion. He states, "Though we are not told in so many words that the Samaritans spoke with tongues. . .there must have been some public evidence of their having received the Spirit. We may therefore agree with our Pentecostal friends at that point that the Samaritans probably did speak with tongues."[7]

Paul Spoke in Tongues

Acts 9 indicates that Paul received the Spirit but it gives no description of this event. As a result, the passage does not mention speaking in tongues. Paul, however, spoke in tongues frequently, for he later said, "I thank my God, I speak with tongues more than ye all" (I Corinthians 14:18). Since he taught that speaking in tongues came by the Spirit (I Corinthians 12:8-10), it is consistent to assume that he first spoke in tongues when he received the Spirit, just as everyone else did.

Like the Ephesian account, Paul's witness demonstrates that tongues was not just a one-time, unrepeatable event in the Early Church. Paul, a Jew, spoke in tongues long after the Jews at Pentecost did, and he continued to do so in his devotion and ministry.

Comparison of the Accounts in Acts

We have investigated all five cases recorded in Scripture where people received the Holy Ghost. In three cases (Pentecost, Cornelius, Ephesus) those who received the Spirit immediately spoke in tongues. A fourth case (Samaria) does not explicitly describe any particular external manifestation but it clearly requires the presence of a miraculous, immediately identifiable outward sign, and most commentators agree this was speaking in tongues. In the fifth case (Paul) the Bible gives no description of the Spirit baptism, but later reveals that the recipient spoke in tongues throughout his Christian life.

What about other possible signs of the Spirit baptism?

Acts 2 records a sound like wind and tongues like fire, but these preceded the first outpouring of the Spirit and are not mentioned in any other account. Acts 8 demonstrates that not all spiritual gifts and miracles were considered as signs. Acts 19 mentions prophecy, but only after it mentions speaking in tongues. Acts 10 mentions magnifying (praising) God, which is not a miraculous sign; more importantly, it clearly identifies speaking in tongues as the one sign sufficient in and of itself to prove that the Spirit had been given. The following table summarizes this comparison:

The Baptism of the Spirit and Tongues

Pentecost	Samaria	Paul	Cornelius	Ephesus
•Sound like wind (filled room). •Tongues like fire (on or over each person). •Speaking in tongues (at individual filling).	•Miraculous, public sign (not named, but evidently tongues).	•No description. •Paul spoke in tongues often as a Christian.	•Speaking in tongues. •Magnification of God (praise).	•Speaking in tongues. •Prophecy (probably inspired praise or testimony).

Speaking in tongues is the only outward manifestation to appear in more than one account and the only one to occur at the actual moment of the individual Spirit baptism. The Book of Acts teaches that a person will speak in tongues when he receives the Holy Ghost. Therefore, speaking in tongues is the initial sign (evidence) that one has received the gift (baptism) of the Holy Spirit.

Other Possible References

Jesus perhaps had speaking in tongues in mind when He said, "The wind bloweth where it listeth [pleases], and thou hearest the sound thereof, but canst not tell whence it cometh, and whither it goeth: so is every one that is born of the Spirit" (John 3:8). Speaking in tongues at least initially fulfills Romans 8:16, which says, "The Spirit itself beareth witness with our spirit, that we are the children of God." It was also probably a factor in Paul's mind when he wrote about confessing with the mouth the Lord Jesus as part of salvation (Romans 10:9-10), for no one can truly confess Jesus as Lord except by the Spirit (I Corinthians 12:3).

Are Tongues Necessary?

Tongues in and of themselves do not save. Nevertheless, the relationship between the Spirit baptism and tongues is similar to that of faith and works. We are saved by faith, not works, yet works always accompany genuine faith. Likewise, tongues cannot save us, yet the Spirit baptism produces tongues as the initial sign.

Do tongues always accompany the baptism of the Spirit? The Book of Acts indicates this to be so; it describes tongues and nothing else as the initial sign associated with the individual filling. A Spirit baptism without tongues is a nonbiblical concept; the Bible does not discuss this possibility. We should always expect speaking in tongues when someone receives the baptism of the Holy Ghost.

The Reasons for Tongues

Why did God choose tongues as the sign of the Spirit baptism? We must realize that God is sovereign; He can establish a plan without explaining His reasons to us. The foolishness of God is wiser than men, and God often uses unusual, foolish, or despised things in the eyes of men to accomplish His will (I Corinthians 1:25-29). Examples are water baptism for the remission of sins and prayer to the invisible God.

We must accept speaking in tongues because God chose this sign. God has historically used outward, physical signs to accompany His covenants with man and the promised blessings under those covenants. Examples are the rainbow to Noah and circumcision to Abraham.

Humans did not invent tongues in a desperate, faithless search for a tangible sign of salvation. God Himself ordained tongues for the church, and we accept His plan by faith. Tongues cannot substitute for faith in the Christian's walk with God, but God gives tongues as the confirmation of faith (Mark 16:17).

Having said this, we can identify several reasons why God chose tongues as the initial sign of the Spirit baptism.

(1) The tongue seems to be the most difficult member of the body to control. It is a small member, but it can direct, control, and defile the whole body (James 3:2-6). "The tongue can no man tame; it is an unruly evil, full of deadly poison" (James 3:8). If a man cannot control his tongue his religion is vain, but if he can control his tongue he can control the whole body (James 1:26; 3:2). Before someone receives the Holy Ghost he must surrender his whole being to God, and the last member he surrenders is the tongue. When this happens, God enters and takes complete control, demonstrating His Lordship by using the most unruly member for His glory. Since the brain controls speech, this actually signifies that God has taken control of our center of consciousness, reasoning, and will—in short, the whole person.

(2) Speaking in tongues symbolizes the unity of the church. After the flood, human beings persisted in disobeying God and tried to compete with God by building the Tower of Babel. To stop their evil schemes and to scatter them, God gave them many languages instead of one (Genesis 11:1-9). Beginning with Pentecost, God reversed the process, taking people from many nations and uniting them into one spiritual family by the sign of tongues. The church contains people of every tribe, nation, and tongue, but all are one through the language of the Spirit. Speaking in tongues becomes the new language associated with citizenship in the kingdom of God.

(3) Speaking in tongues is universal in application and a valid sign under any circumstances. Regardless of a peo-

ple's nationality, language, or location, they can recognize speaking in tongues when it happens among them.

(4) Speaking in tongues provides certainty about one's experience with God since it signifies the baptism of the Spirit at a certain point in time. If one has been baptized in the name of Jesus, has received the Holy Ghost with the initial evidence of speaking in tongues, and continues to obey God's Word, he can know he is saved.

Many churches deny this evidentiary role, and as a result their members struggle with uncertainty about salvation. One Protestant writer stated, "Probably the majority of Christians have a problem with assurance of salvation at some time during their Christian experience. In some cases the difficulty lingers for years. . . .Many are those who continually trip to the altar in search of assurance—and repeatedly leave without finding it."[8] This writer also said, "A Christian may know intellectually, 'I am saved' and yet be overwhelmed by the feeling, 'I am not saved.' "[9] His solution is this: If one believes that Jesus is the Son of God and has asked Him to enter his life as Lord and Savior, then he should ignore all feelings and claim salvation. We acknowledge that salvation does not rest in human feelings, but we should certainly pay attention to conviction from God, especially if our experience does not conform to the biblical pattern.

Comments by another Protestant author demonstrate why many church members still have doubts despite the simplistic formula above: "It is possible to make a public profession of faith in Christ and be baptized and still not experience salvation. It might have been only a historic belief with no personal commitment. Your doubts may mean that you really need to be converted."[10] For example, if a prominent member of a church that teaches unconditional eternal security begins to live in open sin, the church will say he never had a genuine conversion in the beginning. This leads many to wonder how they can ever know if their own conversion is genuine. The writer quoted above often surveyed seminary students to ascertain how many once made a public confession of faith, later became convinced they were not saved, and then had a second experience which they felt to be a genuine conversion. He found that usually twenty percent fall into this category. His conclusion: "This is probably representative of most of our churches. Some of our members struggle with doubts and conclude that they have not been truly converted. It may be true of you."[11] His solution: Turn from sin, ask Christ into your heart as Savior and Lord, and believe in Him. These instructions are fine, but somehow they must be applied spiritually and not just intellectually. The Lord provides objective evidence of full commitment to Him; when one repents from sin and believes on Jesus according to the Scriptures, he will receive the Holy Spirit and speak in tongues.

Not a Sign of the Spirit's Abiding Presence

Speaking in tongues is the initial sign of receiving the Spirit, but by itself it does not prove the abiding presence of the Spirit. Many more important evidences of the Spirit's abiding presence exist, such as the fruit of the Spirit (Galatians 5:22-23). In particular, love is the ultimate test of true discipleship (John 13:34-35). The true child of God will love God, obey His commandments, walk after the Spirit, and be led by the Spirit (I John 2:3-5; Romans 8:4, 14). In the absence of these characteristics, speaking in tongues does not guarantee that the Spirit dwells in one and controls his life.

After one has received the Holy Ghost, a continual ability to speak in tongues indicates only that he has faith for that particular gift and can yield to God for that particular purpose. He might still believe false doctrine, resume a life of sin, or refuse God's leadership in other areas of life. We must always adhere to biblical doctrine, obey biblical instructions, and submit to God's Spirit in order to be saved.

Someone can have the ability to speak in tongues and not be ready to meet God, because God will always honor faith in a certain portion of His Word despite a lack of submission in other areas. This explains why God answers the prayers of sinners, fills people with the Holy Ghost before baptism in Jesus' name, and performs miracles when hypocrites preach. Many people experience miracles and preach in Jesus' name but will not be saved because they do not follow God's Word and will (Matthew 7:21-27).

Romans 11:29 says, "For the gifts and calling of God are without repentance." Although this verse occurs in another context, perhaps it teaches a principle with general application: once God bestows a spiritual gift He never revokes it entirely. Even if the recipient turns from God or abuses the gift, God seems to leave a portion of it to encourage the backslider to repent.

It is also possible that the human mind or spirit can "learn" to speak in tongues. When God enables someone to speak in tongues, He apparently places the words in his brain. God directs the speech but does so by using the person's physical apparatus, including brain cells, nerves, voice box, mouth, and tongue. It is possible, then, that the brain may store these words just as it stores other information. The next time God moves on the individual, He may give new words or He may activate the existing words in memory. This could explain why some people repeat the same phrases when the Spirit moves on them.

Over a period of time the brain can possibly subconsciously "learn" to activate this stored combination of words on its own. If so, even without the moving of the Spirit, the person could utter words that were at one time given by the Spirit. This would explain how some people can "speak in tongues" at will even without the moving of the Spirit or even after the Spirit has left their lives.

In addition, we should not overlook the possibility of false imitations of tongues by men or even counterfeit tongues caused by the power of Satan. Satan has power to perform many miracles, and he often tries to imitate God's work (Exodus 7:10-12; Revelation 13:2, 11-15). Some unbelievers or apostates may "speak in tongues" by the power of Satan. Of course, the existence of counterfeit tongues produced by the spirits of men or devils does not destroy the reality of biblical tongues as given by the Spirit of God.

After the Baptism of the Spirit

The Bible does not teach that speaking in tongues is a necessary sign after the occurrence at the initial Spirit baptism. Just as frequent tongues speaking does not necessarily signify spirituality, so a lack of the same does not necessarily signify unspirituality. Speaking in tongues plays no further evidentiary role, except perhaps as a reminder and confirmation of the previous experience. Of course, Paul spoke in tongues frequently (I Corinthians 14:18), and those who receive the Spirit usually speak in tongues again and again throughout their lifetimes.

The gift of tongues is one of the gifts available to those who have the Spirit (I Corinthians 12:8-10). First Corinthians 12:30 implies that not everyone continues to speak in tongues on a regular basis, although it probably refers primarily to public messages.

A Spirit-filled person who does not continue to speak in tongues is no less a Christian because of it. However, if he will seek the gift of tongues, exercise faith, and yield to the Spirit just as he did at the initial experience, he can speak in tongues again. Since tongues is for private edification, we believe that God desires for him to seek and use the gift of tongues. Once received, a failure to exercise this gift may indicate a drifting away from God. The gift of tongues is available to all Spirit-filled people who ask in prayer, with persistence and faith (Matthew 7:7-11; 21:22; John 14:12-14; I Corinthians 12:31).

The Gift of Tongues

Paul discussed the gift of tongues in I Corinthians 12-14. He wrote the book to saved believers who were all baptized in the Spirit and thus had all spoken in tongues (I Corinthians 1:2; 12:13). His purpose was to instruct them in the use of the gift of tongues, particularly in public meetings. Since these three chapters are so important to any discussion of tongues in the church today, let us summarize their main points relative to this subject.

I Corinthians 12

Verse 1: Paul's purpose is to teach about spiritual gifts.

Verse 2: The Corinthians had been totally ignorant of spiritual things before their conversion.

Verse 3: The Spirit will always exalt Jesus. No one can understand that Jesus is Lord except by the illumination of the Spirit, and no one can actually have Jesus as Lord of his life except through the power of the Spirit.

Verses 4-11: There are many spiritual gifts, but all come from the Spirit of God for the benefit of the church. Paul listed nine: the word of wisdom, the word of knowledge, faith, gifts of healing, the working of miracles, prophecy, discerning of spirits, kinds of tongues, and interpretation of tongues.

Verses 12-27: Born-again believers are all members of one body, the body of Christ. We are baptized into the one body by the one Spirit of God.

Verses 28-30: God has given different functions to various members of the body. Paul listed eight offices and gifts God has placed in the church as a whole: apostles, prophets, teachers, miracles, gifts of healings, helps, governments, and diversities of tongues. Not everyone has these public offices or exercises these public gifts.

Verse 31: We should earnestly desire the best gifts.

However, there is something greater and more important than spiritual gifts.

I Corinthians 13

None of the spiritual gifts is of any value without love. Speaking in tongues (whether human or angelic in origin) is useless without love. Prophecy, tongues, and knowledge will all pass away when perfection comes to the world, but love will remain forever. There are three great things in this world—faith, hope, and love—and the greatest of these is love.

I Corinthians 14

Verse 1: We should follow after love but also desire spiritual gifts, particularly prophecy.

Verses 2-4: Speaking in tongues edifies (builds up, benefits) the speaker, but prophecy (inspired utterance in a tongue known by all) edifies others.

Verse 5: Paul wanted everyone to speak in tongues, but wanted even more for them to prophesy. In the church (public meeting of believers), prophecy is greater than tongues, unless the tongues is interpreted.

Verse 6-11: Without an interpretation, a public message in tongues does not profit the church as a whole.

Verses 12-14: We should seek to exercise spiritual gifts for the benefit of the whole church. Specifically, if someone gives a public message in tongues, we should pray for the interpretation.

Verses 15-19: Paul personally prayed and sang both in the spirit (i.e., in tongues) and in an understandable language. A public, representative prayer should be in the language of the hearers. Paul personally spoke in tongues more than any of the Corinthians, but in the church (public meetings) he spoke in a known language in order to teach others.

Verse 20: We must be mature in understanding when the gift of tongues is and is not appropriate.

Verses 21-22: Tongues are a sign for unbelievers, while prophecy helps believers. In other words, tongues will attract attention and inspire belief, but after that the real teaching must be done in a known language.

Verses 23-25: If everyone continually speaks in tongues in church, observers will think they are insane. However, if everyone prophesies in a known language, listeners can be led to God. Even though tongues will arrest unbelievers' attention initially, it does not benefit them if the whole service is devoted to tongues speaking.

Verses 26-31: Conclusion for public meetings. A normal church meeting can and should include psalms (songs), doctrine, tongues, revelations (spiritual truths in a known tongue), and interpretation of tongues; but all of this must be done for the benefit of everyone.

Some guidelines for implementing this principle are: (1) Let there be two or at most three public messages in tongues. (2) Take turns in giving them instead of everyone speaking at once. (3) Let someone interpret each message. (4) If there is no interpretation, the one speaking in tongues should stop giving public messages but he can speak in tongues quietly for his own private benefit. (5) Let there be two or at most three messages of prophecy.

(6) The listeners should judge for themselves whether the message is of God. (7) Take turns in prophecy; everyone is allowed to prophesy.

Verses 32-33: The gift of prophecy is subject to those who exercise it. God desires that all gifts be exercised in an orderly manner in church.

Verses 34-35: Women should not disrupt church services by asking questions aloud, but should ask their husbands at home. (Of course, women can prophesy in church, I Corinthians 11:5-6 and 14:31.)

Verses 36-38: Let all acknowledge these guidelines to be of God.

Verse 39: Everyone should desire to prophesy and no one should forbid speaking in tongues.

Verse 40: We should do everything decently and in order.

Conclusions about I Corinthians 12-14

(1) Speaking in tongues is a normal part of the New Testament church. Paul spoke in tongues, encouraged other believers to do likewise, gave instructions for the proper use of tongues, and commanded the church not to forbid tongues.

(2) Speaking in tongues is the same phenomenon in I Corinthians as in Acts. The Greek word is the same in both books. Paul talked about literal languages as in Acts 2, not unintelligible, ecstatic gibberish (I Corinthians 13:1).

(3) In Acts, speaking in tongues is the initial sign of the Spirit baptism, but in I Corinthians we find that tongues have two additional purposes. Specifically, speak-

ing in tongues has continuing value for edification of the individual in personal devotion and for edification of the church as a whole when interpreted.

(4) A public message in tongues has little benefit unless it is interpreted.

(5) Tongues are very beneficial in personal devotion.

How Does Speaking in Tongues Occur?

Genuine, biblical tongues speaking comes only as the Spirit of God gives the utterance (Acts 2:4). If one desires to speak in tongues, he must first receive the Spirit. He should not begin by seeking tongues, for tongues themselves are not very important. Speaking in tongues will occur automatically when he receives the Spirit even if he knows little or nothing about the evidence of tongues.

Of course, if one is not familiar with the phenomenon of speaking in tongues, he may unconsciously restrain the utterance. In such a case, the seeker should be encouraged to relax and surrender totally to God's Spirit, but in no case does he need to be "taught" to speak in tongues. Asking him to form nonsense words or repeat unknown syllables is unbiblical and wrong. It seeks to give tongues without the Spirit, and any "tongues" not inspired by the Spirit is vain babbling. Someone who has not received the Spirit should not concern himself too much with tongues but should concentrate on repenting and believing God for the Spirit.

Someone who has received the Spirit can and should seek the gift of tongues as a regular part of his life, but he should also recognize that not everyone will exercise the public gift (I Corinthians 12:28-30). It is much more important to bear the fruit of the Spirit and live a Spirit-filled life than it is to cultivate tongues speaking. Of course, the mature Christian can have both the fruit and the gifts of the Spirit.

Objections

Many people today raise objections to tongues speaking. Here is an analysis of the most prominent ones, as paraphrased from Protestant Professor Anthony Hoekema's book, *What about Tongues Speaking?*[12]

(1) "The Bible does not teach that every believer must seek a postconversion Spirit baptism." This objection applies to many "Pentecostal" groups, but not to the doctrine presented in this book. The Spirit baptism is part of conversion, but tongues still accompany it.

(2) "Pentecostalism implies a nonbiblical subordination of Christ to the Holy Spirit." Again, this does not apply. We believe the Holy Spirit is the Spirit of Christ, and we receive Christ when we receive the Spirit. The doctrine of the Spirit baptism thus magnifies Christ above all.

(3) "Pentecostalism tends to create two levels of Christians: those who have received the Spirit baptism and those who have not." This does not apply to us either. Since the Spirit baptism is part of conversion, it simply distinguishes true apostolic Christians from everyone else.

(4) "Pentecostalism implies that the church has not had the fulness of truth from the end of the first century to the beginning of the twentieth." Chapter 11 will show that speaking in tongues has existed throughout church

history. In any event, history and tradition cannot stand against Scripture. Man's sin, rebellion, error, and ignorance can drastically affect the history of God's people, but this does not mean it is God's will. Israel's backsliding and subsequent captivity does not mean God desired this from the start. Actually, all of Protestantism rests on the belief that for centuries the visible church discarded many essential truths of the gospel.

(5) "A spiritual blessing does not need to be attested to by a physical phenomenon." We can accept this statement, but this does not prevent God from designating one if He so chooses, and in the case of the Spirit baptism He has done so. The Bible describes speaking in tongues as the evidence of the Spirit baptism (Acts 10:46) and as a "sign" (I Corinthians 14:22).

God often chooses a physical sign to accompany a spiritual work. Water baptism consists of both a spiritual blessing (remission of sins) and a physical manifestation that is a necessary part of it (the outward ceremony). Other examples that combine a spiritual blessing with a physical manifestation are prayer, anointing of the sick, ordination, the Lord's supper, holiness of life, and the Second Coming. The long-term evidence of the Spirit baptism is spiritual fruit, but this does not prohibit God from establishing an initial physical sign.

(6) "It cannot be proved that miracles are for the church today." We discuss this objection below in all of its variations.

Miracles Exist Today

The most popular argument against tongues today

is that the days of miracles are over. Chapter 8 established that the baptism of the Holy Spirit is for people today, so logically tongues are for today also. Below we analyze each variant of the argument that miracles, and specifically tongues, no longer occur.

(1) "Miracles were only for the apostles." We can easily disprove this statement by the 120 at Pentecost, Cornelius, and the Ephesians, all of whom spoke in tongues. Stephen and Philip, who were not of the Twelve, also performed many miracles (Acts 6:8; 8:6-7).

(2) "Only the apostles or those commissioned by them (by the laying on of hands) could perform or receive a miracle." This modification to account for the above counterexamples still fails. Ananias prayed for Paul and he received his sight (Acts 9:17-18), but absolutely nothing indicates that Ananias received a special commissioning from the Twelve. Paul and Barnabas were not of the Twelve nor commissioned by them, but God performed many miracles in their ministry (Acts 14:3).

The New Testament promises miracles to all believers without restriction or discrimination. Jesus promised that all believers could speak in tongues and experience other miracles (Mark 16:17-18). All believers can receive answers to prayer, including miracles (Matthew 21:22; Mark 11:22-24; John 14:12-14; 15:7). Local elders can pray successfully for the saints' divine healing and all saints can pray for each other's healing (James 5:14-16). Miracles and tongues are God's gift to the whole church (I Corinthians 12:8-10, 28).

(3) "Miracles were only for the days of the apostles." The passages cited above discredit this statement, for none specify a time limitation. To the contrary, each was

given to all believers or to the church as a whole without restriction as to time. Paul wrote I Corinthians to the entire church of all ages, addressing it "unto the church of God which is at Corinth, to them that are sanctified in Christ Jesus, called to be saints, with all that in every place call upon the name of Jesus Christ our Lord, both theirs and ours" (I Corinthians 1:2). He expressed confidence that they would "come behind in no gift; waiting for the coming of our Lord Jesus Christ" (I Corinthians 1:7). That book discusses the gifts of the Spirit, including gifts of healing, working of miracles, and kinds of tongues (I Corinthians 12:8-10), so Paul clearly expected the church to retain and properly use all the spiritual gifts until Christ's return.

Everyone agrees that the Great Commission applies to the church today, and so must its fulfillment. The Early Church fulfilled it: "And they went forth, and preached every where, the Lord working with them, and confirming the word with signs following" (Mark 16:20); "God also bearing them witness, both with signs and wonders, and with divers miracles, and gifts of the Holy Ghost, according to his own will" (Hebrews 2:4). If we have the same Lord, the same commission, the same gospel, the same faith, and the same needy world, surely we will have the same signs accompanying and confirming our message.

Tongues Have Not Ceased

I Corinthians 13:8-10 states, "Charity never faileth: but whether there be prophecies, they shall fail; whether there be tongues, they shall cease; whether there be knowledge, it shall vanish away. For we know in part, and we prophesy in part. But when that which is perfect is come, then that which is in part shall be done away." Some people use this passage to teach that tongues have ceased, by identifying "that which is perfect" with the completed New Testament. This argument fails for a number of reasons:

(1) The spiritual gifts, including tongues, will reside in the church until the second coming of Christ (I Corinthians 1:2, 7).

(2) This being so, it is logical to identify "that which is perfect" with Jesus Christ or, more specifically, with the Second Coming of Christ. The Greek word translated as "perfect" is *teleion,* which is neuter singular, but the Greek language always refers to the Scriptures in the feminine plural.

(3) Tongues will cease at the same time as prophecy and knowledge, according to verse 8. Prophecy includes inspired preaching, praising, and testifying. Obviously the church still has prophecy and knowledge.

(4) The Bible and miracles do not have interchangeable functions. The Bible presents the Word of God in written form, but God still uses miracles, signs, and spiritual gifts to confirm the Word (Mark 16:20; Hebrews 2:4).

(5) In I Corinthians 13:11-13, Paul compared levels of spiritual growth to physical and mental growth, but he did not label tongues as childish. He compared our partial knowledge to the perfect knowledge we shall have when Christ returns. If we have already reached the ultimate stage, then we are more mature than Paul was,

for he died before the completion of the New Testament. If speaking in tongues be childish, Paul never left the childish stage, for he continually spoke in tongues (I Corinthians 14:18).

(6) The New Testament is God's Word, but we are not yet perfect, nor is the world perfect. Perfection will come only after Christ returns.

(7) It is difficult to see how the completion of the New Testament could have put a halt to tongues, prophecy, and knowledge. Did all tongues suddenly cease when John penned "Amen" to the Book of Revelation? Did each person cease to speak in tongues when he first read the entire New Testament?

Receiving the Spirit without Tongues?

We analyzed all five biblical accounts of the Spirit baptism and concluded that tongues were present in each case. Many other passages describe believers as "filled with the Spirit" without mentioning tongues, but they refer to people who had already been baptized in the Spirit. Tongues do not necessarily accompany all subsequent experiences with God after the initial baptism.

Some conversion accounts in the Book of Acts do not specifically mention tongues. The plan of Acts is to describe a few representative conversions in detail, then briefly mention other conversions. Three very important passages describe tongues, and these detailed accounts set the pattern for the general accounts, not vice versa. No argument from silence can overwhelm or erase these explicit testimonies.

It is not surprising that speaking in tongues is mentioned no more than it is. The important things are repenting, believing, and receiving the Spirit. Tongues simply come along with the Spirit baptism and have no significance apart from this experience. Appropriately, the Bible places more emphasis on believing and receiving the Spirit, letting us know just enough to expect tongues without unduly emphasizing it.

The discussion in *The Tyndale New Testament Commentaries* of speaking in tongues at the conversion of Cornelius (Acts 10:45-46) makes an amazing concession for a non-Pentecostal work: "We cannot tell for certain whether the gift of tongues was the inevitable accompaniment of the coming of the Spirit."[13] In other words, it admits that on the biblical evidence tongues may have always accompanied the outpouring of the Spirit in the apostolic church. It tries to avoid this conclusion by two facts: (1) Speaking in tongues is not mentioned frequently in Acts. (2) In I Corinthians Paul indicates that not all members of the church had the gift of tongues. The first fact is explained as the Bible's way of emphasizing the Spirit baptism without placing too much emphasis on speaking in tongues in and of itself. With respect to the second, Paul was not discussing tongues at the initial Spirit baptism (which all had received). Rather, he implied that not all Spirit-filled believers exercised the subsequent gift of tongues, particularly in the sense of giving public messages in tongues.

Conclusion

Some points from *The Pulpit Commentary* with which

we agree are: (1) Speaking in tongues means the miraculous utterance of a foreign language unknown to the speaker. (2) It is not the gift of a foreign language for missionary purposes. (3) It is a real language, not gibberish. (4) It can be a heavenly or a human language. (5) Speaking in tongues in Corinth was the speaking of real languages. (6) Speaking in tongues is a symbol of the unity the church has in Christ.[14]

In conclusion here are the three functions that speaking in tongues has in the New Testament church:

(1) Speaking in tongues is the initial sign of the baptism of the Holy Spirit (Acts 2:4; 10:46; 19:6). This is to be distinguished in purpose from "the gift of tongues," which God grants to Spirit-filled believers subsequent to conversion.

(2) A Spirit-filled person can exercise the gift of tongues in personal devotions (whether private or congregational) for his own personal edification (I Corinthians 12:8-10; 14:1-5, 14-18, 23, 28).

(3) A Spirit-filled person can exercise the gift of tongues for the edification of the local assembly. This occurs when a public message is given in tongues and interpreted (I Corinthians 12:8-10, 28-30; 14:5, 12-13, 27-28).

If we understand what speaking in tongues is and the purposes for which it is given, we can correctly understand and harmonize all scriptural teaching on the subject. Speaking in tongues is a normal part of the believer's experience with God, the personal devotion of the believer, and the public meetings of the church. Most of all, we can expect a person to speak in tongues when he first receives the Holy Spirit into his life.

FOOTNOTES

[1]Vine, p. 1165.

[2]Norman Geisler and William Nix, *A General Introduction to the Bible* (Chicago: Moody Press, 1968), pp. 270-74, 372; David Otis Fuller, ed., *Which Bible?* (Grand Rapids: Grand Rapids International Publications, 1975), pp. 168-69. For further discussion, see David Otis Fuller, ed., *Counterfeit or Genuine? Mark 16? John 8?* (Grand Rapids: Grand Rapids International Publications, 1975).

[3]*The Pulpit Commentary,* XVIII (Acts), 336.

[4]Vine, p. 903.

[5]*The Pulpit Commentary,* XVIII (Acts), 279-80.

[6]*Ibid.*

[7]Hoekema, *What About Tongues Speaking?,* p. 70.

[8]Charles Solomon, "Counselor's Corner," *Fulness,* November-December 1980, pp. 30-31.

[9]*Ibid.*

[10]James Eaves, "Steps to Blessed Assurance," *Fulness,* November-December 1980, p. 12.

[11]*Ibid.*

[12]Hoekema, *What About Tongues Speaking?,* pp. 103-23.

[13]I. Howard Marshall, *The Acts of the Apostles,* Vol. V of *The Tyndale New Testament Commentaries,* (Grand Rapids: Eerdmans, 1980), p. 194.

[14]*The Pulpit Commentary,* XVIII (Acts), pp. 48-50.

10

THE WITNESS IN CHURCH HISTORY: BAPTISM

"Wherefore seeing we also are compassed about with so great a cloud of witnesses, let us lay aside every weight, and the sin which doth so easily beset us, and let us run with patience the race that is set before us" (Hebrews 12:1).

Since all doctrine must be based on Scripture alone and not on man's traditions, creeds, or philosophies (Galatians 1:8-9; Colossians 2:8; II Timothy 3:16-17), we have based all conclusions in this book on the Bible. However, many people have never heard the doctrines we have presented, and some assume them to be modern inventions. Although history cannot alter or replace biblical truth, the study of these doctrines in church history is very enlightening.

Problems in Studying Church History

There are several difficulties that the student of church history, particularly ancient history, must consider:

(1) Doctrinal bias of church historians. Modern historians often interpret the statements of ancient writers from the perspective of their own beliefs, finding teachings that simply are not there. On the other hand, the doctrinal positions of historians can limit their understanding of doctrines that did exist.

(2) Doctrinal bias of ancient church writers. Consciously or unconsciously, ancient writers sometimes distorted or misrepresented the views of their doctrinal opponents. As a result, we do not always have an adequate presentation of certain ancient views, especially minority views. For example, what concept of Oneness would future generations have if their only source of information were articles written by trinitarians? Likewise, skeptical observers have often described worshipers in ways that made them appear ridiculous, absurd, ignorant, or mentally deranged. For example, what would someone think of Pentecostals if he read only the accounts of cynical opponents?

(3) Possibility of interpolations (additions to ancient manuscripts). Most of our information about church history comes from manuscripts that were copied hundreds of years after the original writings. In many cases the copyists changed or inserted certain lines to create support for particular doctrines. For example, a number of the epistles of the post-apostolic fathers exist in short and long versions. Obviously, one form (probably the

longer one) is corrupt and reflects changes made by generations of editors and scribes. As another example, an ancient Christian writing called the *Didache* was apparently written in the 2nd century, but the only Greek manuscript we have of it dates from the 11th century. This means errors and deliberate changes could have accumulated over 900 years, and the document may reflect teachings from Roman Catholicism.

(4) Existing documents may not reflect the views of the average believer of that time period. In times when many people were not literate and books had to be handwritten, theological documents tended to be written and copied by the educated elite. Then, as now, theologians were frequently more liberal in their doctrines than were the majority of believers.

(5) History is written by the victors. Many who opposed officially accepted doctrines were persecuted so that they had little opportunity to leave an adequate written record of their beliefs. The documents they did write were usually destroyed and not recopied. For evidence of a minority doctrine to survive at all often means it must have been very prevalent in its day. Surviving records probably reveal only a fraction of those who actually held the belief.

(6) False doctrines existed from the earliest times. There is plenty of evidence in the biblical writings of Paul, Peter, John, and Jude that false doctrines abounded even in the days of the apostles and threatened to overwhelm the church. For this reason, the antiquity of a writer is no guarantee of his doctrinal purity.

Repentance and Water Baptism

The church leaders of the early post-apostolic era (A.D. 90-140) taught that baptism was for believers only and that repentance was necessary for baptism to be of any value. Lutheran Professor Otto Heick states, "Baptism, of course, was not meant to work magically. Without repentance and faith it would avail nothing."[1] Lutheran Professor E. H. Klotsche says of the belief in this time: "In closest relation to baptism stands repentance. It is preparatory to baptism."[2] However, when infant baptism began to gain acceptance, theologians began to teach that faith and repentance could follow baptism. This ultimately led to the Roman Catholic sacrament of penance. "When the original sequel of repentance and baptism became inverted by the practice of infant baptism, penance. . .acquired the status of a sacrament."[3]

Water Baptism by Immersion

Church historians generally agree that the early post-apostolic church practiced immersion. Klotsche says, "The practice of immersion was undoubtedly universal in the early church."[4] Kenneth Scott Latourette affirms this view: "Baptism seems to have been by immersion, at least normally."[5] Some historians assert that other modes were practiced in these early times, but they agree that immersion was the predominant and preferred mode even when others began to develop.

Hermas (early 2nd century) described baptism by immersion and Irenaeus (died 202?) denounced baptism by pouring.[6] Tertullian (died 220?) taught baptism by immersion and disapproved of infant baptism. Cyprian (died 258?) is the earliest apologist for sprinkling, but even he considered immersion to be the normal practice. He described baptism as a dipping but advised sprinkling for the sick. The *Didache* teaches baptism by immersion, but permits pouring if much water is not available. The *Constitutions of the Holy Apostles* (2nd or 3rd century), which contains a parallel passage to this portion of the *Didache*, teaches immersion but does not mention pouring.

The Eastern Orthodox still practice immersion even for infants,[7] despite the fact that their counterparts in the West, the Roman Catholics, switched to sprinkling. Many Protestants continue in the Catholic tradition even though most early Protestant leaders recognized that immersion was the biblical method. Martin Luther expressed a preference for immersion based on the Greek word *bapto;* John Calvin acknowledged immersion as the practice of the Early Church; and John Wesley interpreted Romans 6:3-5 to mean immersion.[8]

Water Baptism as Part of Salvation

Early post-apostolic Christians affirmed baptism as part of salvation. Latourette remarked, "Baptism was believed to wash away all sins committed before it was administered. After baptism, the Christian was supposed not to sin."[9] He also said, "Baptism seems to have been regarded as requisite for the 'remission of sins' and for the new birth through which alone one could enter the Kingdom of God."[10]

With respect to baptism in the first and second centuries the *Encyclopedia of Religion and Ethics* states, "The dominant ideas were those of forgiveness of sin, regeneration, and the gift of the Holy Spirit. . .The change effected by baptism was attributed to the 'name' and to the water, which were regarded as actually effective and not merely symbolic."[11] According to Heick, the post-apostolic fathers (A.D. 90-140) taught that "baptism confers the forgiveness of sins."[12] For example, this was the teaching in the *Epistle of Barnabas* and the *Shepherd of Hermas.* For the Greek Apologists (A.D. 130-180) baptism was "a washing of forgiveness and a regeneration."[13] They said it "brings pardon and the new life, and is therefore necessary to salvation."[14]

Other early theologians who taught that God remits sins at water baptism were Justin Martyr, Irenaeus, Origen, Tertullian, and Augustine.[15] Irenaeus, Tertullian, Hippolytus, and Cyprian specifically described water baptism as the birth of the water in John 3:5, and Hippolytus and Cyprian identified water baptism as the laver of regeneration in Titus 3:5. The *Constitutions of the Holy Apostles* paraphrases John 3:5 as, "Except a man be baptized of water and of the Spirit, he shall by no means enter into the kingdom of heaven."[16]

Tertullian taught that at water baptism the believer has his sins washed away, is born in water, and is prepared for the Holy Spirit.[17] He believed that John's baptism pointed towards future remission of sins and that Christ's disciples continued John's baptism during Christ's earthly ministry. He described baptism as a seal of faith that is necessary to salvation, stating that John 3:5 "has tied faith to the necessity of baptism."

These men and writings represent many different theological factions, and we do not endorse all of their doctrines; nevertheless it is interesting to see that all agreed on the necessity of baptism. Third century controversies over heretic baptisms demonstrate that all Christendom of the time agreed that "there can be only one baptism, and that this baptism is essential to salvation."[18]

Roman Catholics have always taught the essentiality of baptism, but have transformed it from an act of faith into a sacramental act by teaching the necessity and validity of infant baptism despite the lack of personal faith and repentance. This incorrectly presumes that regeneration comes by the power of the ceremony itself instead of by grace through faith.

Among Protestants, Martin Luther held that baptism is a necessary part of salvation.[19] Article IX of the *Augsburg Confession* (an early Lutheran creed) states, "Baptism is necessary to salvation."[20]

The *Lutheran Catechism* says, "Baptism is no trifle, but was instituted by God Himself, . . .it is most solemnly commanded that we must be baptized or we cannot be saved."[21] In accordance with his emphasis on justification by faith, Luther taught that baptism was effective only through faith, but still held that God actually forgives sin at the moment of water baptism. Luther even taught the validity of infant baptism, based on the theory that God gives faith to infants. In our estimation, Luther was incorrect in teaching infant faith and infant baptism, but he was correct in simultaneously affirming justification by faith and the essentiality of water baptism.

Most Protestants after Luther began to teach that

baptism is symbolic only, but this is a comparatively new doctrine in church history and not all Protestants accept it. In addition to Luther and his followers, the Churches of Christ teach that water baptism is necessary in order to obtain remission of sins. United Church of Christ theologian Donald Bloesch stated, "Baptism plays a prominent role in our conversion and is not just a symbol of our conversion."[22] He also wrote, "The overall witness of the New Testament seems to be that baptism by itself is not indispensible for salvation, but baptism joined with repentance and faith becomes the means by which people receive the gift of regeneration."[23]

The Earliest Formula

Early post-apostolic Christians administered water baptism by using the name of Jesus in the formula. According to Heick, "At first baptism was administered in the name of Jesus, but gradually in the name of the Triune God: Father, Son, and Holy Spirit."[24] He concluded from a passage in the writings of Justin (which we will analyze shortly) that during the period from about A.D. 130 to 140 the trinitarian baptismal formula gradually received acceptance.[25]

The *Encyclopedia of Religion and Ethics* states: "The earliest form, represented in the Acts, was simple immersion. . .in water, the use of the name of the Lord, and the laying on of hands. To these were added, at various times and places which cannot be safely identified, (a) the trine name (Justin), (b) a moral vow (Justin and perhaps Hermas, as well as already in the NT in I Peter), (c) trine immersion (Justin), (d) a confession of faith (Irenaeus, or perhaps Justin), (e) unction (Tertullian), (f) sponsors (Tertullian), (g) milk and honey (Tertullian).''[26]

It further elaborates: "In connection with the name. . .the question of formula arises. The earliest known formula is 'in the name of the Lord Jesus,' or some similar phrase; this is found in the Acts, and was perhaps still used by Hermas, but by the time of Justin Martyr the trine formula had become general. It is possible that the older formula survived in isolated communities, but there is no decisive contemporary evidence.''[27]

First and Second Centuries

Hastings' *Dictionary of the Bible* admits that one could draw the following conclusion from the historical evidence: "The original form of words was 'into the name of Jesus Christ' or 'the Lord Jesus.' Baptism into the name of the Trinity was a later development. After the one mention of it, Mt. 28:19, we do not find it again until Justin Martyr, and his formula is not identical with that in the Gospel.''[28]

The dictionary preferred one of the following two explanations sometimes given by trinitarians as to the use of the name of Jesus, since they are more consistent with traditional practice: (1) Baptism in the name of one person in the trinity is baptism in the name of the whole trinity and so is valid. (This explanation admits that the original formula actually was "in the name of Jesus.") (2) The phrase "in the name of Jesus" was not meant to be a formula, but only signified that the baptized ones acknowledged Jesus as Lord and Christ. (Of course, this logic could be applied equally as well to Matthew 28:19, leaving us with no formula for Christian baptism.)

In addition to the sources we have cited, most other church historians agree that baptism in Jesus' name was the older formula; further quotations are reproduced in a footnote.[29]

Hermas in the early second century wrote of baptism "in the name of the Lord" and in the "name of the Son of God."[30] He taught that baptism caused an essential change to take place in one's life because of the use of the name, but stressed that the name was not a magical formula and could not be effective in the absence of Christian virtues.[31] He wrote, "If you bear His name but possess not His power, it will be in vain that you bear His name."[32]

The *Didache,* another second century Christian document, speaks of baptism "into the name of the Lord" but also speaks of baptism "into the name of the Father and of the Son and of the Holy Ghost."[33] Some conclude that the *Didache* recognizes both formulas as valid. We must not overlook the possibility of interpolations, for while scholars have variously dated the *Didache* from A.D. 120 to 200 the only existing Greek manuscript of it dates to 1056.[34] Moreover, it teaches other nonbiblical practices relative to baptism such as pouring as an alternative to immersion, fasting before baptism, and triple immersion.

Most scholars assert that Justin Martyr's *First Apology,* written around A.D. 150, contains the oldest historical reference to the trine formula. Here is the key phrase, which describes baptized persons: "For, in the name of God, the Father and Lord of the universe, and of our Saviour Jesus Christ and of the Holy Spirit, they then receive the washing with water."[35] We should note, however, that Justin did not recite the modern trinitarian formula but explicitly included the name Jesus, probably in deference to older practice.

Justin taught that Jesus was a subordinate, second being created by God the Father and did not clearly distinguish the Holy Spirit as a third person. Consequently, it is no great comfort for trinitarians to find evidence of their formula in his writings. In fact, the modern doctrine of the trinity did not become dominant until the councils of Nicea (325) and Constantinople (381). Just because one man in A.D. 150, who did not believe in the full deity of Christ, referred to a baptismal formula similar to the modern trinitarian one does not mean all or even most in his day had abandoned the older Jesus' name formula. Evidence for general usage of the modern trinitarian formula at this early date is not as decisive as some have indicated.

History records a possible reference to Jesus Name baptism shortly after Justin's time. Irenaeus, bishop of Lyons, wrote, "We are made clean, by means of the sacred water and the invocation of the Lord."[36] His last major work, however, describes a baptismal formula that was apparently the same as Justin's.

Closely associated with the baptismal formula is the doctrine of the Godhead. The early post-apostolic fathers, such as Ignatius, Clement of Rome, Polycarp, and Hermas, were certainly not trinitarians.[37] They basically believed in one God and in Jesus as God manifested in flesh. It is hardly surprising, then, to find no reference in their writings to a trinitarian baptismal formula.

The heretic Marcion broke away from the church during this time, and his followers preserved the older baptism "in the name of Jesus Christ."[38] The *Acts of Paul and Thecla,* written by an Asiatic presbyter in the second century, gives an account of baptism "in the name of Jesus Christ."[39]

Third Century

Significantly, we still find references to baptism in Jesus' name long after Justin's time. In the third century, a debate arose over the validity of baptism performed by "heretics." Stephen, Bishop of Rome (Roman Catholics consider him a pope), held such baptism to be valid, while the North African theologian Cyprian held it was not. In opposing Stephen, Cyprian discussed the case of "heretics" who baptized in the name of Jesus. He asked, "Can they who among the heretics are said to be baptized in the name of Christ be judged to have obtained remission of sins?"[40] He argued that the Jews in Acts properly received baptism in the name of Jesus only because they already acknowledged the Father, but that Gentiles who did not acknowledge the Father must be baptized in the full trinity.

> "How, then, do some say, that a Gentile baptized without, outside the Church, yea and in opposition to the Church, so that it be only in the name of Jesus Christ everywhere, and in whatever manner, can obtain remission of sin, when Christ Himself commands the heathen to be baptized in the full and united Trinity?"[41]

Cyprian further argued that heretics deny the Father and blaspheme Him, so baptism in the name of Jesus only cannot save them.

Cyprian's opponents argued that Jesus' name baptism was always valid, even if performed by heretics, because of the power in the name of Jesus. Firmilian, Bishop of Caesarea in Cappadocia, wrote to Cyprian in 256. He quoted Stephen as saying that "the name of Christ is of great advantage to faith and the sanctification of baptism; so that whosoever is anywhere soever baptized in the name of Christ, immediately obtains the grace of Christ."[42]

Cyprian responded to Stephen's view as follows: If this were so then heretics could also receive the Holy Spirit simply by laying on hands and invoking the name of Jesus. This would mean they would be born of the water and Spirit and so would be true Christians, even though they were outside the Catholic Church. Cyprian argued that this could not be correct. Just as the name Jesus could not impart the Holy Spirit outside the Catholic Church, so baptism in the name of Jesus only was not valid outside the Church:

> "If they attribute the effect of baptism to the majesty of the name, so that they who are baptized anywhere and anyhow, in the name of Jesus Christ are judged to be renewed and sanctified; wherefore, in the name of the same Christ, are not hands laid upon the baptized persons among them, for the reception of the Holy Spirit?"[43]

Historians conclude from these writings that many in Cyprian's day used the Jesus' name formula, and that probably Stephen allowed the formula.[44] Some believe that even Cyprian accepted this baptism as long as the catholic church performed it and the trinity was not denied.[45] In any case, the whole debate demonstrates that many people practiced baptism in Jesus' name during the third century A.D.

Striking verification comes from *A Treatise on Re-Baptism by An Anonymous Writer*.[46] Some scholars believe the author was a fourth century monk named Ursinus, but most believe he was a bishop in the third century who opposed Cyprian. The treatise discusses what should be done about persons "who, although baptized in heresy, have yet been baptized in the name of our Lord Jesus Christ" and who turn from their heresy to the catholic church. It concludes that rebaptism is not necessary: "Heretics who are already baptized in water in the name of Jesus Christ must only be baptized with the Holy Spirit."

The author makes a number of interesting points in his discussion: (1) His position had the support of "the most ancient custom and ecclesiastical tradition" and "the authority of so many years, and so many churches and apostles and bishops." (2) "The power of the name of Jesus invoked upon any man by baptism. . .afford[s] to him. . .no slight advantage for the attainment of salvation," citing Acts 4:12 and Philippians 2:9-11. (3) The "invocation of the name of Jesus ought not to be thought futile by us on account of the veneration and power of that very name, in which name all kinds of power are accustomed to be exercised." (4) The invocation of Jesus' name alone does not bring salvation to the heretic, but if he corrects his error, acknowledges the truth, and receives the Holy Ghost, then it becomes effective; the heretic does not "lose that former invocation of the name of Jesus." (5) This teaching does not contradict Matthew 28:19. (6) Not only were heretics baptized by "invoking the name of the Lord Jesus," but many people, both "Jews and Gentiles, fully believing as they ought, are in like manner baptized."

Fourth Century

Even after the Council of Nicea we find mention of Jesus' name baptism, which indicates that it was still a live issue. Ambrose (340-398), although a trinitarian, apparently held it to be valid on the ground that baptism in the name of one person of the trinity is the same as baptism in the name of the whole trinity.[47] An editor's footnote says, "This passage has given rise to the question whether St. Ambrose taught, as some others certainly did (probably on his authority) that baptism in the Name of Christ alone, without mention of the other persons is valid."[48]

The Council of Constantinople in 381 specifically condemned Sabellian baptism, which it described as prevalent in Galatia.[49] A fourth or fifth century addition to the *Constitutions of the Holy Apostles* condemns those who perform only "one immersion, which is given into the death of Christ" and requires all baptism to be performed by three immersions in the trinitarian formula.[50] An Eastern variant of this passage further links the single immersion into Christ with modalism. Therefore, it insists that the baptismal candidate be taught that the Father or the Holy

Spirit did not come in flesh and that the Holy Spirit is not the Father or the Son.

The Medieval Age

The church in Constantinople condemned Sabellian baptism in a letter to Antioch around 450, the Justinian Code of 529 (Byzantine Empire) declared the death penalty for both antitrinitarianism and rebaptism, the Council of Constantinople in 553 again condemned Sabellian baptism, and Martin Dumiun (died 579), bishop of Braga, condemned Sabellian baptism for "retaining single immersion under a single name."[51]

Bede (673-735) of England accepted the validity of baptism in Jesus' name based on the reasoning attributed to Ambrose, as did the Council of Frejus (792) and Pope Nicholas I (858-867).[52] Other medieval writers who mentioned the Jesus Name formula were Peter Lombard (died 1160), Hugo Victor (died 1141), and Thomas Aquinas (1225-1274).[53]

From this evidence we conclude: (1) Throughout church history some people were acquainted with the Jesus Name formula. (2) Many theologians regarded it as valid. (3) Since it reappears repeatedly as an issue, people in various ages apparently maintained the practice.

The Reformation Era Forward

Martin Luther encountered a dispute over the Jesus Name formula in his day.[54] Many sixteenth and seventeenth century Antitrinitarians baptized in Jesus' name. For example, in 1572 George Schomann was baptized in "the name of Christ."[55] Thomas Edwards of England wrote in 1646 about some "heretics" who taught that baptism using the words Father, Son, and Holy Ghost was a man-made tradition and that Christian baptism was "only in the name of Jesus Christ."[56] In the nineteenth century many of the Plymouth Brethren, as well as some other English groups, taught on the authority of Acts 2:38 that baptism should be in the name of Jesus only.[57]

Oneness Believers Throughout History

Throughout history many have affirmed the doctrine of Oneness (the belief in one God with no distinction of persons, who came in flesh as Jesus). Since these Oneness believers denied the trinity, we assume most baptized in Jesus' name, although historical records usually are silent on the subject. Below is a brief list of nontrinitarians recorded in history who believed in the deity of Jesus and probably baptized in His name.[58]

(1) *Ante-Nicene era:* The post-apostolic fathers (including Clement of Rome, Polycarp, Hermas, Ignatius), possibly Irenaeus, some Montanists, Noetus, Praxeas, Epigonus, Cleomenes, probably the Roman bishops Callistus and Zephyrinus, "the majority of believers" in Tertullian's day, Sabellius.

(2) *Nicene era:* Marcellus of Ancyra, Photinus, Commodian, Priscillian, Sabellians.

(3) *Medieval era;* Sabellians, Priscillianists, possibly

unknown "heretics."

(4) *Reformation era:* Michael Servetus (whose doctrine was known to Luther, Zwingli, and Calvin and who was burned at the stake with Calvin's approval), Emmanuel Swedenborg (who recognized the error of the trinity but taught some unusual, nonbiblical doctrines), some Anabaptists, many antitrinitarians, William Penn and many early Quakers.

(5) *Nineteenth century:* John Clowes (England), John Miller (U.S.), some New England Congregationalists.

(6) *Twentieth century:* Oneness Pentecostals, some Sabbatarians, some charismatics.

Twentieth Century

This century has seen a great revival of baptism in the name of Jesus. The modern Pentecostal movement began on January 1, 1901, and its first leader, Charles Parham, began to baptize in the name of Jesus as early as 1901 or 1902.[59] He reasoned as follows: Since baptism identifies us with Christ's death and burial and since Jesus Christ is the only One who died for us, we should be baptized in Jesus' name.

The noted Pentecostal evangelist Andrew Urshan began to baptize in Jesus' name as early as 1910.[60] Beginning in 1913, the doctrines of baptism in Jesus' name and the Oneness of God began to sweep across the North American Pentecostal movement under the leadership of Frank Ewart, R. E. McAlister, Glenn Cook, and others.[61] Each case (Parham, Urshan, the 1913 revival) was independent of the others. Each began with prayerful Bible study and a specific experience in which God gave illumination of His Word.

In 1915 Andrew Urshan brought the Pentecostal message to Russia, where some of his converts asked him to baptize them in Jesus' name, not knowing that Urshan and others had already seen this truth.[62] This began the Pentecostal movement in that land. A few years later, a group of Chinese Christians began to teach Oneness and baptism in Jesus' name based solely on their reading of the Bible, not realizing that anyone else in the world believed it. In 1917 they organized the True Jesus Church, which exists in Communist China and Taiwan today.[63]

Many prominent leaders in the early Pentecostal movement were baptized in Jesus' name, including: A. H. Argue, Frank Bartleman (Azusa Street participant and historian), E. N. Bell (one of two organizers of the Assemblies of God and its first General Chairman), William Booth-Clibborn, Glenn Cook, Frank Ewart (early associate of William Durham and prominent revivalist), Howard Goss (one of two organizers of the Assemblies of God and one of its executive presbyters), L. C. Hall, G. T. Haywood (prominent black leader), B. F. Lawrence, Harry van Loon, R. E. McAlister (prominent evangelist), Aimee Semple McPherson, D. C. O. Opperman (an executive presbyter in the Assemblies of God), and H. G. Rodgers.[64]

Bell later abandoned Jesus Name baptism under pressure from trinitarian colleagues, as did Aimee McPherson, who subsequently founded the International Church of the Foursquare Gospel, and R. G. Hoekstra, who has achieved financial success with his "Chaplain Ray" radio broadcast.[65]

Bell's story is particularly interesting.[66] At first he rejected what he called "The Sad New Issue," but then he was baptized in Jesus' name, giving three reasons why: (1) God had dealt with him personally about it for some time; (2) God took away every other message in his preaching until he would obey; and (3) this is what the apostles taught and practiced.

Bell revealed his rebaptism in a powerful article entitled "Who is Jesus Christ?" but prior to publication the Assemblies of God deleted many parts of it, including the fact of his rebaptism. The article expressed his "brand new vision" of who Jesus really was and the intense emotional experience that accompanied his new understanding and baptism.[67] Eventually, however, Bell suppressed his new baptismal practice in order to maintain fellowship with the Assemblies of God, and in 1920 he became General Chairman a second time.

The position of the Assemblies of God on this issue is also very interesting.[68] In 1915 the group accepted Jesus Name baptism as valid. A short time later it highly recommended a compromise formula that included both the words of Matthew 28:19 and Acts 2:38. Finally, in 1916 it rejected the Jesus Name formula, requiring all to accept use of the titles of Father, Son, and Holy Ghost.

All but one of the Assemblies of God preachers in Louisiana accepted Jesus Name baptism as did almost all the early Canadian Pentecostal leaders, including the founders of the Pentecostal Assemblies of Canada.[69] However, in 1919 the Pentecostal Assemblies of Canada renounced Oneness, accepted trinitarianism, and affiliated with the Assemblies of God.[70]

In all, approximately twenty-five percent of American

Pentecostals believe in Oneness and baptize in the name of Jesus.[71] In addition, some trinitarian Pentecostals baptize in Jesus' name, including: (1) Bethel Temple and Bible School in Seattle, founded by W. H. Offiler; (2) The Pentecostal Church of Indonesia, which resulted from missionary efforts by that group; (3) Bethesda Missionary Temple in Detroit, pastored by James Lee Beall; and (4) Gospel Temple and Northern California Bible College, led by Ernest Gentile.[72] Many modern charismatics have begun to baptize in Jesus' name, including some in the Maranatha Campus Ministries, which exists on more than sixty college campuses.[73] There are approximately fifteen to twenty small Sabbath-keeping groups (apparently non-Pentecostal) that teach Oneness and baptize in Jesus' name.[74]

Conclusion

Baptism in the name of Jesus has evidently existed throughout church history and is now enjoying a great revival.

Chapter 11 will investigate the history of the baptism of the Holy Spirit with tongues. At the end of that chapter we will draw some general conclusions about the apostolic doctrine in church history.

FOOTNOTES

[1]Otto Heick, *A History of Christian Thought* (Philadelphia: Fortress Press, 1965), I, 215.

[2]E. H. Klotsche, *The History of Christian Doctrine,* rev. ed. (Grand Rapids: Baker Book House, 1979), p. 100.

[3]Heick, I, 217, n.17.

[4]Klotsche, p. 99.

[5]Kenneth Latourette, *A History of Christianity* (New York: Harper & Row, 1953), I, 193.

[6]Henry Morris III, *Baptism: How Important is It?* (Denver: Accent Books, 1978), p. 24. For further documentation of this paragraph see *The Ante-Nicene Fathers* [hereinafter *ANF*], Alexander Roberts and James Donaldson, eds. (Rpt. Grand Rapids: Eerdmans, 1977), II, 22 & 49; *ANF,* III, 94 & 678; *ANF,* V, 377 & 400-01, *ANF,* VII, 379, 431 & 469.

[7]Morris, p. 10.

[8]W. H. Murk, *Four Kinds of Water Baptism* (St. Paul, Minn.: Northland Publ. Co., 1947), pp. 16, 17, 100. For Luther's view see also Philip Schaff, *History of the Christian Church,* 3rd ed. (1890; Rpt. Grand Rapids: Eerdmans 1958), VII, 98-99.

[9]Latourette, I, 135.

[10]*Ibid,* p. 194.

[11]"Baptism (Early Christian)," *ERE*, II, 389.

[12]Heick, I, 54; see Klotsche, pp. 20-21, 99.

[13]Heick, I, 62.

[14]Ibid; see Klotsche, p. 27.

[15]Heick, I, 62, 122, 129, 135; "Baptism (Early Christian)," *ERE,* II, 385. For further documentation of this paragraph see *ANF,* I, 444 & 574; *ANF,* III, 674-75; *ANF,* V, 237, 276, & 378.

[16]*Constitutions of the Holy Apostles,* 6.3.15, *ANF,* VII, 457.

[17]Tertullian, *On Baptism, ANF,* III, 669-679.

[18]"Baptism (Early Christian)," *ERE,* II, 391.

[19]Klotsche, p. 180.

[20]*Ibid,* p. 198.

[21]*Ibid,* p. 180, quoting *Lutheran Catechism,* 733.

[22]Bloesch, II, 15.

[23]*Ibid,* p. 12.

[24]Heick, I, 53. See also J. F. Bethune-Baker, *An Introduction to the Early History of Christian Doctrine* (London: Methuen & Co., 1933), p. 25 n.1 & p. 378 n.1.

[25]Heick, I, 87.

[26]"Baptism (Early Christian)," *ERE,* II, 389.

[27]*Ibid.*

[28]"Baptism," *ADB,* I, 241.

[29]Jean Danielou, *The Development of Christian Doctrine Before the Council of Nicaea, Vol. I: The Theology of Jewish Christianity,* John A. Baker, ed. and trans. (London: Darton, Lonman, and Todd, 1964), p. 323 says, "The triune formula and triple immersion" do not come from Jewish Christian practice. Wilhelm Bousset, *Kyrios Christianity—A History of the Belief in Christ from the Beginning of Christianity to Irenaeus,* 5th ed., John Steely, trans. (New York: Abingdon, 1970), p. 292 says, "Baptism in the Pauline age was a baptism in the name of the Lord Jesus." Reed, p. 220 states, "The more archaic formula was undoubtedly some form of Lord Jesus Christ." Williston Walker, *A History of the Christian Church* (New York: Charles Scribner's Sons, 1947), p. 58 asserts, "The trinitarian baptismal formula. . .was displacing the older baptism in the name of Christ." For additional citations, see William Chalfant, *Ancient Champions of Oneness* (1979; Rpt. Hazelwood, Mo.: Word Aflame Press, 1982), Chap. V.

[30]Hermas, *The Pastor [The Shepherd],* 1.3.7 & 3.9.16, *ANF,* II, 15 & 49.

[31]"Baptism (Early Christian)," *ERE,* 385; see Hermas, 3.9.14-16, *ANF,* II, 48-49.

[32]Hermas, 3.9.13, *ANF,* II, 48.

[33]*The Teaching of the Twelve Apostles,* 7.1 & 9.5, *ANF,* VII, 379 & 380.

[34]*ANF,* VII, 372.

[35]Justin, *First Apology,* 61, *ANF,* I, 183.

[36]Irenaeus, *Fragments from the Lost Writings of Irenaeus,* 34, *ANF,* I, 574.

[37]For full discussion and documentation of the beliefs of these men, as well as that of Justin, see David Bernard, *The Oneness of God* (Hazelwood, Mo.: Word Aflame Press, 1983), Chapters 9 and 10.

[38]Cyprian, *Epistles,* 72.4, *ANF,* V, 380.

[39]*Acts of Paul and Thecla, ANF,* VIII, 490.

[40]*Cyprian,* Epistles, 72.17, *ANF,* V, 383.

[41]*Ibid.*

[42]*Ibid,* 74.18, *ANF,* V, 395.

[43]*Ibid,* 73.5, *ANF,* V, 387.

[44]Bethune-Baker, p. 378 n.1.

[45]*Ibid,* p. 25 n.1.

[46]*A Treatise on Re-Baptism By an Anonymous Writer, ANF,* V, 665-78.

[47]Ambrose, *Of the Holy Spirit,* I, iii, 43, *The Nicene and Post-Nicene Fathers* [hereinafter *NPNF*], Philip Schaff and Henry Wace, eds. (Rpt. Grand Rapids: Eerdmans, 1976), 2nd ser., X, 98. See also "Baptism," *ADB,* I, 241; Bethune-Baker, p. 25 n.1. & p. 378 n.1.

[48]*NPNF,* 2nd ser., X, 98 n.2.

[49]Chalfant, p. 78.

[50]*Constitutions of the Holy Apostles,* 47.50, ANF, VII, 503.

[51]Chalfant, pp. 78-80.

[52]"Baptism," *ADB,* I, 241.

[53]*Ibid.*

[54]Vinson Synan, ed., *Aspects of Pentecostal-Charismatic Origins* (Plainfield, N.J.: Logos International, 1975), p. 158, citing John Dillenger, ed., *Martin Luther* (Garden City, N.Y.: Doubleday, 1961), p. 297.

[55]Thomas Weisser, *After the Way Called Heresy* (N.p., 1981), p. 80, quoting Robert Wallace, *Antitrinitarian Biography* (London: E. T. Whitfield, 1850), II, 350.

[56]Weisser, p. 80, quoting Wallace, I, 90.

[57]W. Robertson Nicoll, ed., *The Expositor's Bible* (Grand Rapids: Eerdmans, 1956), V, 330.

[58]See Bernard, Chap. 9; Chalfant, *passim;* "Monarchianism," *ERE, passim;* Weisser, *passim.* For testimony concerning the Montanists see Hippolytus, *The Refutation of all Heresies,* 8.12, *ANF,* V, 123-24.

[59]Fred Foster, *Their Story: 20th Century Pentecostals* (Hazelwood, Mo.: Word Aflame Press, 1981), pp. 120-21, quoting Parham, *A Voice Crying in the Wilderness,* pp. 23-24.

[60]Andrew Urshan, *The Life of Andrew Bar David Urshan* (Stockton, Ca.: Apostolic Press, 1967), p. 141.

[61]Frank Ewart, *The Phenomenon of Pentecost,* rev. ed. (Hazelwood, Mo.: Word Aflame Press, 1975); Foster, pp. 88-90, 102-03.

[62]A. Urshan, pp. 235-37.

[63]David Barrett, ed., *World Christian Encyclopedia* [hereinafter *WCE*] (New York: Oxford University Press, 1982), p. 234.

[64]Foster, p. 107; Walter Hollenweger, *The Pentecostals,* R. A. Wilson, trans. (Minneapolis: Augsburg Publ. House, 1972), pp. 32 & 43 n.21.

[65]N. A. Urshan, Lecture and Personal Interview, July 11-13, 1982, Granby, Colorado.

[66]Reed, pp. 109-123.

[67]Bell's article "Who is Jesus Christ?" is reproduced in Oliver Fauss, *Buy the Truth and Sell It Not* (St. Louis: Pentecostal Publ. House, 1965), Chapt. 2.

[68]Reed, pp. 124-136.

[69]Hollenweger, p. 32, p. 43 n.21, p. 312.

[70]*Ibid,* p. 312; Reed, p. 108.

[71]Tim Dowley et al, eds., *Eerdman's Handbook to the History of the Church* (Grand Rapids: Eerdmans, 1977), p. 619.

[72]Reed, pp. 343-46.

[73]*See* "And Now—Deprogramming of Christians is Taking Place," *Christianity Today,* April 22, 1983, p. 31.

[74]Reed, p. 199, citing, *Directory of Sabbath-Keeping Groups,* 4th ed. (Fairview, Okla.: The Bible Sabbath Association, 1974).

11

THE WITNESS IN CHURCH HISTORY: TONGUES

"We also are compassed about with so great a cloud of witnesses. . ." (Hebrews 12:1).

This chapter investigates the existence of the Holy Spirit baptism with tongues in church history and draws conclusions about the complete apostolic message throughout history. We should keep in mind all the difficulties associated with such a study, as discussed in Chapter 10. The words of *Encyclopedia Britannica* serve well as our central proposition: "[P]ost-apostolic instances of glossolalia have been recorded throughout the history of the Christian church."[1]

First and Second Centuries

The post-apostolic fathers of the first two centuries believed in the gift of the Holy Spirit, practiced the laying on of hands to receive the Spirit, and testified that the gifts of the Spirit, including tongues, existed in their day.[2] In the following quotations from these men, the English word *gifts* represents the Greek word *charismata* in the original texts,[3] the same word Paul used for the nine gifts of the Spirit including tongues (I Corinthians 12).

Clement of Rome (died 100?) reminded the Corinthians that "a full outpouring of the Holy Spirit was upon you all."[4]

Ignatius (died 107?) wrote to the church at Smyrna: "Ignatius. . .to the Church of God the Father, and of the beloved Jesus Christ, which has through mercy obtained every kind of gift, which is filled with faith and love, and is deficient in no gift, most worthy of God, and adorned with holiness. . . .Be ye strong, I pray, in the power of the Holy Ghost."[5] He also admonished Polycarp to pray so that he might "be wanting in nothing, and. . .abound in every gift."[6]

The *Didache* says, "For the Father desireth that the gifts be given to all" and also describes prophets who speak "in the Spirit."[7]

Justin Martyr wrote, "For the prophetical gifts remain with us, even to the present time. . .Now it is possible to see amongst us women and men who possess gifts of the Spirit of God."[8]

Irenaeus (130?-202?), Bishop of Lyons, wrote, "[T]hose who are in truth His disciples, receiving grace from Him, do in His name perform (miracles). . .It is not possible to name the numbers of the gifts which the Church (scattered) throughout the whole world, has received from God, in the name of Jesus Christ."[9] He taught the necessity of receiving the Spirit and specifically described speaking in tongues as evidence of the Spirit:

> "[T]he perfect man consists in the commingling and the union of the soul receiving the spirit of the Father. . .For this reason does the apostle declare, 'We speak wisdom among them that are perfect,' terming those persons 'perfect' who have received the Spirit of God, and who through the Spirit of God do speak in all languages, as he used [h]imself also to speak. In like manner we do also hear many brethren in the Church, who possess prophetic gifts, and who through the Spirit speak all kinds of languages. . .whom also the apostle terms 'spiritual,' they being spiritual because they partake of the Spirit."[10]

Celsus, a pagan, wrote near the end of the second century that Christians in his day spoke in tongues. The theologian Origen (died 254?) preserved his testimony without denying the existence and validity of tongues, and accepted the gifts of the Spirit for his day.[11]

A group called the Montanists emphasized the Holy Spirit and spoke in tongues.

Third Century

Tertullian wrote against the heretic Marcion shortly after A.D. 200: "[T]he Creator promised the gift of His Spirit in the latter days; and. . .Christ has in these last days appeared as the dispenser of spiritual gifts."[12] Tertullian specifically mentioned the gift of tongues and quoted I Corinthians 12:8-11 and Isaiah 28:11 as applicable in his day. He regarded speaking in tongues as one of the marks of a true church:

> "Let Marcion then exhibit, as gifts of his god, some prophets, such as have not spoken by human sense, but with the Spirit of God. . .let him produce a psalm, a vision, a prayer—only let it be by the Spirit, in an ecstasy, that is, in a rapture, whenever an interpretation of tongues has occurred to him. . .Now all these signs (of spiritual gifts) are forthcoming from my side without any difficulty."[13]

Novatian (died 257?), a presbyter in Rome, wrote about the Holy Spirit:

> "This is He who places prophets in the Church, instructs teachers, directs tongues, gives powers and healings, does wonderful works, offers discrimination of spirits, affords powers of government, suggests counsels, and orders and arranges whatever other gifts there are of *charismata;* and thus makes the Lord's Church everywhere, and in all, perfected and completed."[14]

Sabellius apparently taught the baptism of the Holy Spirit with tongues. None of his writings have survived, but Epiphanius said that Sabellius taught regeneration by the Holy Ghost and Pseudo-Athanasius records that Sabellius taught on the spiritual gifts of I Corinthians 12.[15]

Asterius Urbanus (c. 232) indicated that the Christians of his day expected the spiritual gifts to remain permanently in the church. Writing against the later Montanists, he asked why they no longer had prophets after their prophet Montanus and his co-workers died. Urbanus noted that the true church would always have the prophetical gifts (prophecy, tongues, interpretation of tongues): "For the apostle [Paul] deems that the gifts of prophecy should abide in all the church up to the time of the final advent."[16]

Fourth and Fifth Centuries

Hilary (died 367), bishop of Poitiers, mentioned both tongues and interpretation of tongues, describing them as "agents of ministry" ordained of God.[17]

Ambrose (340-98), bishop of Milan, taught that all the gifts of I Corinthians 12 were part of the normal Christian experience.[18]

By the late fourth century and early fifth century, Christendom had for the most part evolved into what came to be known as the Roman Catholic Church. Apparently, speaking in tongues had practically disappeared from most places in the backsliding church, but the memory of it remained to some extent. John Chrysostom (345-407), bishop of Constantinople, wrote a comment on I Corinthians 12:

> "This whole place is very obscure: but the obscurity is produced by our ignorance of the facts referred to and by their cessation, being such as then used to occur but now no longer take place. . .Well: what did

happen then? Whoever was baptized he straightway spoke with tongues. . .They at once on their baptism received the Spirit. . .[They] began to speak, one in the tongue of the Persians, another in that of the Romans, another in that of the Indians, or in some other language. And this disclosed to outsiders that it was the Spirit in the speaker."[19]

Augustine (354-430) testified that the church in his day did not expect to speak in tongues when receiving the Holy Spirit, but admitted that this used to be the case:

> "For the Holy Spirit is not only given by the laying on of hands amid the testimony of temporal sensible miracles, as He was given in former days. . .For who expects in these days that those on whom hands are laid that they may receive the Holy Spirit should forthwith begin to speak with tongues?"[20]

Evidently some "heretics" in Augustine's day believed in receiving the Holy Spirit with evidence of speaking in tongues. He sought to refute them by the following argument: (1) Tongues are valueless without love (I Corinthians 13); (2) love comes only by the Spirit (Romans 5:5); (3) they did not have the Spirit because they did not belong to the Catholic Church; and (4) no one expected tongues any longer anyway.[21]

The Medieval Age

Evidence of tongues in medieval times is sparse, probably because the Roman Catholic Church was so effective in silencing "heretics." Nevertheless, there are reports of speaking in tongues among the following groups:

(1) Waldenses, 1100's, Europe.[22] A group that rejected papal authority and attempted to base their beliefs solely on the Bible.

(2) Albigenses, 1100's, Europe.[23] Another group that rejected papal authority and emphasized purity of life.

(3) Franciscans and possibly other mendicant orders, 1200's, Europe.[24] Catholic monks who embraced a very simple lifestyle and traveled throughout the countryside preaching.

The Reformation Era Forward

Reports of speaking in tongues increase greatly after the Protestant Reformation, due to several factors: (1) greater religious freedom, (2) renewed emphasis on Bible study, apostolic doctrine, conversion, and spiritual experiences, (3) the invention of printing, and (4) the closer proximity to our time. According to respected historians, speaking in tongues has occurred among many groups (from 1500 to 1900):

(1) Anabaptists, 1500's, Europe.[25] One of the four main branches of the early Protestant movement (along with Lutherans, Reformed, and Anglicans). Unlike other Protestants, the Anabaptists emphasized the restoration of apostolic patterns of worship and lifestyle, the importance of a conversion experience, baptism of believers only, baptism by immersion, total separation of church and state, the power to overcome sin after conversion, and

the need to live a holy life. A prominent Anabaptist leader named Menno Simons, whose followers became known as Mennonites, wrote about speaking in tongues as if it were expected evidence of receiving the Holy Ghost.[26] Many early Anabaptists worshiped quite demonstratively; in the words of a secular history text some participated in "very excited, 'enthusiastic,' evangelical practices. . .what Americans know as 'holy rolling'. . .The congregation sometimes shouted and danced, and always sang hymns with great fervor."[27] In view of their doctrine and worship, it is not at all surprising that speaking in tongues occurred among early Anabaptists.

(2) Prophecy movement, 1500's, England.[28]

(3) Camisards, 1600's and 1700's, southern France (often called the Prophets of the Cevennes).[29] A group of Huguenots (French Protestants), mostly peasants, who resisted the attempts of Louis XIV's government to convert them to Roman Catholicism. Many were imprisoned, tortured, and martyred. Observers reported tongues, uneducated peasants and young children prophesying in pure, elegant French, enthusiastic, demonstrative worship, and people "seized by the Spirit."

(4) Quakers, 1600's, England.[30] A group that emphasized spiritual experience and waited on the moving of the Spirit in their services. The early Quakers received their name because they literally "quaked" under the power of the Spirit.

(5) Jansenists, 1600's and 1700's, France.[31] A Catholic reform movement.

(6) Pietists (including Moravians), late 1600's, Germany.[32] The Pietists emphasized spiritual experience and Christian living.

(7) Converts of Camisards, early 1700's, England.[33] Some Camisards fled to England to avoid persecution, making converts there.

(8) Methodists, 1700's, England, particularly in the revivals of Wesley and Whitefield and in later American revivals.[34]

Wesley himself believed that the gifts of the Spirit had practically disappeared but that a fully restored church would have them again.[35] When a certain Dr. Middleton wrote that the gift of tongues was absent from later church history, Wesley replied that (1) many ancient writings are no longer extant, (2) many Christians wrote no books, (3) the ante-Nicene fathers do not say tongues ceased with the apostles, and (4) just because tongues was not specifically recorded does not mean it was not practiced.[36] He said, "Many may have spoken with new tongues, of whom this is not recorded; at least, the records are lost in a course of so many years."[37] In reply to the objection that tongues did not exist in his time, Wesley replied, "It has been heard of more than once, no farther off than the valleys of Dauphiny" [southern France].[38]

We should also note the strong emphasis on repentance and physical demonstrations in the Methodist revivals. One hostile historian wrote, "Extreme emotional disturbances, ecstasies and bodily seizures of various sorts were common in the Wesleyan Revival of the eighteenth century in England," with people in Wesley's meetings exhibiting "violent motor reactions. . .convulsions and shakings" and screaming.[39] Similar phenomena occurred in the Great Awakening, a period of American revival in the 1700's led by Jonathan Edwards, George Whitefield, and others.[40]

(9) Revivals and Camp Meetings, 1800's, America. It is reported that physical demonstrations occurred in later American revivals, called the Second Awakening, which began with camp meetings in Kentucky and swept across the American frontier.[41] In the camp meetings people "shouted, sobbed, leaped in the air, writhed on the ground, fell like dead men and lay insensible for considerable periods, and engaged in unusual bodily contortions," in addition to manifesting the "holy laugh," the "barks," and the "jerks."[42] Observers at various American revival meetings reported sobbing, shrieking, shouting, spasms, falling, rolling, running, dancing, barking, whole congregations breathing in distress and weeping, and hundreds under conviction and on the ground repenting.[43]

These meetings were conducted by Methodists, Baptists, some Presbyterians, and later the Holiness movement. With such a strong emphasis on repentance and free, demonstrative worship, it is not surprising that many people received the Holy Spirit and spoke in tongues. A great revival swept the University of Georgia in 1800-1801, and the students "shouted and talked in unknown tongues."[44]

In many cases tongues speaking went unreported because observers did not recognize it or its significance and did not distinguish it from other physical phenomena. One historian said, "Throughout the nineteenth century speaking in unknown tongues occurred occasionally in the revivals and camp meetings that dotted the countryside. Perhaps the phenomenon was considered just another of the many evidences that one had been saved or sanctified."[45]

(10) Lutherans, early 1800's, Germany.[46] This began among followers of Gustav von Below.

(11) Irvingites, 1800's, England and America.[47] The Spirit fell among the London congregation of a prominent Church of Scotland pastor named Edward Irving, beginning with Mary Campbell and James and Margaret MacDonald. Soon after, Irvingites formed the Catholic Apostolic Church, which emphasized the gifts of the Spirit. This revival also gave birth to the Christian Catholic Church and the New Apostolic Church, and there were Irvingites in the traditional denominations. Unfortunately, these groups gradually lost the gifts of the Spirit, degenerated into ritualism, suffered rapid decline, and are almost nonexistent today. Church historian Philip Schaff (1819-1893) wrote of observing speaking in tongues in an Irvingite church in New York:

> "Several years ago I witnessed this phenomenon in an Irvingite congregation in New York; the words were broken, ejaculatory, and unintelligible, but uttered in abnormal, startling, impressive sounds, in a state of apparent unconsciousness and rapture, and without any control over the tongue, which was seized as it were by a foreign power. A friend and colleague (Dr. Briggs), who witnessed it in 1879 in the principal Irvingite church in London, received the same impression."[48]

(12) Plymouth Brethren, 1800's, England.[49]

(13) Readers (Lasare), 1841-43, Sweden.[50]

(14) Revivals, 1859, Ireland.[51]

(15) Holiness people, 1800's, Tennessee and North Carolina.[52]

We should note that one German historian attributed speaking in tongues to Martin Luther, and a friend of Dwight Moody described some of Moody's followers speaking in tongues.[53] However, it is unclear whether either source definitely meant speaking in tongues as we know it. The *Westminster Confession,* an important statement of Presbyterian Calvinism adopted by English Puritans in 1648, specifically required that prayer be made in a known tongue.[54]

Twentieth Century

The modern Pentecostal movement began on January 1, 1901, in a small Bible college in Topeka, Kansas, operated by Charles Parham, a minister with a background in the Holiness movement. The students began to seek the baptism of the Spirit with tongues, and Agnes Ozman was the first student to experience speaking in tongues. The revival soon spread to many denominations and around the world. Since then speaking in tongues has been verified and documented many times.[55]

In the late 1950's a revival of tongues speaking, known as the charismatic or neo-Pentecostal movement, began among non-Pentecostal churches and has spread throughout the Protestant, Roman Catholic, and Orthodox world.[56] Some charismatics have joined Pentecostal churches, others have formed their own churches, and many have remained in their traditional denominations.

Statistics on Pentecostals Today

According to the *World Christian Encyclopedia,* in 1970 there were 160,509 Pentecostal congregations, 18,694,038 adult adherents, and total affiliation of 36,794,010; by 1980 total affiliation had reached an estimated 51,167,187 worldwide.[57] As *Time Magazine* noted, this means Pentecostals are larger than any single bloc of Protestants in the world today.[58] In addition to these figures, total charismatics or neo-Pentecostals numered 1,587,700 in 1970 and 11,005,390 in 1980.[59]

As defined by this source, affiliation is much more than membership or regular attendance; it includes adult adherents, children, attending sympathizers, and irregular attenders.

Below is a chart of the major Oneness Pentecostal groups in the United States today.[60]

Oneness Pentecostals, USA (1970)

Name	Churches	Adults	Affiliated *(estimate)*
Apostolic Assembly of the Faith in Jesus Christ (Spanish speaking)	195	24,000	55,000
Apostolic Overcoming Holy Church of God (black)	300	30,000	75,000
Assemblies of the Lord Jesus Christ	300	25,000	60,000
Associated Brotherhood of Christians (spiritual communion)	100	2,500	6,000
Bible Way Churches of Our Lord Jesus Christ World Wide (black)	350	30,000	42,000
Church of Our Lord Jesus Christ of the Apostolic Faith (black)	200	45,000	60,000
Pentecostal Assemblies of the World (majority black)	550	45,000	60,000
United Pentecostal Church International (majority white; many blacks, Hispanics)	2,300	250,000	450,000

In addition to these figures, a number of smaller organizations, independent churches, and charismatic groups embrace Oneness Pentecostal doctrine. It should be noted that these figures from 1970 are out of date since most Pentecostal groups are experiencing rapid growth.

In September 1983, the UPCI estimated a constituency of approximately 500,000 in the United States and Canada and 500,000 overseas.[61] At that time it had 3295 churches in the United States and Canada, with 500 considered as home missions churches and with about four new churches being started per week.[62] Foreign missions statistics at that time included: works in 90 countries, 5998 churches and preaching points, 53 established Bible colleges, and an increase in twelve months of 534 churches and 86,686 constituents.[63] Major foreign missions fields as of 1984 are listed below.[64]

Major UPCI Mission Fields (1984)
(multiply *constituents* by 2 or 3 to obtain affiliation)

Country	Churches	Constituents
Brazil	226	11,000
Burma	160	9,000
El Salvador	439	14,000
Ethiopia	445	95,278
Ghana	102	9,000
Haiti	135	13,181
India, N.E.	613	53,356
India, South	175	10,000
Indonesia	203	12,901
Jamaica	160	23,000
Kenya	212	28,000
Madagascar	122	10,000
Pakistan	208	15,000
Philippines	1,375	60,000
Venezuela	608	40,000

Many other Oneness Pentecostal groups exist outside the United States. The following table lists those with over 10,000 adult adherents as of 1970:[65]

Jesus Name Pentecostals, Non-US, Non-UPCI (1970)

Country	Organization	Churches	Adults	Affiliation
Canada	Apostolic Church of Pentecost in Canada	100	12,000	30,000
China (PRC)	True Jesus Church	1700	15,000	35,000
Colombia	United Pentecostal Church of Colombia	570	47,000	95,000
Indonesia	Pentecostal Church of Indonesia*	1500	750,000	1,000,000
Mexico	Apostolic Church of the Faith in Christ Jesus	954	16,034	48,192
Mexico	Light of the World Church	20	15,000	30,000
Taiwan	**True Jesus Church**	**187**	**25,000**	**50,000**
Japan	Spirit of Jesus Church	453	37,000	62,726

*The PC of I is officially trinitarian but baptizes in Jesus' name.

The True Jesus Church is an indigenous church formed by mainland Chinese in 1917 without any prior contact with other Oneness Pentecostals. Just before the Communist takeover, it had 1260 churches and 125,000 affiliated; since then its members have gone underground in secret house meetings.[66] It is one of the few churches to resist successfully the government's efforts to merge all Protestants into one registered body called the Three-Self Patriotic Movement.[67] The True Jesus Church teaches that birth of water is water baptism, that using the name of Jesus at baptism is for remission of sins, that birth of the Spirit is receiving the Spirit, and that the evidence of receiving the Spirit is speaking in tongues.[68]

The UPC of Colombia is a completely autonomous church founded by UPC missionaries. It is the fastest growing and the largest non-Catholic denomination in the country. Its amazing progress had been the subject of two scholarly books by non-Pentecostal researchers.[69]

Many smaller Oneness Pentecostal bodies exist around the world including several in Mexico, many in the Caribbean, many among Caribbean immigrants to England, and the Church of the Spirit (Footwashing) in Yugoslavia.

For the U.S.S.R., the *World Christian Encyclopedia* lists a single Oneness Pentecostal body, an underground group known as the Evangelical Christians in the Apostolic Spirit. They are the oldest Russian Pentecostals, dating back to Andrew Urshan's revivals of 1915, and they practice footwashing. The only officially registered church which contains Pentecostals is the Union of Evangelical Christians-Baptists (AUCECB).

In the 1940's the Oneness people were forced to join this government controlled organization, but many soon left, preferring to become an illegal sect.[70] Apparently, many remained in this group, for in 1974 a Oneness believer named Peter Shatrov was elected to the presidium of the AUCECB, thereby becoming the major Pentecostal spokesman in the AUCECB and in the U.S.S.R. as a whole.[71] We assume, then, that many groups classified as trinitarian could have significant numbers of Oneness believers. Below are statistics for Russian Pentecostals:[72]

Russian Pentecostals (1970)

Name	Churches	Adults	Affiliation
Christians of Evangelical Faith (underground, classified as trinitarian)	600	80,000	320,000
Evangelical Christian Pentecostal Zionists (underground, classified as trinitarian)	100	10,000	20,000
Evangelical Christians in the Apostolic Spirit (underground, all Oneness)	50	2,000	5,000
Christians of Evangelical Faith (AUCECB) (registered church, classified as trinitarian but elected a Oneness leader)	400	40,000	160,000
Other Pentecostal Bodies (underground, not specified as Oneness or trinitarian)	900	80,000	160,000

The *World Christian Encyclopedia* lists these total statistics for Oneness Pentecostals worldwide in 1970: 13,350 churches; 1,593,999 adults; 2,682,248 affiliated; and 4,205,428 projected affiliated by 1985.[73]

Conclusion

We do not agree with all the doctrines of every individual or movement discussed in this chapter, but our investigation has demonstrated a basic truth: through the ages people have believed, preached and experienced repentance, baptism by immersion, baptism for the remission of sins, baptism in Jesus' name, receiving the Holy Spirit, and speaking in tongues. These are not modern day inventions; the Bible teaches them and many throughout history have followed them.

In particular, it can be stated that some groups adhered simultaneously to baptism in Jesus' name and the baptism of the Spirit with tongues. We find both doctrines among the early post-apostolic fathers (1st and 2nd centuries), the early Sabellians (3rd century), and modern Pentecostals (20th century). The historical evidence also indicates that both doctrines existed among Montanists (2nd and 3rd centuries), later Sabellians (4th, 5th, 6th centuries), various "heretics" (3rd and 4th centuries, middle ages), Anabaptists (16th century), Antitrinitarians (16th and 17th centuries), and Plymouth Brethren (19th century). No doubt Satan has tried to suppress the facts, but there is enough evidence to indicate that God has always had some people who taught the full apostolic doctrine. We are confident that the apostolic church, as defined by message and experience, has never been absent since the days of the apostles.

Church history alone can never prove the validity of doctrine, but it provides insight into how these key doctrines were altered or lost over the centuries. It helps to dispel the myth that these doctrines are of recent origin. The clear teaching of Scripture is enough to tear away the shrouds of nonbiblical tradition, but perhaps this brief historical survey can aid in the process.

In these latter days, the full apostolic truth is proclaimed around the world. This century has seen a miraculous revival of the baptism of the Holy Spirit with tongues. In less than one century, the Pentecostal movement has grown from a small group to the largest single grouping of Protestants in the world, and it has affected every branch of Christendom. We firmly believe a revival of the name of Jesus will match the outpouring of His Spirit. The history of the church is not over; we believe the best is yet to come!

FOOTNOTES

[1]"Pentecostal Churches," *Encyclopedia Britannica* [hereinafter *EB*] (Chicago: William Benton, 1976), XIV, 31.

[2]Heick, I 47; Latourette, I, 194.

[3]"Charismata," *ERE,* III, 371.

[4]Clement of Rome, *First Epistle to the Corinthians,* 2, *ANF,* I, 5.

[5]Ignatius, *Epistle to the Smyrnaeans,* superscription & 12, *ANF,* I, 86 & 92.

[6]Ignatius, *Epistle to Polycarp,* 2, *ANF,* I, 99.

[7]"Charismata," *ERE,* III, 371. See *The Teaching of the Twelve Apostles,* 1.5 & 11.7; *ANF,* VII, 377 & 380.

[8]Justin, *Dialogue with Trypho,* 82 & 88, *ANF,* I, 240 & 243.

[9]Irenaeus, *Against Heresies,* 2.32.4, *ANF,* I, 409.

[10]*Ibid,* 5.6.1, *ANF,* I, 531.

[11]Origen, *Against Celsus,* 7.9, *ANF,* IV, 614, quoting Celsus, *True Discourse.* Origen, *Commentary on John,* 2.6, *ANF,* X, 329.

[12]Tertullian, *Against Marcion,* 5.8, *ANF,* III, 446.

[13]*Ibid,* III, 446-47.

[14]Novatian, *Treatise Concerning the Trinity,* 29, *ANF,* V, 641.

[15]Chalfant, pp. 133, 135.

[16]Asterius Urbanus, *Extant Writings,* 10, *ANF,* VII, 337.

[17]Hilary, *On the Trinity,* 8.33, *NPNF,* 2nd ser., IX, 147.

[18]Ambrose, *Of the Holy Spirit,* 2.8, *NPNF,* 2nd ser., X, 134.

[19]John Chrysostom, *Homilies on First Corinthians,* 29, *NPNF,* 1st ser., XII, 168.

[20]Augustine, *On Baptism,* Against the Donatists, 3.16.21, *NPNF,* 1st ser., IV, 443.

[21]*Ibid,* IV, 442.

[22]Carl Brumback, *What Meaneth This?* (Springfield, Mo.: Gospel Publ. House, 1947), p. 92.

[23]*Ibid.*

[24]"Tongues, Gift of," *ADB,* IV, 796; "Tongues, Gift of," *Smith's Dictionary of the Bible* [hereinafter *SDB*], H. B. Hackett, ed. (1870; Rpt. Grand Rapids: Baker Book House, 1971), IV, 3310-11.

[25]Bloesch, II, 115-16; Michael Hamilton, *The Charismatic Movement* (Grand Rapids: Eerdmans, 1975), pp. 73-74; "Pentecostal Chur-

ches," *EB,* XIV, 31.

[26]Hamilton, p. 74.

[27]Crane Brinton et al, *A History of Civilization,* 3rd ed. (Englewood Cliffs, N.J.: Prentice-Hall, 1967), I, 472, 480.

[28]"Tongues, Gift of," *SDB,* IV, 3310-11.

[29]*Ibid;* "Camisards," *ERE,* III, 175-176; "Pentecostal Churches," *EB,* XIV, 31; Schaff, I, 114; "Tongues, Gift of," *ADB,* IV, 796.

[30]Bloesch, II, 115-16; "Charismata," *ERE,* III, 370; Schaff, I, 114.

[31]"Charismata," *ERE,* III, 370; "Pentecostal Churches," *EB,* XIV, 31; "Tongues, Gift of," *ADB,* IV, 796; "Tongues, Gift of," *SDB,* IV, 3310-11.

[32]Bloesch, II, 115-16; Hamilton, p. 77.

[33]"Tongues, Gift of," *SDB,* IV, 3310-11.

[34]*Ibid;* "Tongues, Gift of," *ADB,* IV, 796.

[35]Howard Snyder, *The Radical Wesley* (Downers Grove, Ill.: Inter-Varsity Press, 1980), p. 96.

[36]John Wesley, "A Letter to the Reverend Dr. Conyers Middleton," *The Works of John Wesley,* 3rd. ed. (Rpt. Grand Rapids: Baker Book House, 1978), X, 54-55.

[37]*Ibid,* p. 55.

[38]*Ibid,* p. 56.

[39]Clark, pp. 111-12.

[40]*Ibid,* pp. 112-13.

[41]*Ibid,* pp. 114-17.

[42]*Ibid,* pp. 116-17.

[43]William Sweet, *The Story of Religion in America* (Grand Rapids: Baker Book House, 1950), pp. 133, 227-31.

[44]Vinson Synan, *The Holiness-Pentecostal Movement in the United States* (Grand Rapids: Eerdmans, 1971), p. 25, quoting E. Merton Coulter, *College Life in the Old South* (New York, 1928), pp. 194-95.

[45]Synan, p. 25 n.29.

[46]Hamilton, pp. 84-85.

[47]"Irving and the Catholic Apostolic Churches," *ERE,* VII, 422-25; "Pentecostal Churches," *EB,* XIV, 31; "Tongues, Gift of," *ADB,* IV, 796; "Tongues, Gift of," *SDB,* IV, 3310-11.

[48]Schaff, I, 115.

[49]Bloesch, I, 115-116.

[50]"Tongues, Gift of," *SDB,* IV, 3310-11; Schaff, I, 114.

[51]*Ibid.*

[52]"Pentecostal Churches," *EB,* XIV, 31.

[53]Brumback, pp. 92-94, quoting Souer [or Sauer], *History of the Christian Church,* III, 406 and R. Boyd, *Trials and Triumphs of Faith* (1875), p. 402.

[54]Justo Gonzalez, *A History of Christian Thought* (Nashville: Abingdon, 1975), III, 271.

[55]Robert Dalton, *Tongues Like as of Fire* (Springfield, Mo.: Gospel Publishing House, 1945); Ewart, pp. 59-93; Foster, pp. 41-69; Stanley Frodsham, *With Signs Following* (Springfield, Mo.: Gospel Publishing House, 1941).

[56]Don Basham, *Face Up with a Miracle* (Springdale, Pa.: Whitaker House, 1967); Hamilton, *passim;* John Sherrill, *They Speak with Other Tongues* (New York: McGraw-Hill, 1964).

[57]*WCE,* pp. 6, 14.

[58]"Counting Every Soul on Earth," *Time Magazine,* May 3, 1982.

[59]*WCE,* p. 6.

[60]*WCE,* pp. 720-25. In the spring of 1983 the author sent a survey to most of these groups, but only received responses from the UPCI and from the Apostolic Overcoming Holy Church of God, which reported 198 churches. For a description of these and several smaller Oneness Pentecostal groups, see J. Gordon Melton, *The Encyclopedia of American Religions* (Wilmington, N.C.: McGrath Publishing Co., 1978), pp. 287-94 and Arthur Piepkorn, *Profiles in Belief: The Religious Bodies of the United States and Canada* (San Francisco: Harper & Row, 1979), III, 195-219.

[61]"Profile: General Superintendent, Reverend Nathaniel A. Urshan," *UPCI Press Release of September 1983,* p. 14.

[62]*Financial Reports, UPCI, Year ending June 30, 1983* (Hazelwood, Mo.: Pentecostal Publishing House), pp. 8, 78.

[63]*Ibid,* pp. 71-72.

[64]Annual Field Report from UPCI, Foreign Missions Division, 1984.

[65]*WCE,* pp. 216, 234, 243, 327, 386-87, 490-91.

[66]"Churches in China: Flourishing from House to House," *Christianity Today,* June 18, 1982, pp. 24-25.

[67]*WCE,* p. 234.

[68]John Yang, *The Essential Doctrines in the Holy Bible,* M. H. Tsai,

trans. (Taichung, Taiwan: The General Assembly of the True Jesus Church in Taiwan, 1970), pp. 113, 119, 157-58.

[69]Cornelia Butler Flora, *Pentecostalism in Columbia: Baptism by Fire and Spirit* (Cranbury, N. J.: Associated University Presses, 1974); Donald Palmer, *Explosion of People Evangelism* (Chicago: Moody Press, 1974).

[70]Walter Sawatsky, *Soviet Evangelicals Since World War II* (Scottsdale, Pa.: Herald Press, 1981), p. 95.

[71]*Ibid,* p. 434.

[72]*WCE,* pp. 695-96.

[73]*WCE,* pp. 792-93.

12
ARE THERE EXCEPTIONS?

"How shall we escape, if we neglect so great salvation; which at the first began to be spoken by the Lord, and was confirmed unto us by them that heard him; God also bearing them witness, both with signs and wonders, and with divers miracles, and gifts of the Holy Ghost, according to his own will?" (Hebrews 2:3-4).

Can there be any exceptions to the New Testament plan of salvation we have studied in this book? This chapter will analyze some proposed exceptions in the light of Scripture.

Basic Principles

At the outset, we must establish some basic principles to guide our discussion:

(1) God alone will judge the salvation of each person (Romans 2:16; Hebrews 12:23). No human being can condemn a soul to hell or guarantee him a place in heaven, for salvation is a matter between the individual and God.

The Lord taught us not to judge each other, but to judge ourselves and leave the judgment of others to God (Matthew 7:1-5; Luke 6:37). Jesus did not come to condemn the world but to offer salvation (John 3:17), and we should do likewise. We should proclaim the gospel, encourage obedience to it, and warn of the biblically prescribed consequences for disobedience, but the final results rest in God's hands.

We should not be quick to reject those who reverence the name of Christ, but who apparently do not have the fulness of truth. The disciples rebuked a man who cast out devils in Jesus' name because he was not part of them, but Jesus said, "Forbid him not: for there is no man which shall do a miracle in my name, that can lightly speak evil of me. For he that is not against us is on our part" (Mark 9:39-40). People such as these are not necessarily saved (Matthew 7:21-23), but they may still help to spread the Word of God and the name of Jesus (Philippians 1:15-18). Instead of opposing them, we should be thankful for what good they do and endeavor to lead them to more truth. If we preach the full gospel in a positive way, the truth will speak for itself and be its own defense.

(2) God is sovereign in His bestowal of mercy. He said, "I will have mercy on whom I will have mercy, and I will have compassion on whom I will have compassion" (Romans 9:15). Nevertheless, He has voluntarily chosen a plan of salvation and will abide by it; He has clearly established the conditions upon which He will grant mer-

cy. Paul first taught God's sovereignty in salvation (Romans 9:14-24), but then explained that God will grant salvation to everyone who believes on Jesus, confesses Him as Lord, calls upon His name, and obeys His gospel (Romans 10:9-17).

(3) The Bible is the sole authority for doctrine and instruction in salvation. Jesus told the Jews, "Search the scriptures; for in them ye think ye have eternal life: and they are they which testify of me. And ye will not come to me, that ye might have life" (John 5:39-40). He did not rebuke their reliance on the Scriptures to find eternal life, but their refusal to believe on Him for eternal life when the Scriptures pointed so clearly to Him.

The Bible contains the only gospel we can preach. Paul stated, "But though we, or an angel from heaven, preach any other gospel unto you than that which we have preached unto you, let him be accursed. As we said before, so say I now again, If any man preach any other gospel unto you than that ye have received, let him be accursed" (Galatians 1:8-9).

All true doctrine must rest upon the Bible. "The holy scriptures. . .are able to make thee wise unto salvation through faith which is in Christ Jesus. All scripture is given by inspiration of God, and is profitable for doctrine, for reproof, for correction, for instruction in righteousness: That the man of God may be perfect, throughly furnished unto all good works" (II Timothy 3:15-17).

We cannot impose demands that the Bible does not support, nor can we make exceptions that the Bible does not grant. Precisely because God is sovereign in granting salvation, we must limit ourselves to the clear teaching of Scripture. If God has plans that go beyond what He has revealed to us in the Bible, that is His prerogative, but we have authority only to teach the plan God gave to us in the Scriptures. We have no right to offer false or uncertain hopes based on wishful thinking, speculations, reasoning, philosophy, or doubtful interpretations of difficult passages. We cannot make exceptions for situations that arise from failure to follow biblical teachings and examples.

(4) We must not formulate doctrinal teaching on the basis of unusual or hypothetical situations. Human sympathy may sway us, but if we try to establish any exception we undercut the authority of God's Word. For example, God could have chosen to remit sins without water baptism, but we exceed our authority if we assert that He will or list circumstances under which He will. If we make an exception for one who was not baptized, then logically speaking baptism is not necessary for anyone.

By playing judge in this manner we will encourage disobedience or a casual approach to the Word of God. God alone is qualified to be Judge, and as such He will apply general principles to specific facts in order to reach a fair and legally correct decision. We should obey the full gospel to the utmost of our understanding and capacity, encourage everyone else to do the same, and leave eternal judgment to God.

(5) God is the most loving, merciful, and just Judge anyone could have. His love, mercy, and sense of fairness are perfect, while ours are not: "For the LORD is good; his mercy is everlasting; and his truth endureth to all generations" (Psalm 100:5); "Great and marvelous are thy works, Lord God Almighty; just and true are thy ways, thou King of saints" (Revelation 15:3). When it

comes to salvation, our concept of justice is faulty, because no one deserves salvation. Only God has the right to grant mercy. Only He knows what is fair in each situation because only He has perfect knowledge. Only He knows the condition of the heart, the opportunities of the past, and what an individual will do if given future opportunities.

(6) We cannot compromise God's plan because only a few follow it. "For what if some did not believe? shall their unbelief make the faith of God without effect? God forbid: yea, let God be true, but every man a liar" (Romans 3:3-4). Jesus said, "Strait [small] is the gate, and narrow is the way, which leadeth unto life, and few there be that find it" (Matthew 7:14). Someone asked Him, "Lord, are there few that be saved?" (Luke 13:23). He replied, "Strive to enter in at the strait gate: for many, I say unto you, will seek to enter in, and shall not be able" (Luke 13:24).

In Noah's day God saved only eight souls out of the entire world because only they believed Him and obeyed His plan. In the first century, almost all of God's chosen people (Israel) rejected His plan, prompting Paul's statement in Romans. Almost all the religious leaders and religious community rejected the gospel. Should we be surprised if the same is true today?

Are the Heathen Lost?

Applying these principles, let us investigate the possibility of an exception for those who have never heard the gospel.

No one can inherit eternal life outside the gospel of Jesus Christ: "Except a man be born of water and of the Spirit, he cannot enter into the kingdom of God" (John 3:5). Jesus said, "I am the way, the truth, and the life: no man cometh unto the Father, but by me" (John 14:6). He also said, "If ye believe not that I am he, ye shall die in your sins" (John 8:24). Paul wrote, "And to you who are troubled rest with us, when the Lord Jesus shall be revealed from heaven with his mighty angels, In flaming fire taking vengeance on them that know not God, and that obey not the gospel of our Lord Jesus Christ: Who shall be punished with everlasting destruction from the presence of the Lord, and from the glory of his power" (II Thessalonians 1:7-9).

Even those who have never heard the gospel have a sufficient witness of God in His creation: "Because that which may be known of God is manifest in them; for God hath shewed it unto them. For the invisible things of him from the creation of the world are clearly seen, being understood by the things that are made, even his eternal power and Godhead; so that they are without excuse" (Romans 1:19-20). God holds everyone accountable to glorify Him as God and to be thankful to Him (Romans 1:21).

God has also given a conscience to all. The heathen may not have full knowledge of God's will, but they have enough conscience that (1) if they follow it God will lead them farther into His will and (2) if they do not follow it they will be condemned. Everyone knows some things are morally wrong and that the proper penalty for these sins is death (Romans 1:32). Those who had the Law of Moses will be judged by it, and those who did not will be judged by the law of conscience (Romans 2:12-16). This does not mean anyone will be saved on the basis of conscience alone, because no one has ever lived up to the minimum demands of conscience. Everyone has transgressed at least once (Romans 3:10, 23). No one will be saved by works, or by adherence to law, including the law of conscience (Romans 3:20; Ephesians 2:8-9). Conscience, then, will serve as a just basis for condemnation, not as a basis for salvation outside of Jesus Christ.

If someone sincerely attempts to follow conscience and diligently seeks after God, we believe He will reveal enough truth to him so that he can be saved. God "is a rewarder of them that diligently seek him" (Hebrews 11:6). He will always honor a broken and contrite heart (Psalm 34:18; 51:17), and He always reveals Himself to the seeker (I Chronicles 28:9; Jeremiah 29:13-14; Matthew 7:7).

God does not save outside of truth; it is God's will for "all men to be saved, and to come unto the knowledge of the truth" (I Timothy 2:4). Cornelius is a good example. He was a devout man who feared God, gave alms to the poor, and prayed to God constantly (Acts 10:1-2). In short, he did everything within his power to seek, worship, and obey God. His actions became a memorial before God, and as a result God sent an angel to him (Acts 10:3-6). The angel did not design a special plan of salvation for him or preach the gospel to him, but the angel gave him instructions so that he could find a preacher of the gospel. Cornelius was not already saved, for the angel told him, "Call for Simon, whose surname is Peter; who shall tell thee words, whereby thou and all thy house shall be saved" (Acts 11:13-14).

There was a woman in Seoul, Korea, whose mother was a shamaness (witch doctor). The mother's superstitious practices and constant communication with evil spirits caused the daughter to become so depressed that she attempted suicide. While near death she had a vision of two Americans. She recovered, and one day she passed by the First Pentecostal Church. Attracted by the noise of worship, she looked inside and saw the two American faces that had appeared in her vision. They were Elton and Loretta Bernard, the founders of the church. As a result of this miracle, the young woman began attending services, repented from her sins, was baptized in Jesus' name, received the Holy Ghost, and eventually won her mother to the Lord. She had known nothing of the gospel of Jesus Christ, but God apparently saw a longing in her heart for more than superstition and saw a sincere desire to worship Him. As a result, He led her to the truth.

If the heathen are saved without the gospel, then Christ's death was unnecessary and Christ's command to preach the gospel to every creature was a mistake. If the heathen are saved before hearing the gospel, then missionaries actually cause saved people to be damned, because many reject the gospel when they do hear it. In this case, Christ's commission would actually cause more people to be lost, contrary to God's stated will (II Peter 3:9).

Paul said, "For whosoever shall call upon the name of the Lord shall be saved. How then shall they call on him in whom they have not believed? and how shall they believe in him of whom they have not heard? and how shall they hear without a preacher? And how shall they preach, except they be sent? . . .So then faith cometh by hearing, and hearing by the word of God'' (Romans 10:13-15, 17). The truth is that all men are lost until they hear, believe, and obey the gospel of Jesus Christ.

God is not unfair to base salvation totally upon the gospel, for everyone deserves to be lost. God was not responsible for man's sin and had no obligation to design a plan of salvation. Since salvation is by His grace, He can offer it on His own terms. Furthermore, God is not to blame that many people do not know about Him. Beginning with Adam and again with Noah, God revealed His will to all humanity. In our age He has commissioned the church to bring the gospel to everyone. It is not God's fault that men have repeatedly failed to transmit the knowledge of God to their descendants and to their fellow men. God is more than fair—He is gracious—to give every man a witness of Himself through creation and conscience.

Moral and Sincere People

No one is righteous in himself, no one is good in God's sight, all are sinners, and no one will be saved on the basis of his good works (Romans 3:10-12, 23, 27-28; Ephesians 2:8-9). One sin is enough to condemn the soul, and no matter how good a person may be, without God he is still a sinner. No one can earn salvation; it is a free gift of God and must be received on God's terms, which include faith in Christ and obedience to His gospel. No matter how morally a person attempts to live, if he does not follow God's plan he cannot be saved.

Morality and good works are not the determinants

of salvation, for there have been Moslems, Jews, Buddhists, Hindus, and others who have rejected Christ but who have manifested morality and good works equal to or greater than that of many professing Christians. No doubt many of the Jews who rejected Jesus were highly moral, obeying the Law of Moses in every detail. Paul was blameless as far as the righteousness of the Law, but he still needed a conversion (Philippians 3:5-7).

Sincerity is not enough either, for false religionists, Communists, atheists, and others are often highly sincere in their beliefs. It is absolutely necessary to worship God both in spirit and in truth (John 4:24). God demands obedience above sacrifice (I Samuel 15:22), and no one will be saved who does not obey the gospel, regardless of sacrifice.

Only God sees the heart of a man and knows what he is truly like (Jeremiah 17:9-10). We must not make exceptions for those who seem to deserve salvation based on their goodness as perceived by faulty human judgment.

Those Who Profess Christ

Sincere profession based on a faulty concept of Christ is not enough; one must believe and obey the gospel. False prophets and cultists profess Christ, but they are not saved. According to Jesus, some people will sincerely profess Him, believe that they are saved, and even profess to perform miracles in His name, but they will not be saved because they did not obey His Word (Matthew 7:21-27). Many will profess to know Him and even to have enjoyed His presence but will not be saved (Luke

13:25-27).

Where does this leave those who have a certain degree of faith in Christ but have not obeyed the full gospel? We must recognize that they have responded to God's Word in some measure and that God has dealt with them. God seeks to lead them to the full truth, and if they continue to follow His Word and Spirit they will be saved. We must not belittle any genuine experience with God they may have. These people have begun to follow God's Word, but at this point in their experience they are not apostolic believers; they have not been born again of water and the Spirit according to John 3:5 and Acts 2:38.

Apollos is a biblical example of someone in this situation (Acts 18:24-28). He was an eloquent man, mighty in the Scriptures, instructed in the way of the Lord, and fervent in the spirit. He taught diligently the things of the Lord and spoke boldly in the synagogue, but he knew only the baptism of John. When Aquila and Priscilla heard him, they took him aside and expounded the way of God unto him more perfectly. Apparently, they taught him baptism in the name of Jesus Christ and the baptism of the Holy Ghost, because that is what Paul taught twelve other disciples of John in the very next chapter.

From this account, we see that someone may have a deep knowledge of the Scriptures, a powerful ministry, and a spiritual fervency and still not be born again. Basically such people are pre-Pentecost believers, not part of the apostolic church. Despite their valid religious experience with God, they need to be led to further truth.

Perhaps one way to describe their position is to say they are in the conception stage and have not yet had the new birth. Pioneer Pentecostal leaders such as A. D.

Urshan and G. T. Haywood used this analogy.[1] The Word has been planted and conception has taken place as a result (Luke 8:11; I Peter 1:23), but the actual birth has not yet occurred. They are in the formative stages of being a Christian and need to be led to the fulness of truth so they can have a normal, healthy birth.

Professing Christians in Church History

The Bible reveals only one plan of salvation for the entire New Testament church age, and the Bible has been available throughout church history. Historical accounts from the early post-apostolic age have also been available to later generations, and they confirm the apostolic message of baptism in Jesus' name and the baptism of the Holy Ghost with tongues. Furthermore, it appears that these doctrines have existed throughout church history.[2]

We do not know everything about the spiritual lives of important church leaders during the Reformation period. Some possibly received the Holy Ghost and spoke in tongues without fully comprehending the significance of this experience. In many cases there is evidence that certain Protestant leaders were aware of key apostolic doctrines. For example, during the Reformation a noted Spanish physician named Michael Servetus proclaimed the oneness of God, the full deity of Jesus, and the need for rebaptism. Luther, Zwingli, and Calvin all knew of his doctrine. In particular, Luther was aware of a controversy over the Jesus Name baptismal formula. Speaking in tongues occurred among early Anabaptists and the

Reformers could have heard of this experience. Luther definitely knew of the "enthusiasts," a group that emphasized the moving of the Spirit and communication with God through prophecy and inspiration (probably including tongues and interpretation). They opposed Luther as being a man of letter only; in turn Luther and the Lutheran Formula of Concord (1577) rejected them.[3] Apparently, then, the Reformers were exposed to at least some apostolic doctrines.

The Reformers certainly were not infallible doctrinally, for they held such false doctrines as predestination of the individual soul, infant baptism, sprinkling, and the trinity. Neither were they always noble examples of Christian principles. Luther condoned and even recommended that a certain German ruler practice bigamy, believed that all Anabaptists were heretics and endorsed their execution, questioned the value of the Book of James and called it "an epistle of straw," endorsed violent persecution of the Jews, and strongly supported the German feudal princes in crushing peasant revolts.[4] He wrote a tract condemning the peasant revolts, entitled "Against the Murderous and Thieving Hordes of Peasants," which said, "Let everyone who can, smite, slay, and stab" them.[5] Zwingli died in battle attempting to extend Protestant rule to Catholic portions of his native Switzerland.[6] Calvin consented to the execution of Servetus, allowing him to be burned at the stake near Geneva.[7]

The basic noble character of these men and their significant contributions to church history are well documented, but it is equally true that none of them were perfect or infallible.

We cannot make special exceptions based on personal

courage, zeal, or insight into certain areas of Scripture. Many people have demonstrated courage, zeal, determination, and sacrifice for false religions, politics, and nationalism. Many have been persecuted, cruelly tortured, and martyred for the sake of Judaism, Buddhism, Islam, Communism, revolutionary causes, and anarchism. Many heretics and cultists have suffered because of their profession of Christ. Men have lived and died for noble causes and even for causes important to God, such as democracy, freedom of religion, belief in Jehovah, and belief in the Bible. However, none of these people were saved because of their suffering or sacrifice. Under no circumstances should we allow the life of a pious ancestor or a noble leader in church history to dissuade us from believing, obeying, and proclaiming what we know to be God's will today.

Extra-biblical Speculations

All other schemes and speculations concerning salvation for those who do not experience the new birth are outside the boundaries of Scripture and must be treated as such.

A Second Chance after Death?

Some people, including Mormons and Jehovah's Witnesses, teach the possibility of a chance to be saved after death, at least for those who did not have a "full" opportunity in this life. These theories may be interesting to speculate upon, but the Bible does not give us the authority to preach them as gospel. The Bible nowhere teaches the doctrine of a chance to accept the gospel after this earthly life is over, but if anything, it indicates there is no such chance: "It is appointed unto men once to die, but after this the judgment" (Hebrews 9:27); "Marvel not at this: for the hour is coming, in the which all that are in the graves shall hear his [the Son's] voice, And shall come forth; they that have done good, unto the resurrection of life; and they that have done evil, unto the resurrection of damnation" (John 5:28-29); "And the sea gave up the dead which were in it; and death and hell delivered up the dead which were in them: and they were judged every man according to their works" (Revelation 20:13).

Two passages have been used to support the doctrine of a second chance. One is Paul's allusion to baptism for the dead (I Corinthians 15:29), which was explored in Chapter 6. The other passage states that the Spirit of Christ preached to spirits in prison who were disobedient in Noah's day (I Peter 3:18-20). Here are some alternative explanations for this verse: (1) The Spirit of Christ preached in Noah's day through Noah to those who are now in prison. The wording and tense of I Peter 4:6 support this interpretation. (2) The Spirit of Christ went to the underworld while His body lay in the tomb and announced His victory over death to the fallen angels in prison (II Peter 2:4) or to all the satanic forces. (3) The Spirit of Christ made this announcement to human spirits in the underworld but did not offer anyone a second chance to be saved.

The last two explanations receive support from the Greek word translated "preached," which is not the usual word *euangelizo,* meaning to preach the good news of salvation, but *kerusso,* meaning to proclaim as information. Both explanations fit in well with the doctrine of Christ's descent into hell (*hades*), when He won the keys of hell and death and led captivity captive (Acts 2:25-32; Romans 10:7; Ephesians 4:8-10; Revelation 1:18).

A Subnormal New Birth?

Instead of teaching salvation today without the new birth, some hold that one can be born again with less than full conformity to the apostolic pattern. For support of this concept they point to examples in which God saved people within His plan for their day, but fulfilled His plan in an unconventional or unexpected way. Old Testament examples are Jethro, Balaam, and Nineveh. Also, the thief on the cross was saved under the Law, but with Jesus being his priest and sacrifice. This shows that God has the liberty to fulfill His plan in His own way, but we must not make too much of this example since it occurred in a unique situation and time period.

There are two possibilities raised with respect to New Testament salvation: (1) Some could be born of the Spirit without the sign of tongues because they did not know about it or did not understand it and so did not have faith for it. (2) Some could be born of water without orally uttering the name Jesus at baptism because they never heard it taught or did not understand it. This presupposes that at baptism they had genuine faith in Jesus as Savior and understood practically (if not theologically) that He is the fulness of the Godhead.

Although these arguments seem more logical and internally consistent, there are at least two serious difficulties: (1) The Bible itself teaches the complete apostolic experience without alluding to exceptions; (2) Throughout church history and today many sincere people have received the Holy Ghost with the evidence of tongues, including many who were not expecting tongues, and many have been baptized in the name of Jesus who had never heard anyone teach baptism in Jesus' name. In view of these difficulties, our clear responsibility is to receive and proclaim the complete apostolic experience, expecting to see the apostolic pattern repeated exactly.

Destiny of Infants

Our discussion has not treated the case of children who die before they are old enough consciously to believe God and repent from sin, nor has it dealt with the mentally incompetent. Several views have been proposed:

(1) They cannot go to heaven due to their sinful natures (Psalm 51:5; Romans 5:12-21). This presupposes that the sinful nature includes not only a compulsion to sin but also an inherited guilt apart from personal acts. Roman Catholics hold this view, teaching infants must be baptized to wash away original sin. They have invented a nonbiblical place for unbaptized infants, called limbo, where there is neither pleasure nor pain.

(2) They will go to heaven. Jesus used little children as examples to illustrate the kingdom of heaven (Matthew 18:1-10; 19:14); perhaps this implies they are part of the kingdom. This view presupposes that based on Christ's

atonement God will automatically eliminate their sinful nature.

(3) They will be resurrected in the Millennium and given an opportunity to accept or reject salvation. Jehovah's Witnesses teach this, but there is no biblical support.

(4) God will judge infants based on His foreknowledge of what they would have done had they lived. This raises unanswerable questions about the freedom of the will and the factors contributing to an individual's decision.

(5) An infant's salvation is determined by that of his parents. The problem here is that God would condemn some infants because of their parents' sin and their own inability to believe. There are Old Testament examples in which children suffered because of their parents' sin, such as in the Flood. This does not necessarily mean those children were eternally damned, but simply demonstrates that children often suffer in this life as a result of their parents' actions.

First Corinthians 7:14 states that an unbelieving spouse is sanctified (separated) by a believing spouse and the children of that union are made holy (separated from the world to God). If this refers to salvation, arguably the unbelieving spouse and adult children are included. It seems clear, however, that it alludes to the godly influence that believers have on their families, which certainly may be a powerful factor in leading them to salvation.

We conclude that the Bible simply does not say what happens to infants and the mentally incompetent. This is not surprising, for the Bible is a very practical book and addresses only those who are able to respond. Perhaps the Bible does not address this subject because God does not want us to withhold the gospel from any age group. The Bible teaches us to train children in the ways of the Lord (Proverbs 22:6), and we should do this from the earliest ages. God fills even small children with His Spirit; members of families have been filled at ages 6, 7, 9, and 10. The Bible specifies no age limitation, perhaps because the age of accountability may vary considerably depending on the individual child's rate of development, capabilities, and training.

The lack of clear teaching regarding infants and the mentally incompetent should not disturb us. We should have faith in God, believing that He has a gracious plan for them even as He does for us. Having experienced God's grace, mercy, and love in our own lives, we can entrust them into His care without reservation.

Degrees of Punishment

The Bible indicates that sinners will suffer differing degrees of punishment based on the knowledge and opportunity they had on earth. This does not minimize, however, the reality of punishment that all sinners will have or the greatness of the salvation that they will forfeit. It may help us understand the justice of God a little better, and encourage us not to make exceptions to the gospel out of sympathy for those who seem to deserve punishment less than others. God will fairly evaluate every sinner's degree of responsibility and will mete out punishment accordingly. The Bible does not explain exactly how God will implement this principle, but the following passages teach it:

(1) Jesus taught, "For unto whomsoever much is given, of him shall be much required" (Luke 12:48). By way of illustration, He told a parable about a master who unexpectedly returned to his possession. The servant who knew his lord's will but did not follow it was beaten with many stripes, while the servant who did not fully comprehend what his lord required but also committed deeds worthy of punishment received few stripes (Luke 12:42-48).

(2) Hypocrites will receive a greater damnation than others (Mark 12:38-40).

(3) Backsliders will be punished more severely than if they had never known the truth (Matthew 12:43-45; II Peter 2:20-22).

(4) The saints, who are saved by faith, will receive rewards according to their good works (I Corinthians 3:11-15). If the same principle applies to sinners, they will be punished according to their works.

(5) Everyone will be judged according to his works as evaluated by the knowledge available to him (Romans 2:6, 11-16). No one will be saved outside the gospel, but sinners who followed the law of conscience in certain areas will be excused in those areas, while those who transgressed will be punished (Romans 2:14-15). This distinction has meaning only if there are different levels of punishment.

(6) If any man does a good deed for the gospel or for a Christian, he will not lose his reward under any circumstances (Matthew 10:40-42; Mark 9:41). Possibly, some unsaved people will not receive their full reward in this life but will somehow reap benefits in the life to come.

Conclusion

The Bible does not teach any exceptions to the simple new-birth message, which is repentance from sin, water baptism in the name of Jesus, and the baptism of the Holy Ghost. We should not teach extra-biblical theories and speculations as revealed truth, but we should base all doctrine solely on the clear teaching of God's Word. God will save anyone who sincerely seeks truth with his whole heart and places complete faith in Jesus Christ.

We should preach the full gospel, which includes Acts 2:38 as the norm for the new birth.

FOOTNOTES

[1]Andrew Urshan, *Apostolic Faith Doctrine of the New Birth* (Portland, Or.: Apostolic Book Publishers, n.d.), pp. 3, 15; G. T. Haywood, *The Birth of the Spirit in the Days of the Apostles,* pp. 10-11, 21-22, Rpt. in Paul Dugas, ed. and comp., *The Life and Writings of Elder G. T. Haywood* (Stockton, Ca.: WABC Apostolic Press, 1968).

[2]For documentation of information in this section, see chapters 10 and 11.

[3]Rene Laurentin, *Catholic Pentecostalism,* Matthew J. O'Connell, trans. (Garden City, N. J.: Doubleday & Co., 1977), pp. 133-34.

[4]Roland Bainton, *Here I Stand* (Nashville: Abingdon, 1978), pp. 259, 292-97.

[5]*Ibid,* pp. 216-17.

[6]Latourette, II, 749.

[7]Klotsche, p. 224.

13

FOUR ASPECTS OF SALVATION

"And such were some of you: but ye are washed, but ye are sanctified, but ye are justified in the name of the Lord Jesus, and by the Spirit of our God" (I Corinthians 6:11).

The salvation that God provides will cure every problem created by sin. Ultimately, it will restore everything lost by Adam and more (Romans 5:15-21) and will remake us in the image of Christ (Romans 8:29; I John 3:2).

This chapter discusses four major aspects of salvation: justification, regeneration, adoption, and sanctification.

Justification

Justification is the act by which God declares the sinner to be righteous. The sinner does not actually become righteous within himself at this point, but God counts, reckons, or considers him as righteous, without regarding his past sins. Justification is a legal term denoting a change of standing in the sight of God.

Justification consists of two elements: (1) God forgives the sinner, removing the guilt and penalty associated with his sins (Romans 4:6-8; 8:1). (2) God imputes (transfers) the righteousness of Christ to the sinner, so that he can partake of everything the sinless Christ is entitled to receive because of His righteousness (Romans 3:22; 4:3-5; II Corinthians 5:20-21). As a result of this two-fold work, the justified man is fully reconciled to God (Romans 5:1, 9-10) and entitled to inherit all His promises, including eternal life (Romans 5:9; 8:30; Galatians 3:10-14; Titus 3:7).

Justification originates in God's grace, having been purchased for us by the blood of Christ: "Being justified freely by his grace through the redemption that is in Christ Jesus: whom God hath set forth to be a propitiation through faith in his blood" (Romans 3:24-25). It comes only through faith in Jesus Christ and not by works of the law: "Therefore we conclude that a man is justified by faith without the deeds of the law" (Romans 3:28); "But to him that worketh not, but believeth on him that justifieth the ungodly, his faith is counted for righteousness" (Romans 4:5).

The blood of Christ signifies His total redemptive work, including His death (which satisfied the requirements of God's law) and His resurrection (without which the death would have no effect). "For us also, to whom it [righteousness] shall be imputed, if we believe on him that raised up Jesus our Lord from the dead; who was delivered for our offenses, and was raised again for our justification" (Romans 4:24-25). God's grace is the source of justification, Christ's blood (death, burial, and resurrection) is the ground of justification, and faith is the condition upon which we receive justification.

Since justification comes through faith, it occurs when a person fully exercises saving faith, which includes obedience to the gospel (Chapter 2). Therefore, the full work of justification comes by faith as one repents, is baptized in Jesus' name, and receives the Holy Spirit.

In I Corinthians 6:9-10 Paul listed ten categories of unrighteous people who will not inherit the kingdom of God. He continued: "And such were some of you: but ye are washed, but ye are sanctified, but ye are justified in the name of the Lord Jesus, and by the Spirit of our God" (I Corinthians 6:11). In other words, justification occurred when they were baptized in Jesus' name and baptized with the Holy Spirit. Although this verse does not specifically mention the word *baptism, Smith's Dictionary of the Bible* explains it as referring to baptism: "It is generally believed that here is an allusion to being baptized in the name of the Lord Jesus Christ. . .[T]he reference to baptism seems unquestionable."[1] A Baptist theologian asserted that, "The voice of scholarship is unanimous in affirming the association with baptism."[2]

Further examination of the purposes of repentance, water baptism, and the Spirit baptism demonstrates that the work of justification takes place in all three. At repentance, man and God begin to form a personal relationship, which lays a foundation for water and Spirit baptism. At water baptism, God remits sin (Acts 2:38), which corresponds to the first element of justification.

The Holy Spirit imparts the righteousness of Christ, for the Spirit is Christ in us: "That the righteousness of the law might be fulfilled in us, who walk not after the flesh, but after the Spirit" (Romans 8:4); "But ye are not in the flesh but in the Spirit if so be that the Spirit of God dwell in you. Now if any man have not the Spirit of Christ, he is none of his. And if Christ be in you, the body is dead because of sin; but the Spirit is life because of righteousness" (Romans 8:9-10). The indwelling Spirit enables us to receive future salvation (Romans 8:11). Through the Spirit we qualify for God's blessings and promises (Romans 8:15-17; Galatians 3:14). In short, the baptism of the Spirit corresponds to the second element of justification.

The work of justification begins at initial repentance from sin and is completed at the time of water and Spirit baptism. Therefore, justification is instantaneous at the time of the new birth as a whole. It would be incorrect to identify justification solely with one aspect of the new birth, because the new birth must be regarded as a single whole. In one sense, however, justification is available on a continuing basis for sins committed and repented of after the new birth experience.

Regeneration

Regeneration means a new birth. It is more than a reformation of the old nature; the regenerated man receives a new, holy nature that has power over the old, sinful nature. The new birth involves two elements: (1)

destroying the power of the old nature (II Corinthians 5:17) and (2) imparting a new nature, which is actually the nature of God Himself (Ephesians 4:24; Colossians 3:10; II Peter 1:4).

The new nature brings a change of desires and attitudes (Ephesians 4:23-32) and power to live a new life (Acts 1:8; Romans 8:4). The new birth does not eliminate the sinful nature; the Christian has two natures, the flesh (sinful or carnal nature) and the Spirit. If he follows after the desires of the flesh or depends upon the power of the flesh, he cannot live an overcoming, holy life (Romans 7:21-25; 8:12-13; Galatians 5:19-21). If he lives after the Spirit, he can enjoy a life of victory over sin (Romans 8:1-4; Galatians 5:22-23; I John 3:9). No man can be saved without the work of regeneration in his life (John 3:3-7; Galatians 6:15).

Regeneration originates in God's grace (John 1:13; Titus 3:5; James 1:18) and comes through man's faith (John 1:12-13). We are begotten (conceived) by the Word of God, the gospel of Jesus Christ (I Corinthians 4:15; James 1:18; I Peter 1:23). Hearing the Word plants the seed of our salvation, but for this to develop into the new birth we must respond in faith by obeying Acts 2:38. At repentance and water baptism our old man is killed and buried, which means our old lifestyle and the dominion of sin over us are destroyed (Romans 6:1-7). The baptism of the Holy Spirit imparts the new nature and permanent power to keep the old man dead (Romans 8:8-9, 13). Thus the baptism of water and the baptism of the Spirit correspond to the two elements of regeneration; both are part of the new birth.

Regeneration, then, occurs at the time we repent, are

baptized in the name of Jesus, and receive the Holy Spirit. The work of regeneration benefits us throughout our Christian walk by bestowing godly desires, spiritual guidance, and power to overcome sin daily.

Adoption

Adoption is the act of choosing and placing a child. *Regeneration* indicates that we are children of God by reason of a new, spiritual birth; *adoption* signifies that we become God's adult sons and heirs by His conscious choice. Adoption, then, refers to our position as sons of God with all the rights associated with that status.

In Galatians 4:1-7, Paul contrasted life under the Law before Christ and life in the Spirit after Christ. Before the death of Christ, people lived under bondage to the world. God's people lived under subjection to the Law, just as a child who has not yet reached the age of maturity lives under the control of guardians and tutors. After Christ's redemptive work, however, God's children came of age, received the Spirit of Christ, and became entitled to the inheritance God had planned for them all along. Paul used the word *adoption* to describe this change of status, since an adoption confers rights and privileges upon a person that he has never before enjoyed.

In Romans 8:14-17, Paul used the adoption analogy in a somewhat different way. At our conversion we were adopted in God's family, becoming younger brothers and sisters of the man Christ. As adopted children we obtain all the legal rights and privileges of a natural born son. Christ is the only begotten of the Father and the only One originally entitled to be an heir, but by adoption we, too, become heirs of the Father and, therefore, co-heirs with Christ.

We have not yet inherited all the benefits of adoption; we are still awaiting the full revelation of our position as children of God and the redemption of our physical bodies (Romans 8:23).

Adoption originates in God's grace and choice (Ephesians 1:4-5) and comes through faith (Galatians 3:26). The Scriptures indicate that adoption occurs by water baptism and the Spirit baptism, for this is what places us into the family of God: "For ye are all the children of God by faith in Christ Jesus. For as many of you as have been baptized into Christ have put on Christ" (Galatians 3:26-27); "For by one Spirit are we all baptized into one body" (I Corinthians 12:13); "For ye have not received the spirit of bondage again to fear; but ye have received the Spirit of adoption, whereby we cry, Abba, Father" (Romans 8:15). The Spirit is both the agent of adoption and the first benefit of adoption.

Adoption into God's family, then, occurs instantaneously at the new birth. In one sense, it is a past event since we are already called the sons of God (I John 3:1). We already enjoy the firstfruits of our inheritance, which is the Spirit of God (Romans 8:23; Galatians 4:6; Ephesians 1:13-14), and we have the assurance of a future inheritance. In another sense, however, adoption is still future. We are yet awaiting the revelation of our position before all creation, the redemption of our bodies, and the fulness of our inheritance, all of which we will receive when Christ returns.

Sanctification

Sanctification literally means separation. In the context of our present discussion, it is basically equivalent to holiness, which means separation from sin and consecration to God. Sanctification is the process of becoming righteous—actually becoming like Christ.

At the new birth, God sets us apart from sin (I Corinthians 6:11), but this is only the beginning of the process. God continues to work in us to perfect us and make us holy. The Bible teaches that we can attain maturity and perfection in this life (II Corinthians 3:18; 7:1; Ephesians 4:11-15; II Peter 3:18). This is not absolute, sinless perfection as exemplified by Christ but a relative perfection, for the sinful nature and the possibility of sin still reside within.

We can all be equally perfect in a relative sense even though we may have attained different levels in an absolute sense, just as two children at different stages of development can both be perfectly normal and healthy. God evaluates our lives on the basis of where we have come from, what our abilities are, what He has given us, and what our potential is (Matthew 13:23; 25:14-30). He expects us to undergo a growth process (Mark 4:26-29). If we have been born again, grow at the proper rate in our relationship, use everything God has given us, live a repented life, and progressively become more Christlike, we can be perfect in His sight. The goal He has given us to strive for is absolute perfection (Matthew 5:48). If we submit to the sanctifying process, ultimately Christ will transform us into absolute, sinless perfection at His coming (Philippians 3:12-14; I Thessalonians 3:13; I John

3:2).

Our sanctification comes by grace through faith on the basis of Christ's sacrifice (Acts 26:18; I Thessalonians 5:23; Hebrews 10:10). The initial act of sanctification comes at the time of repentance, water baptism, and Spirit baptism (I Corinthians 6:11). The continuing work of sanctification comes by the operation of the indwelling Spirit (II Thessalonians 2:13; I Peter 1:2) as we live daily by faith (Romans 1:17).

In sum, sanctification is first of all an instantaneous work that takes place at the new birth, when we are first set apart from sin to God. Sanctification continues progressively throughout the Christian's life and will be completed at Christ's coming for the church.

God's Eternal Plan of Salvation

Romans 8:28-30 describes five steps in God's eternal plan of salvation for fallen mankind:

(1) *Foreknowledge.* God foreknew man would sin and would need salvation. He also foreknew that when He provided salvation, some would accept it.

(2) *Predestination.* Because God foresaw this response, He planned from the foundation of the world to provide salvation through Christ's atoning sacrifice (I Peter 1:18-20; Revelation 13:8). Those who choose God's plan are predestined to be conformed to the likeness of Christ. The church is ordained to be successful, but each individual must choose whether to be part of this foreordained plan or not.

(3) *Calling.* Acting upon His plan, God has extended

a call to all mankind ("whosoever will") to be part of it. Romans 8 speaks of an effectual calling; only those who respond to God's universal call actually become part of the church (Greek *ekklesia,* literally meaning "the called out ones").

(4) *Justification.* God then justifies those who accept His call. He declares them to be righteous, which entitles them to all the benefits of salvation.

(5) *Glorification.* The last step is glorification, which is the ultimate work of sanctification. Romans 8 speaks of it in the past tense because in God's mind it is an absolutely certain, predestined event for His church. At that time we will receive glorified bodies with absolutely perfect and sinless natures. When God's plan is complete, we will have complete, eternal deliverance from all the power and effects of sin.

Summary

This chapter has investigated four important aspects of our salvation: (1) justification, the act by which God declares us to be righteous; (2) regeneration, the act by which we are born again and receive a new nature; (3) adoption, the act by which we are placed into God's family and chosen as His heirs; and (4) sanctification, the act by which we are separated from sin and the process by which we actually become righteous.

All these works of salvation originate in God's grace, are purchased by Christ's blood, and come to us through faith in Christ. Furthermore, all four occur when we repent, are baptized in the name of Jesus, and are filled with the Holy Spirit. Thus our study has reaffirmed two basic truths: (1) salvation is by grace through faith and (2) both water baptism and Spirit baptism are part of the salvation experience.

Justification, regeneration, adoption, and the initial act of sanctification all occur simultaneously at the new birth experience. We have described them as instantaneous, in recognition of the fact that God considers the new birth to be a single whole. Since the Bible teaches the unity of water and Spirit baptism (Chapter 4), we believe the work is not complete until both baptisms take place. The normative pattern in Acts is for both to occur together (Acts 2:38; 10:44-48; 19:1-6).

If people have faith and are taught to expect the Spirit baptism at the time of water baptism, it will happen just as it did in the days of the apostles. Either they will be baptized in Jesus' name and receive the Spirit when they come up out of the waters of baptism (Acts 19:1-6), or they will receive the Spirit and immediately obey the command to be baptized in Jesus' name (Acts 10:44-48).

In view of this, we have based our discussion on the typical case of one who repents, is baptized in water, and is baptized with the Spirit, all at the same time. It is marvelous to see how God has designed it so that all the various aspects of salvation will be fulfilled when we obey the simple message of John 3:5 and Acts 2:38.

FOOTNOTES

[1]"Baptism," *SDB,* I, 238.

[2]Beasley-Murray, p. 163.

14

AN HONEST ANSWER

At the close of this book we return to our original question: "What must I do to be saved?" The New Testament answer is to exercise faith in the Lord Jesus Christ, by repenting from sin, being baptized in the name of Jesus for the remission of sins, receiving the Holy Ghost with the initial sign of speaking in tongues, and continuing to live a holy, separated life by the power of the indwelling Spirit.

All avenues of biblical study lead to this answer. The Bible presents this answer in response to direct questions about salvation (Chapter 1). This is the biblical definition of saving faith (Chapter 2). This is the gospel of Jesus Christ, since it applies His death, burial, and resurrection to our lives, and it is the gospel proclaimed by all the New Testament preachers (Chapter 3). This is the new birth, which consists of water and Spirit (Chapter 4).

Repentance is a turn from sin to God, involving the intellect, the emotions, and the will, and it includes recognition of sin, confession of sin, contrition for sin, and a decision to forsake sin (Chapter 5). The proper mode for Christian water baptism is immersion in water, and God remits the sins of the repentant believer at that time (Chapter 6). The proper formula for Christian water baptism includes an oral invocation of the name Jesus, since Jesus is the only saving name and the highest name by which God has revealed Himself to mankind (Chapter 7). The baptism of the Holy Ghost is a part of salvation, since God imparts His Spirit to the believer at that time (Chapter 8). The biblical evidence of the Spirit baptism is speaking in tongues; tongues is also available as a gift to Spirit-filled believers for both personal and congregational edification (Chapter 9).

Not only did the apostles preach this message, but the early post-apostolic church also preached it; moreover, it has appeared throughout church history, and it has enjoyed a remarkable revival in the twentieth century (Chapters 10 and 11).

The Bible presents no clear-cut exceptions to this full gospel message; as a result, we should not be satisfied with receiving or preaching anything less (Chapter 12).

The various works of salvation, including justification, regeneration, adoption, and sanctification, all manifest themselves in our lives when we obey the gospel completely (Chapter 13). However, the new birth experience is only the beginning of a Christian's relationship with God; thereafter he must continue to walk by faith and live a holy life separated from sin in order to enjoy eternal salvation in the future. (See *In Search of Holiness* by Loretta

Bernard and David Bernard.)

We do not reject those who have not received the New Testament experience, but we simply encourage them to receive what God has for them. Instead of dwelling on negative questions such as, "Do I have to receive this?" we should ask "Is this available for me today?" and "Does God want me to receive this?" Living for God should not be a question of minimum requirements for salvation; instead we should actively seek to please Him in every way possible and to do His perfect will.

Our experience and doctrine should conform to the complete biblical, apostolic pattern; those who serve God without fulfilling this pattern will answer to God. Our responsibility is clear: we must act on what we know to be the truth.

Sometimes people ask, "Am I going to hell if I have not received the New Testament experience?" We do not presume to play God or to judge anyone's ultimate salvation on our own authority. However, we can and must present the Word of God. When we analyze the Word of God, we find that God has instructed everyone to obey the simple message of salvation. The words of Peter still ring true today: "Repent, and be baptized every one of you in the name of Jesus Christ for the remission of sins, and ye shall receive the gift of the Holy Ghost. For the promise is unto you, and to your children, and to all that are afar off, even as many as the Lord our God shall call" (Acts 2:38-39).

In conclusion, we have honestly presented our understanding of the biblical doctrine of the new birth. In everything we have studied to ascertain the true message of God's Word, and we have prayed that His Spirit would illuminate His Word. Our doctrinal presentation affirms that the atoning death, burial, and resurrection of Jesus Christ is the only necessary and sufficient basis for our salvation and that we are saved by grace through faith in the Lord Jesus Christ. The application of grace and the expression of faith come to us as we obey from our hearts the doctrine delivered to us from God's Word, and experience the new birth of water and the Spirit.

BIBLIOGRAPHY

Amplified Bible, The. Grand Rapids: Zondervan, 1965.

"And Now—Deprogramming of Christians is Taking Place," *Christianity Today.* April 22, 1983.

Ante-Nicene Fathers, The. Alexander Roberts and James Donaldson (eds.). Rpt. Grand Rapids: Eerdmans, 1977.

Asimov, Isaac. *The Human Body.* New York: The New American Library, Inc., 1963.

Bainton, Roland. *Here I Stand.* Nashville: Abingdon, 1978.

"Baptism," *A Dictionary of the Bible.* James Hastings (ed.). New York: Charles Scribner's Sons, 1898.

"Baptism," *The Interpreter's Dictionary of the Bible.* Nashville: Abingdon, 1962.

"Baptism," *Smith's Dictionary of the Bible.* H. B. Hackett (ed.). 1870, Rpt. Grand Rapids: Baker Book House, 1971.

"Baptism (Early Christian)," *Encyclopedia of Religion and Ethics.* James Hastings (ed.). New York: Charles Scribner's Sons, 1951.

Barrett, David (ed.). *World Christian Encyclopedia.* New York: Oxford University Press, 1982.

Basham, Don. *Face Up with a Miracle.* Springdale, Pa.: Whitaker House, 1967.

Beall, James Lee. *Rise to Newness of Life.* Detroit: Evangel Press, 1974.

Beasley-Murray, G. R. *Baptism in the New Testament.* Grand Rapids: Eerdmans, 1962.

Bernard, David. *The Oneness of God.* Hazelwood, Mo.: Word Aflame Press, 1983.

Bernard, Loretta and Bernard, David. *In Search of Holiness.* Hazelwood, Mo.: Word Aflame Press, 1981.

Bethune-Baker, J. F. *An Introduction to the Early History of Christian Doctrine.* London: Methuen & Co., 1933.

Bloesch, Donald. *Essentials of Evangelical Theology.* San Francisco: Harper and Row, 1978.

Bonhoeffer, Dietrich. *The Cost of Discipleship,* 2nd ed., trans. R. H. Fuller. New York: Macmillan, 1959.

Bousset, Wilhelm. *Kyrios Christianity—A History of the Belief in Christ from the Beginning of Christianity to Irenaeus,* 5th ed., trans. John Steely. New York: Abingdon, 1970.

Brinton, Crane et al. *A History of Civilization,* 3rd ed. Englewood Cliffs, N. J.: Prentice-Hall, 1967.

Bruce, F. F. *Answers to Questions.* Exeter, U. K.: Paternoster Press, 1972.

Brumback, Carl. *What Meaneth This?* Springfield, Mo.: Gospel Publishing House, 1947.

Buswell, James Jr. *A Systematic Theology of the Christian Religion.* Grand Rapids: Zondervan, 1980.

"Camisards," *Encyclopedia of Religion and Ethics.*

Chalfant, William. *Ancient Champions of Oneness.* Hazelwood, Mo.: Word Aflame Press, 1982.

"Charismata," *Encyclopedia of Religion and Ethics.*

"Churches in China: Flourishing from House to House," *Christianity Today.* June 18, 1982.

Clark, Elmer. *The Small Sects in America.* Nashville: Cokesbury Press, 1937.

Clarke, Adam. *Commentary on the Bible,* abr. by Ralph Earle. Grand Rapids: Baker Book House, 1967.

"Counting Every Soul on Earth," *Time Magazine.* May 3, 1982.

Dalton, Robert. *Tongues Like as of Fire* (Springfield, Mo.: Gospel Publishing House, 1945.

Danielou, Jean. *The Development of Christian Doctrine Before the Council of Nicaea, Vol. I: The Theology of Jewish Christianity,* ed. and trans. John Baker. London: Darton, Lonman, and Todd, 1964.

Demarest, Bruce, "How to Know the Living God," *Christianity Today.* March 18, 1983.

Dowley, Tim et al (eds.). *Eerdmans' Handbook to the History of the Church.* Grand Rapids: Eerdmans, 1977.

Dugas, Paul, (ed. and comp.). *The Life and Writings of Elder G. T. Haywood.* Stockton, Ca.: WABC Apostolic Press, 1968.

Eaves, James. "Seven Steps to Blessed Assurance," *Fulness.* November-December 1980.

Erdman, Charles. *The Epistle of Paul to the Romans.* Philadelphia: Westminster Press, 1966.

Evans, William. *Great Doctrines of the Bible.* Chicago: Moody Press, 1974.

Ewart, Frank. *The Phenomenon of Pentecost,* rev. ed. Hazelwood, Mo.: Word Aflame Press, 1975.

Fauss, Oliver. *Baptism in God's Plan.* St. Louis: Pentecostal Publishing House, 1955.

Fauss, Oliver. *Buy the Truth and Sell It Not.* St. Louis: Pentecostal Publishing House, 1965.

Financial Reports, United Pentecostal Church International, Year ending June 30, 1983. Hazelwood, Mo.: Pentecostal Publishing House, 1983.

Flora, Cornelia Butler. *Pentecostalism in Columbia: Baptism by Fire and Spirit.* Cranbury, N. J.: Associated University Presses, 1974.

Foster, Fred. *Their Story: 20th Century Pentecostals.* Hazelwood, Mo.: Word Aflame Press, 1981.

Frodsham, Stanley. *With Signs Following.* Springfield, Mo.: Gospel Publishing House, 1941.

Fuller, David Otis (ed.). *Counterfeit or Genuine? Mark 16? John 8?* Grand Rapids: Grand Rapids International Publications (Kregel, Inc.), 1975.

Fuller, David Otis (ed.) *Which Bible?* Grand Rapids: Grand Rapids International Publications (Kregel, Inc.), 1975.

Geisler, Norman and Nix, William. *A General Introduction to the Bible.* Chicago: Moody Press, 1968.

Gonzalez, Justo. *A History of Christian Thought.* Nashville: Abingdon, 1975.

Hall, William Phillips, *Remarkable Biblical Discovery or "The Name" of God According to the Scriptures.* 1929; Rpt. St. Louis: Pentecostal Publishing House, 1951.

Hamilton, Michael. *The Charismatic Movement.* Grand Rapids: Eerdmans, 1977.

Heick, Otto. *A History of Christian Thought.* Philadelphia: Fortress Press, 1965.

Henry, Matthew. *Commentary.* Old Tappan, N. J.: Fleming H. Revell, n.d.

Hesselgrave, David. *Communicating Christ Cross-Culturally.* Grand Rapids: Zondervan, 1978.

Hoekema, Anthony. *Holy Spirit Baptism.* Grand Rapids: Eerdmans, 1972.

Hoekema, Anthony. *What About Tongues Speaking?* Grand Rapids: Eerdmans, 1966.

Hollenweger, Walter. *The Pentecostals,* trans. R. A. Wilson. Minneapolis: Augsburg Publishing House, 1972.

Holy Bible, The, King James Version.

Holy Bible, The, New International Version. Grand Rapids: Zondervan, 1978.

"Irving and the Catholic Apostolic Churches," *Encyclopedia of Religion and Ethics.*

Klotsche, E. H. *The History of Christian Doctrine,* rev. ed. Grand Rapids: Baker Book House, 1979.

Lange, John Peter. *Commentary on the Holy Scriptures.* Grand Rapids: Zondervan, 1960.

Latourette, Kenneth. *A History of Christianity.* New York: Harper & Row, 1953.

Laurentin, Rene. *Catholic Pentecostalism,* trans. Matthew J. O'Connell. Garden City, N. J.: Doubleday and Company, 1977.

Laurin, Robert. "Typological Interpretation of the Old Testament," in Bernard Ramm et al, *Hermeneutics.* Grand Rapids: Baker Book House, 1967.

Marshall, Alfred (ed.). *The Interlinear Greek-English New Testament.* Grand Rapids: Zondervan, 1958.

Melton, J. Gordon. *The Encyclopedia of American Religions.* Wilmington, N. C.: McGrath Publishing Company, 1978.

Morris, Henry III. *Baptism: How Important is It?* Denver: Accent Books, 1978.

Murk, W. H. *Four Kinds of Water Baptism.* St. Paul, Minn.: Northland Publishing Co., 1947.

Nicene and Post-Nicene Fathers, The. Philip Schaff and Henry Wace (eds.). Rpt. Grand Rapids: Eerdmans, 1976.

Nicoll, W. Robertson (ed.). *The Expositor's Bible.* Grand Rapids: Eerdmans, 1956.

Palmer, Donald. *Explosion of People Evangelism.* Chicago: Moody Press, 1974.

Paterson, John. *The Real Truth About Baptism in Jesus' Name.* St. Louis: Pentecostal Publishing House, 1953.

Pentecost, J. Dwight. *The Words and Works of Jesus Christ.* Grand Rapids: Zondervan, 1981.

"Pentecostal Churches," *Encyclopedia Britannica.* Chicago: William Benton, 1976.

Piepkorn, Arthur. *Profiles in Belief: The Religious Bodies of the United States and Canada.* San Francisco: Harper and Row, 1979.

Pugh, J. T. *How to Receive the Holy Ghost.* Hazelwood, Mo.: Pentecostal Publishing House, 1969.

Reed, David Arthur. *Origins and Development of the Theology of Oneness Pentecostalism in the United States.* Ann Arbor, Mich.: University Microfilms International, 1978.

Reynolds, Ralph. *Truth Shall Triumph.* Hazelwood, Mo.: Word Aflame Press, 1965.

Rushdoony, Rousas John. "Baptism and Citizenship," *Chalcedon Position Paper No. 37.* Vallecito, Ca.: Chalcedon, n.d.

Sawatsky, Walter. *Soviet Evangelicals Since World War II.* Scottsdale, Pa.: Herald Press, 1981.

Schaff, Philip. *History of the Christian Church,* 3rd. ed. 1890; Rpt. Grand Rapids: Eerdmans, 1958.

Sherrill, John. *They Speak with Other Tongues.* New York: McGraw-Hill, 1964.

Smedes, Lewis. *Union with Christ.* Grand Rapids: Eerdmans, 1983.
Snyder, Howard. *The Radical Wesley.* Downers Grove, Ill.: Inter-Varsity Press, 1980.
Solomon, Charles. "Counselor's Corner," *Fulness.* November-December 1980.
Spence, H. D. M. and Exell, Joseph (eds.). *The Pulpit Commentary.* Rpt. Grand Rapids: Eerdmans, 1977.
Strong, James. *Exhaustive Concordance of the Bible.* Nashville: Abingdon, 1890.
Sweet, William. *The Story of Religion in America.* Grand Rapids: Baker Book House, 1950.
Synan, Vinson (ed.). *Aspects of Pentecostal-Charismatic Origins.* Plainfield, N. J.: Logos International, 1975.
Synan, Vinson. *The Holiness-Pentecostal Movement in the United States.* Grand Rapids: Eerdmans, 1971.
Tasker, R. V. G. (ed.). *The Tyndale New Testament Commentaries.* Grand Rapids: Eerdmans, 1960-80.
Thiessen, Henry. *Lectures in Systematic Theology.* Grand Rapids: Eerdmans, 1979.
Thomas, W. H. Griffith. *St. Paul's Epistle to the Romans.* Grand Rapids: Eerdmans, 1974.
"Tongues, Gift of," *A Dictionary of the Bible.*
"Tongues, Gift of," *Smith's Dictionary of the Bible.*
Urshan, Andrew. *Apostolic Faith Doctrine of the New Birth.* Portland, Or.: Apostolic Book Publishers, n.d.
Urshan, Andrew. *The Life of Andrew Bar David Urshan.* Stockton, Ca.: Apostolic Press, 1967.
Vaughan, Curtis (ed.). *The New Testament from 26 Translations.* Grand Rapids: Zondervan, 1967.
Vine, W. E. *An Expository Dictionary of New Testament Words.* Old Tappan, N. J.: Fleming H. Revell, 1940.
Walker, Williston. *A History of the Christian Church.* New York: Charles Scribner's Sons, 1947.
Webster's Third New International Dictionary of the English Language, unabr. Philip Gove et al (eds.). Springfield, Mass.: G. & C. Merriam Co., 1976.
Weisser, Thomas. *After the Way Called Heresy.* N.P., 1981.
Wesley, John. *The Works of John Wesley,* 3rd. ed. Grand Rapids: Baker Book House, 1950.
Yang, John. *The Essential Doctrines in the Holy Bible,* trans. M. H. Tsai, Taichung, Taiwan: The General Assembly of the True Jesus Church in Taiwan, 1970.

Scripture Reference Index

John

Acts

II Corinthians

Galatians

Ephesians

Philippians

Colossians

Subject Index

Prayer List

Brian & Family
Laurie & F
Sara & F.
Dallants & F.
Mike Beatty
Jim Travis & F. Venassa
Wopats F
Pastor & F.
Ann Nassa & F. Kenny
Bobby Allen
Terri Perdue
Eric Harden
Barbara Hoffman
Jimmy Hill
Jay Bates & F.
David & Beth
Kelly
Sis Reese & Jan.
Church Board.
Pres. George Bush.
Gary W. "Donut"
Sandy Cunning (Grey)
Fill my 18 chairs
Rob Abbinett
Jim Wells
Shirley & Paul Strole
May Gibson. F
Joe Gregory

Acts 8
Acts 2
Acts 10
Acts 19

July 19. 04
Dreamed about Gary
Brian's house!